D1251513

A Layman's Guide to Naval Strategy

A Layman's Guide
to Naval Strategy

BY

BERNARD BRODIE

PRINCETON UNIVERSITY PRESS · PRINCETON

LONDON: HUMPHREY MILFORD, OXFORD UNIVERSITY PRESS

1943

FIRST EDITION, *August 1942*
Revised Printing, September 1942
Revised Printing, October 1942

SECOND EDITION, *March 1943*
25th thousand

MAPS AND DRAWINGS BY
RICHARD D. BUTTERFIELD

To Fawn

Preface

THERE are many good reasons for not writing a treatise on naval strategy at the present time. The greatest war in history is now in progress. The next two or three years are bound to produce many events from which important lessons will be drawn. Tactics are in an extraordinarily fluid state, and pronounced tactical changes are bound to exercise some influence on strategy—sometimes a profound influence. Certain tactical trends have appeared, and whether these trends will halt, proceed further, or reverse themselves, time alone will tell. Only the biased can have fixed opinions. Battles have been reported to us in one-sided, fragmentary, and sometimes purposely deceptive fashion. No belligerent knows just what damage it has inflicted on the opponent, and none is willing to announce gratuitously its own injuries. Above all, we lack perspective.

On the other hand, the reasons for writing at this date are compelling. The perplexities of today cannot wait upon the sounder insight of tomorrow. It is necessary to make sense out of vast confusion in order to fight the war more efficiently. New theories of war are flowering all over the landscape, and they must be scrutinized intelligently. Strategic dogmas spring into being almost overnight and gather amazing political force. In so far as they are in error, they are a distraction and diversion from our war effort.

This book is addressed directly to the layman. That fact should need no justification, yet it is unfortunately true that the study of war is of all human pursuits the one which laymen have most generally abandoned to professionals. The idea persists that strategy can be comprehensible only to people who wear uniforms. Yet for better or for worse, the layman plays a great part in determining the military strategy of a nation. In a democracy during wartime he rightly insists on speaking his mind, and he probably underestimates the degree to which military and political leaders respond to his demands. His very optimism or despondency creates situations which the authorities cannot afford to ignore. Prior to the outbreak of war he elects to office politicians whose policies may either further or hopelessly compromise the country's security, or at least greatly affect the price of victory.

I should be loath, however, to leave the impression that civilian influence upon the determination of strategy is in any sense regrettable. Clemenceau had good enough reasons for his famous statement that "War is too important to be left to the generals." The greatest generals have themselves expressed that very opinion. Everyone is familiar with the dictum of Clausewitz that war is a continuation of politics, but its implications are not so generally recognized. Yet we have on the authority of that great philosopher of war himself just what he meant by it.

"To leave a great military enterprise," he said, "or the plan for one, to *a purely military judgment and decision* is a distinction which cannot be allowed . . . and when people speak, as they often do, of the prejudicial influence of policy [i.e. politicians] on the conduct of a war, they say in reality something very different from what they intend. It is not this influence but the policy itself which should be criticized."

For a democracy, the corollary of that idea can be best expressed in the words of Captain Russell Grenfell of the British Navy: "Though the Government may often be forced by the exigencies of the case to come to vital decisions concerning the conduct of the war without previously taking the public into its confidence . . . it will be greatly strengthened in making those decisions if it can feel that it has behind it an instructed public opinion on strategical matters; a public opinion which is capable of forming a just and reliable estimate of the soundness or otherwise of the strategy adopted as it is seen to develop."

It might be added that those who are now devoting themselves to the worthy effort of planning a lasting peace can afford no more than others to dismiss the study of war as irrelevant. Thus far most peace planners have approached the problem of war with the technique of the medicine man rather than the physician, and have sought to prescribe cures without troubling to study the disease. The result has been a long list of proposed remedies which have been utterly fantastic in view of the realities of war.

The manner in which I have treated naval strategy in this book might be classified as "orthodox." That approach may not prove popular in a day when we are being told on every hand that we must repudiate all the ideas of the past and develop a whole new strategy overnight. Modified and amended our theory must certainly be if it is to fit modern conditions. But what is required is an attitude of fine discrimination and adjustment, not nihilism. The war of today is being fought with new weapons, but so was the war of yesterday and the day before. Drastic change in weapons has been so persistent in the last hundred years that the presence of that factor might be considered one of the constants of strategy. Only those to whom the study of war is novel permit themselves to be swept away by novel elements in the present war.

One who reads General Sir Frederick Maurice's *Principles of Strategy* or Colonel Hermann Foertsch's *Kriegskunst heute und morgen* (translated under the title, *The Art of Modern Warfare*), penetrating books both and written before the present conflict, will be impressed to find scarcely a passage which either author would have to retract at this date. Yet both lean heavily on their predecessors of the nineteenth century. By contrast, many people who write or speak from day to day with a new whim on each occasion are proved wrong from week to week. In the field of naval strategy, the underlying value of the teachings of men like Mahan, Corbett, and Castex is still largely intact. Undoubtedly in the end the bulk of their theory will decay, will have only an antiquarian interest, but we live and fight in the present.

The colleagues (past and present) and authors who helped me indirectly in the preparation of this work are too numerous to mention. The persons who helped me directly are few, but my indebtedness to each of them is correspondingly great.

I must mention first Mr. Datus C. Smith, Jr., of the Princeton University Press, who looks upon the duties of a publisher in a manner that can be described only as creative. He urged me to undertake the work, watched over it at every stage, and gave me the benefit of his astute judgment.

Dr. Herbert Rosinski favored me with criticisms and suggestions based on his phenomenal command of naval history and strategy. His comments enabled me to effect some marked improvements in the manuscript.

Vice-Admiral William L. Rodgers has in the same generous fashion as on an earlier occasion helped me with his alert mind and broad knowledge. Captains C. C. Gill and H. M. Briggs kindly consented to read the proof and contributed several valuable suggestions.

My wife not only served as a typical intelligent layman, offering her usual steady and trustworthy criticism, but also helped me considerably in the more onerous labor involved in preparing the book.

A condensed version of Chapter VIII has been published in the *Saturday Evening Post*.

B. B.

Dartmouth College
Hanover, N. H.
July 25, 1942

Preface to Second Edition

To PRESENT a second edition of a book only seven months after its first printing is perhaps presumptuous at best and in normal times would be wholly unpardonable from any sound standard of publishers' or authors' ethics. But if the times are times of war and if one's work is on the subject of war, seven months may be equivalent to a good number of years of less agitated character. Considering the many controversial subjects upon which I had ventured to express convictions, my publishers and I in first sending this book to press were taking the risk that in seven months' time the tenets it expounded might look very foolish. The fact that a second edition is offered at all indicates that the events of war have on the whole dealt gently with my conclusions, and that the temerity of rushing in where admirals fear to tread may have its rewards—if only negative ones.

However, various changes made for the second printing and again for the third when added to those made for the present issue constitute a fairly substantial revision, and justify our naming this a new edition. The pagination, however, has remained unchanged.

Chapter VIII, as was anticipated, was the chapter which received the most attention from the majority of the reviewers. If it were to be written anew today, its argument would be presented with at least as much conviction and firmness though possibly with a shade less vehemence. After the Solomon Islands and North African campaigns, it should no longer be necessary to plead to unbiased readers the continuing utility of the surface warship and especially of the battleship. One of the great tactical revolutions of the past year has been the enormously enhanced effectiveness of the anti-aircraft armament mounted on United Nations warships. The excellent news, reported in the press on this very day, of the total destruction of a Japanese convoy by General Mac-Arthur's air forces, with negligible loss to ourselves, appears to confirm the pleasant conclusion that in this vital matter of anti-aircraft fire our Japanese enemies are greatly inferior to us.

Inasmuch as I have recently become an officer in the United States Naval Reserve, it becomes incumbent upon me to state that the opinions expressed in this book are those solely of the author and in no way reflect the official views of the Navy Department.

B. B.

Washington, D. C.
March 4, 1943

CONTENTS

CHAPTER I

Sea Power in Modern War

WHEN Japan struck at the American battle fleet at Pearl Harbor on the morning of December 7, 1941, the immediate thought of the average American was that the Japanese had run completely amuck. The word "hara-kiri" was much in the air. How could it be other than suicidal for this oriental nation of limited resources to challenge to mortal conflict the greatest industrial power in the world, and by that challenge to give unity and resolution to its previously vacillating people? How could a political event so portentous for Japan possibly be offset by the disabling of a few battleships thousands of miles away from Japanese territories? Would the Japanese not have been shrewder to have ignored our fleet and by-passed our possessions in their pursuit of conquest?

We are confident that the Japanese miscalculated, but we know now that they were goaded to their fateful act not by desperation but by faith in victory. They knew that regardless of the ultimate magnitude of our strength we could not bring it to bear in the western Pacific save through the instrumentality of sea power. They knew that regardless of their own strength in infantry and mechanized divisions, in bombing and torpedo planes, they could not seize the advanced bases they needed for the operation of these planes and armies, they could not move their divisions across the water to new fields of conquest and keep them supplied with ammunition and fuel, if they were opposed by a superior sea power. Our battle fleet was the most concentrated, the most potent, and the most readily available force which could oppose their purposes, and it was our battle fleet at which they struck first.

Never before had the world seen such a gigantic demon-

3

stration of sea-borne invasion as the Japanese forces presented in the months following the Pearl Harbor attack. Never before had the offensive potentialities of command of the sea been so forcefully demonstrated. Yet curiously, at that particular moment it became most fashionable to decry that apostle of modern sea power, Admiral Mahan, as a false prophet, to assert that he belonged among the scholastics of the Middle Ages. The general conviction was that while sea power in the past had been invariably decisive in war and had determined the course of history (which was never claimed for it), it was now a clearly obsolescent factor. The new air arm had displaced it from its proud preeminence.

Unfortunately for Mahan's memory, he is much more often criticized than read. For on the second page of his most famous work he pointed out that "the unresting progress of mankind causes a continual change in the weapons; and with that must come a continual change in the manner of fighting." He would have been the first to welcome the modern airplane to the arsenal of naval weapons; and he would have been the first to reject doctrines which confuse the aims of military power with the tools for carrying them out.

Sea power has never meant merely warships. It has always meant the sum total of those weapons, installations, and geographical circumstances which enable a nation *to control transportation over the seas during wartime*. If the airplane plays an important part in such control, which it obviously does, it is functioning as an instrument of sea power. All naval enterprise—with the exception of bombardments of land objectives from the sea, which is only an incidental use of sea power—is directed toward the single aim of affecting the movements of the lowly freighter or transport in which is carried nearly all the commodities and the men that move across the sea. If in the future the greater part of ocean transport is carried in aircraft rather than in ships, or if the transfer of men and commodities across the seas becomes unimportant, sea power as such will cease to have meaning. At the present time, however, because of the most telling economic and engineering considerations, neither of these contingencies seems near at hand; at any rate, they have no bearing on present circumstances.

Even if one insists on regarding as a separate branch of military power the forces which move through the air rather than upon land or water, it is a rather limited outlook which concentrates upon the spectacle of the airplane over its target to the exclusion of the long chain of circumstances which are responsible for putting it there. The air forces which so vitally aided the Japanese armies in their quick conquests of Malaya, the East Indies, and Burma operated from airdromes which in almost every instance had been seized by Japanese armies landed from ships. Many of the aircraft involved, especially the fighter planes, and all their fuel, cargoes, and maintenance crews and supplies were brought to the scene of operations in ships. Their local air superiorities, in other words, were derived from sea power. Most of the materials that went into the construction of the British aircraft which hurled back the Luftwaffe in the Battle of Britain of 1940 and which took the offensive in 1942 were brought to the British Isles in ships. So, too, was all the fuel which those aircraft used, as well as most of the food which fed the men and women who made the planes and the crews that flew them. The island base from which these aircraft operated would have been untenable without British command of the sea approaches from the west.

It does not therefore detract in the least from the marvelous power of air forces to say that command of the sea is still as likely as formerly to be decisive in great wars, and that in fact the greatly increased quantity and complexity of the equipment used in modern war has made control of the sea

5

lanes more important than ever before. The question of whether the airplane or the warship is the best means of exercising maritime control is of course another matter, and one which will be examined at some length in subsequent chapters. For the moment it is enough to bear in mind the distinction between issues which are too generally confused. In scoffing at navies the extreme air enthusiasts are prone to forget the purpose for which navies exist. If they could avoid that error, questions such as whether additional airplanes are more necessary at the moment than additional warships or whether aircraft have made battleships obsolete could be threshed out somewhat more dispassionately and fruitfully.

The ability of the United States to wage the war abroad rather than at home, to win the war rather than merely to avoid being conquered, and to win it at a minimum of cost in blood and treasure, depended on our ability to aid our allies first to sustain themselves and second to carry the fight to the enemy. Except for large bombers—minus their ground crews and supplies—that aid could go to them only by sea. It is an old axiom among the armed forces of America that the Navy is "our first line of defense," but it is just as true and somewhat more meaningful to say that the Navy is our first line of offense. No war can be won simply by standing interminably on the defensive, unless the word "victory" be given a hollow content indeed. Regardless of how impregnable our defenses are, and they can never be perfectly so, our security in the world is jeopardized if we cannot inflict vital injury on any nation which menaces us or our legitimate interests. And for this our Navy is indispensable.

In the two great wars which we have had to fight during a single generation, the fact that we have had strong allies who were contiguous with our enemies has been an incalculable benefit to us. It has enabled us to hit our enemies hard, and to do so on their own thresholds rather than on ours. It is foolish to talk, as some do, about winning the war from our own shores, whether by air power or any other means, when we have allies whose position makes it possible for us to expend our offensive strength upon our enemies far more generously than would otherwise be the case.

No development in aircraft or any other weapons of war thus far has nullified the tremendous bearing upon strategy of the factor of distance. Aerial bombardment can be carried on far more effectively at 250 miles than at 500, and immeasurably more effectively at 500 miles than at 1,000, even though the ranges of available aircraft much exceed the latter figure. And the experience of Europe and China during 1939–1942 ought to make us cautious about relying too much upon aerial bombardment alone to win a decision. Our ability to defeat the enemy will depend upon armies as well as air forces, and these can be brought to the enemy in large numbers only by sea.

A navy thus has defensive and offensive uses, which are sometimes indistinguishable and always mutually supporting. By denying the seas to the enemy while assuring the overseas transfer of one's own men and munitions, a navy may be defending one's own territories from invasion at the same time that it is carrying through an offensive. And the fact that it is defending one's territories means that a much greater quantity of men and materials of war can be dispatched abroad for offensive uses than would otherwise be the case. Even when England was alone and desperately in peril, Churchill's faith in the Royal Navy was such that he sent to Egypt men, planes, tanks, and munitions which except for the protection of that Navy would have been needed at home. For the first year that Russia was in the war, England was sending abroad five planes and fifteen tanks for every one she received from America. England has always resorted to such strategy in war,

7

and it explains why she has always accomplished so much with small armies.

If the chief purpose of a navy is control of sea-borne transportation, the vehicles of such transportation must be considered not as incidental to sea power but as an essential part of it. It would be as unreasoning to consider sea power in terms of warships alone as it would be to consider railroad trains in terms solely of locomotives. A locomotive without cars attached represents power well enough, but power without functional meaning. Since the warship has meaning mostly as it affects the movements of cargo carriers, lack of such carriers makes the sea as much a barrier as does a superior hostile fleet —more so, perhaps, for a hostile fleet may frequently be evaded, but the consequences of a shortage of shipping cannot be evaded. Without sufficient shipping, naval efforts can be only negative; one can keep the enemy from using the sea but cannot use it for oneself.

In autumn of 1942, the limiting factor in the efforts of the United Nations was not so much men and weapons as the shipping to carry them. Russia had to be supplied through her Arctic ports and the distant Persian Gulf. The battle front in North Africa had to be approached mainly by a voyage round the Cape of Good Hope, a voyage which the average freighter could make only thrice in one year. By the devious routes that had to be followed, the ports of Australia were 7,000 miles from the coast of the United States. There was not yet an active front in western Europe, but the British and Americans had the patent ambition of opening one. Any one of those theaters would make enormous demands on shipping resources if given the full attention it deserved, and to give such attention to all of them simultaneously was out of the question. Concentration of offensive effort regionally was less a matter of principle judiciously chosen than of stark necessity in the face of a shortage of bottoms.

The event which suddenly immersed us in total war in the Pacific brought us also into the European war, but for a while it was difficult for Americans to think of anything but the necessity of dealing a crushing blow to the Japanese. The manner in which war came to us, the galling defeats suffered at the hands of a power obviously inferior in total strength, the undeniable strategic importance of the campaigns in the Pacific and Indian oceans, and the knowledge of the terrible costs that would be required to retrieve what was being lost there made it easy to forget that the most decisive theater in this all-encompassing war was Europe and the sea lanes leading to it.

Of the three great powers in the Axis camp, Germany was unquestionably the most formidable and in the long run the most dangerous to the security and well-being of the United States. The Atlantic is after all much narrower than the Pacific, and American cultural and economic affinity with Europe has always been incomparably greater than any attachments to Asia. And quite apart from ultimate goals, it was clear in 1942 that victory over Japan would be an empty victory indeed if it were coupled with a United Nations defeat in Europe at the hands of Germany, whereas the defeat of Japan might reasonably be regarded as inevitable—though by no means automatic—once Nazi power was liquidated.

The question of whether it was best to attack the stronger or the weaker enemy first might be dismissed as entirely academic so far as concerned United Nations strategy. Russia and Great Britain were already engaged to the hilt in Europe, with the enemy at their very throats. It was impossible to mark time in Europe in order to concentrate an overwhelming offensive strength against Japan. It was entirely logical, on the other hand, to pursue a defensive strategy in the Pacific and to gather all available strength for a knock-out blow against Germany. Only one of the major powers among the

United Nations was *vitally* engaged in the Orient. The ideal of concentrating the maximum of power against each of the main enemies in turn could be realized far more fully by taking Germany first. The defense of China was of extreme importance, but that still did not mean the same thing as a full-scale offensive against Japan.

Those to whom the word "defensive" has now become malodorous must be reminded that simultaneous offensives against two powerful and widely removed enemies are usually impossible and always foolish. "One at a time" is always a good strategy to follow if at all possible—one can go farther in much shorter time and consequently with a much greater economy of blood and treasure. It is a mistake to regard the defensive and the offensive as mutually exclusive; the latter always implies some measure of the former, for to make the offensive most effective where it is launched it is necessary to assume the defensive elsewhere.

Of course, a defensive strategy by no means excludes aggressive action. The battles of the Coral Sea and of Midway were examples of defensive strategy on the part of the United Nations carried out through vigorously offensive tactics. The numerous raids by American naval forces on Japanese-held islands and even the sea-borne invasion of the Solomon Islands carried out by American forces in August 1942 were primarily intended not as a part of a far-reaching offensive but as a means of disturbing Japanese offensive plans both in the Pacific and the Indian oceans.

The first problem facing the United States, therefore, was to sustain Russia and Britain until all-out offensives could be launched against Germany. In this scheme of strategy Britain occupied what was essentially the key position. Her geographical position combined with her naval strength made it possible for the United Nations to control shipping lanes across the Atlantic, which the United States and Russia together could not do without her aid. That same geographical position made Britain the logical base for the gigantic sum of Anglo-American offensive strength that was being built up. So long as a large Russian Army remained in being on the eastern front, the chances for dealing a death blow against Germany from the west were certain to increase, and the heart of German power was much closer to Britain than to Russia.

The Battle of the Atlantic, which opened on the first day of the war, was thus the key naval campaign of the whole war. Its outcome could be determined not by the result of a decisive engagement but by a score on a tally sheet—of ships lost against ships built, of shipping available against shipping required. By the middle of 1942 the total score of German successes was all too impressive. And when those successes are considered in the light of the facts that Britain and her Allies had entered the war much weaker in shipping than they had been in the first World War and that the lines of communications to the active fronts were much longer, the compelling reasons for the fantastically large 1942–1943 shipbuilding program which the United States had set for herself are apparent.

For the enemy there were stringencies no less acute. It is curious that upon the entrance of Japan and the United States into the war, the daily press, while full of comparisons of the naval strength of the two new belligerents, entirely neglected the equally important item of shipping tonnage. Yet Japan was carrying on campaigns over a great maritime area with shipping which on December 1, 1941, totaled less than 6,000,000 tons. With such limited resources, Japanese shipping losses in the offensive against the East Indies were of the greatest strategic importance.

After she gained access to the rich oil-producing fields of Malaysia, Japan no longer had to fear a shortage of oil, but none of her conquests alleviated her shipping difficulties. On the contrary, the more extended her lines became, the more difficult the problem. The enormous disparity in shipbuilding resources between Japan and the United Nations was perhaps the largest single advantage of the latter powers.

The sea-borne communications of the European Axis partners were shorter but vitally important. Germany needed shipping in the Baltic and the North Sea for her campaign against Russia and for communications with Scandinavia. To Italy, shipping was an indispensable means of coastwise transportation and of military communications with the Axis armies in North Africa. But the proportion of losses suffered by the Axis powers relative to their total fund of shipping was extremely severe, much more so than that suffered by their enemies. Churchill was able proudly to report to the House of Commons in June 1941 that "the destruction of enemy tonnage is proceeding at a most rapid and satisfactory rate."

The ugly little tramp steamer thus occupies an important quarter of the shield of naval power. It is less splendid but no less vital than the great battleship. But both are ships, and to all the embattled nations in the Second World War there was nothing quite so valuable as a ship.

It is one thing to have the implements of sea power and quite another to use them wisely to achieve the purpose for which they are provided. This general handling of the tools of war to realize their purpose is what is known as "strategy." The term is often confused with "tactics," which refers to the localized business of fighting. Admiral Mahan proposed a simple criterion to distinguish the two concepts—the fact of contact. Where the adversaries are in contact we have tactics, but strategy transcends contact to include the whole conduct of a war. Ideally, all tactical problems should be handled in a manner to further the strategic end. Thus, strategic considerations may demand on the one hand that a warship avoid an engagement with a force to which it is not especially inferior (as for example when it is on a commerce raiding or reconnaissance mission), and on the other hand that it attack and fight to the bitter end even when hopelessly outclassed.

There are certain basic ideas about fighting a war which have such general validity as to be known as "principles" of strategy. Contrary to popular belief, there is nothing especially esoteric about the basic principles of warfare. They have been garnered by intelligent reading of military history. The general treatise on naval strategy happens to be a very recent invention, and the great admirals of the past attained their stature without benefit of catechisms. They thought their problems through on the basis of common sense and experience and arrived at wise decisions.

However, common sense is not an abundant commodity, and the practice of thinking problems through is exceedingly rare, especially among persons whose conclusions are untrammeled by responsibility. The layman unacquainted with the prevailing ideas of strategy will, when confronted with a strategic problem, frequently venture unwise proposals. Yet intelligence and an inclination to think are indispensable even when one is conversant with the principles—among professionals as well as laymen. Adherence to one principle frequently demands violation of another, and there is no principle but admits of exceptions. Wars cannot be fought according to books of rules. The admiral or general who adheres inflexibly to any set of preconceived commandments is hardly likely to be a victor against a resourceful opponent.

As a matter of fact, it is easier to speak of principles of strategy than to catalog them. The outstanding treatises of the last hundred years on the strategy of war show a remarkable diversity respecting the ideas which are elevated to the status of "principles." The less imaginative among military men have long been fond of reiterating the old dictum: "Methods change but principles are unchanging," yet when asked to describe immutable principles they are often at a loss for an answer. It is true that modern land and naval campaigns bear certain marked similarities in broad outline to those of earlier times, but these similarities, while important, can usually be described in absurdly simple terms.

The Chinese general Sun Tzu wrote about 500 B.C. that the essence of war is deception, by which he meant simply that it is well to keep your enemy guessing about your intentions and preferably to make him guess wrongly; by doing so you may strike him when and where he is least prepared. No one can deny the universal validity of this idea, but neither can one deny that it is an intellectual commonplace. It may be important enough to merit being regarded reverently as the "principle of surprise," but it is hardly an abstruse point to be comprehended only by specialists. It is true that many of the fundamental ideas of strategy are not obvious until they are pointed out—there would otherwise be no purpose in this book—but all are easily understood by an alert mind. There is no need for a complicated terminology in strategy.

However, to say that the basic principles of war are easy to understand is not to say that it is easy to comprehend the finer points, or what is more important, to determine upon a wise plan of strategy and then carry it out. The great commander must of course have a profound insight into all the ramifications of strategic principle, but that is only the first requirement of military leadership. He must also thoroughly understand tactics, which with modern arms is bound to be exceedingly complex and to require long training and experience. He must know how to solve problems of supply or "logistics," he must know human nature, and he must have certain qualities of character and personality which transcend mere knowledge. He must be able to stick to his course despite a thousand distractions and yet be sufficiently elastic to recognize when a change in circumstances demands a change in plan. He must above all be able to make adjustment to the inevitable shocks and surprises of war.

Unfortunately, the very preoccupation of commanders with specific and inevitably complex problems sometimes tends to make them impatient with the age old verities. Long-tested doctrines which are utterly simple are rejected in part because of their very simplicity, and in part too because of the dogma of innovation so prevalent in our age. The French High Command in the summer of 1940 found out too late that the side which carries the ball makes the touchdowns, and that all the maxims of the great military leaders of the past relative to the merits of initiative had not been outmoded by modern arms. We live in an age when the basic theories of naval warfare are being rejected out of hand by responsible officials on the wholly unwarranted assumption that they do not fit modern conditions. One can say about theory what Mahan said of materiel: "It is possible to be too quick in discarding as well as too slow in adopting."

Naval warfare differs from land warfare in the objectives aimed at, the implements used, and the characteristics of the domain on which it is waged. These are major determinants indeed, and we must therefore expect maritime strategy to differ materially from the strategy of land warfare. Certain ideas are common to both, but it is a mistake to carry over wholesale into the realm of the sea concepts which govern the conduct of war on land. The purpose of naval operations is usually much more limited than that of land warfare; as a rule navies exist chiefly to aid and sustain armies and air forces, and it is the latter which achieve the final decision. The warship, which is still the chief instrument of sea power, has no counterpart among the implements of land warfare for mobility and for tactical and strategic independence—the tank, for example, falls far short of it in self-sufficiency. Finally, the sea has few of the terrestrial complexities of land. It has nothing resembling railroads or highways; it has no mountains, forests, or rivers; it has no centers of population or industry. It is only a flat waste to be traversed, and it is almost uniformly traversable throughout. The sea even imposes a relative uniformity upon the weather conditions prevailing over it. True, different areas of the sea vary tremendously in strategic importance, but these variations are imposed upon the maritime areas by the lands which delimit them.

In saying that sea power is intended to control transportation—or communications, as military men prefer to call it—over the seas during wartime, we mean that it fulfils the following functions:

(a) It protects the transfer over water of land and air forces and their supplies to those areas where they may be used effectively against enemy forces. This may mean bringing an army to a hostile coast, which is sea-borne invasion, or to a friendly shore for operations in nearby territories.

(b) It protects also the transfer of the commodities of ordinary sea-borne trade, including those generally termed "strategic raw materials." Considering the complex technology of modern war, this falls not far short of including all raw materials.

(c) It prevents the enemy from using the sea to transport his own armies on a large scale. This means, among other things, that it defends one's homeland and overseas territories against invasion.

(d) It exerts economic pressure on the enemy by preventing him from importing overseas commodities which are scarce or lacking in the region under his control. It prevents him also from exporting his products, the proceeds of which might be used to pay for commodities received from contiguous neutrals or for various services (propaganda, etc.) abroad. A navy also adds to the strain upon the enemy's system of internal transportation by interfering with coastwise or other shipping which normally relieves the burden on his internal transport. During peacetime, for example, much of the trade between Italy and Germany goes through Gibraltar Strait and round the Iberian Peninsula. Severance of this route throws a great burden on the railroads running between those countries.

The only other important use of a navy is as a mobile heavy artillery (or aircraft base) in the direct assault against land objectives, either in covering a landing, in cooperating with armies already ashore but operating near the coast, or merely in the independent bombardment of enemy coastal installations. British strategists have long had a fondness for land campaigns which enable them to utilize the great firepower of their fleet, since it enables British armies—always small during the early part of a war—to be effective far beyond their numerical strength. The British offensives in Libya during 1941 and 1942 illustrated this type of strategy. But the fleet will usually not be used against land objectives if such use threatens its ability to perform its primary function of controlling maritime communications. One of the maxims of naval strategy is that important warships should not be risked against strong land batteries or within close range of land-based air forces while an enemy fleet remains in being.

However, before one can understand how a navy fulfils these various functions, one must examine the instruments which make up a navy. The tools one uses for a job have certain potentialities and certain limitations, which together determine the scope of one's operations. The story of sea power at work is told in terms of ships, guns, torpedoes, and bombers, and upon the characteristics of these tools may depend the survival of nations.

CHAPTER II

The Tools of Sea Power

WHATEVER sea power may now mean in its entirety, traditionally it has chiefly meant ships. And at least since the seventeenth century warships have tended to evolve into specialized types. Frequently this tendency has been temporarily reversed by a desire, particularly on the part of the weaker naval power, to build vessels stronger than the corresponding types in the enemy fleet. Our own *Constitution* class frigates, which were far more powerful than British frigates, and which could pull away from line-of-battle ships, are a case in point, and the German *Panzerschiffe* or "pocket battleships" are a more recent example. But it is usually found in the long run that the best warship is the cheapest one which will fulfil its specific strategic function adequately.

For many purposes it may be better to have a large number of light ships than a smaller number of heavier ones. Much of course depends on what the potential enemy is doing, but it is well not to try to outdistance him too far in each class. Otherwise one will have a number of intermediate types which are too weak for some purposes and needlessly expensive and therefore too few in numbers for other purposes. Even in the case of the most powerful type of fighting ships —battleships—there are strategic, tactical, and economic considerations which tend to impose both minimum and maximum limits upon size and fighting power. It must always be remembered that the resources available to any nation for naval purposes are never unlimited, and it is incumbent upon that nation to allocate those resources wisely.

Every navy has distinctive needs, depending upon the duties which will devolve upon it in wartime and the geographical and climatic conditions under which it expects to fight. England's fleet must be prepared to carry on operations all over the globe and to protect a vast shipping; the American Navy, like the Japanese, has been built with an eye particularly to war in the broad Pacific; the Italian fleet, on the other hand, has been designed in the main for short-range operations in the Mediterranean; and the German Navy, whose High Seas Fleet of the First World War was designed primarily for operations in the North Sea, has now created a fleet adapted chiefly to the war against commerce.

Within these special circumstances, however, each navy seeks to get out of the money and materials available to it the maximum in all-weather, all-purpose fighting strength. This involves a balanced fleet, balanced in accordance with the soundest and yet most advanced tactical and strategic theories of the time. Those theories cannot be fully tested until war comes, which means that errors are inevitable, and the nation which has made the fewest mistakes has a tremendous advantage. Some important adjustments may be made during the course of a war, but in doing so it is imperative to avoid the pitfalls of hasty generalization from inconclusive data. Ordinarily it takes years of hard thinking and debate and the most exhaustive examination of accumulated evidence to digest even the tactical lessons of a war. No such luxury is permitted during wartime. Every engagement must, however, be considered in the light not only of what *did* happen but also of what *might* have happened had various controlling circumstances been somewhat different. Future events are as likely to follow the pattern of the alternative "might have" as they are the recorded reality—more so, in fact, since history has a horror of exact repetition.

The Battleship

THE battleship represents the hitting power of a navy in its most copious, compact, and durable form. It has traditionally constituted, in company with its like, the navy's chief means of defeating the largest concentrated force which the enemy can place at sea; and the fulfilment of that objective is the primary purpose of the battleship, some would say its exclusive purpose. It is clearly too much to say, as some do, that the isolated battleship has no strategic meaning, that it is always intended to form part of a battle fleet; but it ought not be appraised in terms of its lack of adaptability to functions for which it has never been intended. One could do without battleships if the enemy had none. Or one could do without them even if the enemy had some, provided those the enemy had could *with certainty* be defeated or sunk by other and cheaper means whenever they attempted to dispute the control of communications. But if those other means are relatively unreliable or in the aggregate more costly than a battleship fleet superior to the enemy's, the battleship remains the key to command of the sea.

Many who have been impressed with the striking successes against battleships scored by much smaller vessels and particularly by airplanes have questioned the utility of the battleship. They point to Taranto, to Pearl Harbor, and to the destruction of the *Prince of Wales* and *Repulse* off Malaya. The battleship, they insist, is definitely outmoded. It is the sentimental fetish of the purblind admirals, the weak reed of the nations who have leaned upon it. As one air enthusiast put it, "What have battleships been able to do in this war but sink?" These questions will be dealt with more adequately in a later chapter; but the very examples cited, when looked at from another point of view, bear out the momentous role of the battleship.

The disabling of three battleships at Taranto upset the entire strategic position in the Mediterranean; it gave the British for the first time, a clear, even though temporary, ascendancy in that sea. At Pearl Harbor only a handful, relatively, of all the warships in the United States Navy were injured or destroyed; but since that handful included a number of battleships, the whole strategic situation in the Pacific was catastrophically altered. The Pacific Fleet was unable to advance into the western Pacific where it was most needed, and a whole train of tragic events inexorably followed. Japan made enormous political sacrifices in order to be able to inflict that damage, and congratulated herself after the event on what she had accomplished. And the destruction of the *Prince of Wales* and the *Repulse* greatly hastened the fall of Singapore.

Moreover, it must ever be remembered that British-American control of the North Atlantic, which is the keystone to the entire strategy of the United Nations, rests fundamentally on a battleship superiority over the Axis. Never, it might be said, have so many nations owed so much to so few ships.

Battleships have sometimes proved vulnerable to torpedo attack, whether by airplane or other means; they have also proved able for the most part to carry on their traditional functions. Loss of two capital ships off Malaya must not obscure the fact that by far the greater part of British battleships have remained afloat and active. Great naval wars have never been fought without loss of important ships.

Since its chief purpose is to fight the strongest forces which the enemy can send to sea, the battleship is designed to give and take the heaviest blows that modern science can devise and to be able to assert its strength almost anywhere on the high seas. But maximum firepower, maximum protection, and maximum mobility are conflicting ends. The only way they can be at all reconciled is by giving the vessel great size. The characteristics which identify the battleship are thus its great size, tremendous weight of armor, and huge guns.

The replacement of wood by iron in shipbuilding about the middle of the nineteenth century made the large modern ship possible, and the application at about the same time of iron armor to the fighting vessel made large dimensions desirable. Nevertheless, the great growth in the size of the battleship since the introduction of those changes has on the whole been remarkably gradual. The chief reason for this has been what the economist calls the principle of diminishing returns, which in plain language means the principle of getting the most for your money. Weighing the cost of a ship against its military utility will usually indicate roughly its proper dimensions. If, for example, a 60,000-ton ship would cost twice as much as a 40,000-tonner, as it well might, and if under expected conditions of warfare it would have less military value than two of the 40,000-ton size, the lesser size will obviously be preferable.

Naturally, a great many other factors will limit the size of the battleship, such as the depth of strategic canals and harbors, the length and width of locks (the beam of American battleships is limited by the 110-foot locks of the Panama Canal, though the German *Bismarck's* have a 118-foot beam), the size of available drydocks, and above all the characteristics of existing ships, both in rival navies and in one's own. During wartime or imminent threat of war, considerations of building time come to the fore, since a vessel in commission may be worth infinitely more than a better one on the building ways.

Curiously enough, international agreement has played a rather small role historically in limiting the size of the battleship. The first such agreement was made in 1922 in the Treaty of Washington and was continued in several subsequent treaties. Yet by the beginning of the Second World War, only the British *Rodney* and *Nelson* had been directly affected by those treaties, which imposed a limit of 35,000 tons standard displacement. All but a few existing battleships had been built before those treaties went into effect, and the few built during the treaty period were of considerably less tonnage than the limits permitted. On the other hand, though the battleships under construction in 1939 had for the most part been begun after the treaties had ceased to be effective, the blueprints for them had been drawn up during the treaty regime. Moreover, the agreements which limited size had also limited building, or a great many more battleships would have been affected.

In recent ships the proportion of tonnage devoted to armor has gone above the 40 per cent mark. The 35,000-ton *Richelieu*, for example, was given 15,000 tons of armor, and there is every indication that the new battleships in the American, British, and German navies have a comparable or perhaps even greater weight of protection. This prodigious burden of armor is, however, by no means spread over the entire vessel, for in order to make the plating thick enough where it is most needed, it is necessary to restrict its coverage. The side armor on some ships, such as the *Nelson* or the new *North Carolina*, is taken up mostly by a belt over the long central portion which houses the barbettes and the ship's vitals, with perhaps a few offshoots to protect propeller shafts and the like, but very little elsewhere.

The heaviest armor on the vessel is found on the faces of the gunhouses or turrets, and on the conning tower, where it may reach as much as 18 inches in thickness. The belt along the waterline may be 14 to 16 inches thick, but the portion of maximum thickness is only about nine feet wide. Just below the waterline the armor begins to taper down to more slender proportions. Most of the remaining vertical armor

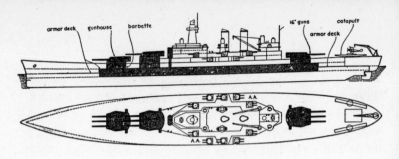

U.S. BATTLESHIP "NORTH CAROLINA"

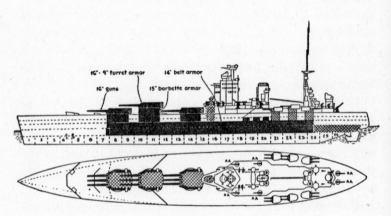

BRITISH BATTLESHIP "NELSON"

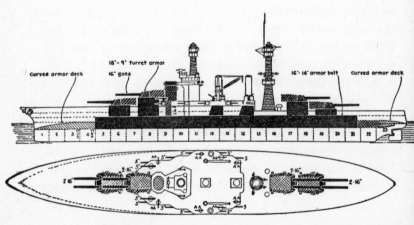

U.S. BATTLESHIP "WEST VIRGINIA"

on the ship is found on the barbettes, which are the vertical cylinders atop which the gunhouses are perched and which open below to the magazines. The actual gauge of armor applied at any place depends always on the importance of the position protected, its exposure to fire, and the probable angle of impact of shells which may strike it.

As a protection against aerial bombs and against high-angle shell fire there are two "protective decks," the heavier of which, called the "principal armored deck," used to be placed at the waterline where it covered the ship's vitals. Above the principal armor deck (third deck) was the armored main deck, which was more lightly plated and intended mainly to stop light case air bombs and light shell and bring them to explosion. Naturally, it also helped the lower deck to withstand the impact of heavy bombs and of heavy plunging shell. In the later types of battleships, however, the upper armored deck has become the heavier of the two. On the *North Carolina* class the upper armored deck is 6 inches and the lower deck 4 inches thick.

It is worth noting that armor decks were used on warships long before the development of the airplane bomber, and even now the heaviest impact which the armor decks are called upon to bear is not from bombs but from plunging shell. Since the modern battleship has a very broad beam and since combat today is characterized by long-range fire, which means highly arched trajectories, horizontal armor is increasing in importance as compared to belt armor. In fact, it is likely that the battleship of the future will abandon belts of side armor altogether in favor of an arched or "turtle-back" protective deck, the sloping sides of which would be heavily plated. This would mean a return to the type of armor defense which characterized the so-called "protected cruisers" of the latter nineteenth century.

Modern armor is relatively little improved over the fa-

mous Krupp's Cemented or "K.C." armor which revolutionized the ballistic standard about forty-five years ago. The
term "cemented" refers to the process by which the tough
special alloy steel is given an exceedingly hard face to break
up projectiles striking it. There are, however, several kinds
of armor, or "ballistic steel" as the naval architect likes to
call it. Three or four different kinds will be used on the same
vessel, depending mostly on the position, purpose, and thickness of the plating used. Modern armor plates have a resistance to shot about three times that of wrought iron,
which formed the plating of the original armorclads and
which remained in use until about 1881. Heavy ballistic plate
is extraordinarily expensive and difficult to manufacture, and
the problem of providing it has presented one of the chief bot-
tlenecks in the current American naval building program.

As a defense against torpedo or mine damage the battleship is provided with a "protective layer," popularly called
the "bulge," though the bulge or "blister" of the modernized
older vessels is only a small part of the protective layer (comparable to compartment A in the accompanying diagram).
This layer, which is more akin in its operation to a shock ab-
sorber than to a plate of armor, is of considerable depth and
runs along the side of the vessel just inside the skin. It should
be noticed that even when a deep and especially effective protective layer prevents the flooding of the interior of the ship,
the portion which absorbs the shock is usually destroyed in
the process and must be repaired.

For further protection against underwater explosions, the
whole length of the lower hull including the protective layer
on each side is subdivided by transverse bulkheads into twenty-
five to thirty compartments, each of which extends across the
hull. Any flooding of the interior resulting from a rupture on
either side will thus affect only a restricted portion of the
vessel and will be partially distributed across the ship (i.e. to

26

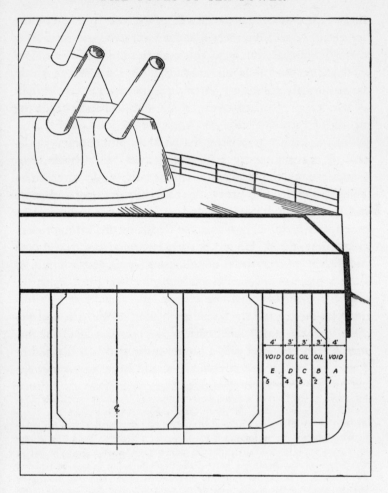

4' 3' 3' 3' 4'

VOID OIL OIL OIL VOID

E   D   C   B   A

5   4   3   2   1

The above diagram shows the 17-foot deep protective layer on the *West Virginia*. The layer is divided by longitudinal bulkheads into five compartments inside the skin of the ship, of which the three center ones (B, C, D) are filled with fuel oil while the two outer ones (A, E) are left as air spaces. The skin brings the torpedo to explosion and is ruptured. The compressible air in compartment A tends to absorb the expanding gases vented into the ship by the explosion and to distribute their force against bulkhead No. 1. The oil in compartments B, C, and D takes up much of the inside limit of the opposite protective layer). On the underside of the ship there is at least a double and sometimes a triple bottom. The subdivision of the hull into numerous compartments extends also above the waterline, where it is in fact especially extensive, particularly in unarmored portions of the hull. The effects of exploding shell or bombs inside the vessel are thus localized.

Recent events have proved that the contemporary battleship is not sufficiently protected against the torpedo, particularly since the airplane has joined the ranks of torpedo-launching craft. This proves not that the battleship is obsolete but that its anti-torpedo protection must be improved. This can clearly be done, provided the designers are willing to sacrifice some speed. Under existing circumstances, the 27- to more than 30-knot speed of the more recent battleships is of little avail. The *Bismarck* was slowed down from about 30-knot top speed to something approaching zero knots by a torpedo hit on her rudder which jammed it to one side, and the 23-knot *Rodney* was able easily to overtake her. Had the *Bismarck* been provided with a tunnel stern, that is, an enclosure round her rudder and screws, she would have been somewhat

---

the shock by its inertia, and by its incompressibility causes bulkheads 2, 3, and 4 to help withstand the shock simultaneously with bulkhead 1. Compartment E is left as a compressible void so that bulkhead 5 does not share in withstanding the major shock but serves as a flooding boundary in case bulkheads 2, 3, and 4 are ruptured, which they usually are. The oil in the center compartments is a part of the ship's fuel, but it may be replaced by water as it is consumed. Water serves even better than oil, because it absorbs much of the terrific heat of the explosion and thus reduces its intensity. Notice that if the skin is not heavy enough to withstand rupture—which it never is in present models—it must be very thin. Any intermediate gauge of steel would simply add large fragments to the torpedo fragments which help to destroy the bulkheads. The *West Virginia* represents only one type of protective layer. There are others, some of which comprise a more minutely divided cellular construction with "blow-out" patches on each cell, or perhaps some filler like cork or corn-pith in place of air, especially in the interior compartments.

slower to begin with but probably would have escaped her fate. Three of the four torpedo hits scored against her by British aircraft were taken on her exceptionally deep and effective protective layers and did comparatively minor damage.

The 30-knot *Prince of Wales* also was stopped and made an easy target for destruction by a torpedo hit in the stern. The sacrifice of protection for speed is hardly a profitable transaction when speed vanishes so quickly in the face of attack. Of course, with greater dimensions or power the necessary protection can be acquired without giving up recent gains in speed.

It is likely, too, that the protection of the future will have to be designed not only to keep the battleship from sinking but also to keep it from being laid up for prolonged periods after each torpedo hit. This could be done either by having some device bring the torpedo to explosion *before* it hit the ship's side (several devices which promise to accomplish that end are being developed) or by extending the armor belt to the bottom of the ship.

Despite the great emphasis on protection in the battleship, it is armament and not armor that makes a fighting ship. The battleship is a mobile, floating gun platform. It is built around the guns it carries, and its protection is provided for the sole purpose of keeping those guns in action or available for action. The guns for which it is built are the few large rifles which comprise its primary armament. The so-called "secondary armament" and anti-aircraft guns are essentially defensive in character, intended primarily to help protect the vessel against torpedo and bombing attack.

In 1905 the British laid down a vessel, the *Dreadnought*, which carried ten of the heaviest naval guns then being made, the 12-inch caliber. Up to that time the armament of the standard battleship had consisted of four heavy guns and several medium guns, besides the light caliber quick-firers. The "all-big-gun" *Dreadnought* revolutionized naval design. All battleships laid down since its completion in 1906 have carried a primary armament of eight to fourteen [1] identical guns of large caliber. The *Dreadnought* gave its name to the general type of capital ship which it inaugurated, and when guns larger than 12-inch caliber were introduced on the British *Orion* class (1909), the term "super-dreadnought" also came into use. During the first World War marked distinctions were drawn between the many existing predreadnoughts and the dreadnoughts (the latter term usually included super-dreadnoughts), which differed greatly in fighting qualities. But since no battleships of predreadnought type survive among the major powers, the use of the terms "dreadnought" or "super-dreadnought" in reference to modern ships is mere rhetorical flourish.

The lightest primary armament on any recently built battleship are the 11-inch guns of the German *Gneisenau* and *Scharnhorst*. These ships are to a degree atavisms. Their gun caliber is a throw-back to the pre-1914 period; and by their contrast with other modern battleships they revive memories of the latter nineteenth century, when battleship designs were usually carried out in two sizes, the smaller being known as "second-class battleships." They are hardly a match, ship for ship, for other modern battleships, and cannot be explained except as super commerce raiders.

On the other hand, the *Gneisenau* and *Scharnhorst* have proved useful to the Axis powers and Japan far beyond their actual fighting power, not only by sinking the British aircraft carrier *Glorious* and other ships but particularly by the fact that their threat value, added to that of the *Tirpitz* and her

[1] The British *Agincourt* which fought at Jutland carried fourteen 12-inch guns, but no battleship existing at this writing carries more than twelve heavy guns, and most newer types carry from eight to ten.

sisters, neutralized modern British and American battleships which might otherwise have been sent to the Mediterranean or Pacific. The many efforts made against them by British aircraft and other vessels, particularly during their dash up the English Channel on February 12, 1942, when the British lost at least forty-two aircraft, show the concern of the British over these two ships. They do not have the power of other contemporary battleships, but since they are quite heavily armored, they cannot be neutralized by vessels of less than capital ship size; and since they are fast they require the attention of the newest battleships.

The newer battleships of the British and American navies carry guns of either 16-inch or 14-inch caliber. All naval guns are of the type called "rifles," a term which nowadays distinguishes them not from smoothbores but from the shorter-barreled and shorter-ranged howitzers and mortars common in land artillery.[2] The large naval rifle is a weapon of almost fantastic range, accuracy, and striking power. The British 16-inch gun can hurl a shell weighing 2,460 pounds to a distance of over 40,000 yards. The 15-inch gun used on several of the older vessels of the British Navy fires a shell weighing 1,920 pounds, and the new 14-inch guns of the *King George V* class fire a projectile of 1,560 pounds. The American guns of equivalent caliber have somewhat different characteristics— the American 16-inch gun, for example, fires a projectile of 2,100 pounds—but they are generally comparable in power to the British. The 14-inch type is not necessarily of lesser range and accuracy than the 16-inch gun, but is bound to have a lesser hitting power. After their experience with the *Bismarck*, the British probably regret building five new battleships with only 14-inch guns.

---

[2] It has been reported, however, that some of the Japanese lighter ships are fitted with howitzers for use in landing operations. It is more likely that guns of the usual type are fitted for high angle, *i.e.* howitzer-like, fire.

The guns of the battleship are calibrated to fire in exact parallel alignment (or with slight, pre-determined convergence or divergence), and since they are usually aimed together, a salvo (two or more shells fired at once) will produce a compact pattern of shot in the vicinity of the target. This pattern is then shifted as a unit until it is centered on the target, at which time the target is said to be "straddled." The observation of the fire to secure the proper adjustments in range and bearing, which is called "spotting," may be done not only from the control tower of the battleship itself but from a cruiser or aircraft. The latter will usually have a much better vantage point out of the smoke of battle, though recent developments are reducing dependence on visual spotting.

The amazing accuracy of long-range fire is due primarily to the spotting, but wastage of shells and loss of effectiveness in the initial stages of the firing are kept down by aiming the first salvos as accurately as possible. The process of laying the guns before opening fire involves all sorts of abstruse data, including even an allowance for the rotation of the earth during the time of flight of the projectile, but the computation is done almost automatically in amazingly brief time. A gyroscopic device can be used to regulate the firing so that it occurs always at the same stage of the ship's roll. The gunnery officer in the director tower gives the guns their bearing and fires them not by mere verbal directions to the turrets but by automatic control. He manipulates a sort of super-gunsight called the "director" with which the turret is synchronously connected and by which the guns are laid. The fire-control gear which includes such devices must of course consist of the most elaborate and costly mechanisms. The gear of the *King George V* laid down in 1939 cost £213,000, which happens to be about twenty times the cost of the fire-control gear for the *King George V* of 1912. The large naval gun itself has not changed very materially in the last thirty years, but fire control has been totally transformed—and a wholly new device which has completely revolutionized gunnery control, including anti-aircraft fire, has been perfected.

The battleship distinguishes its own shots in the vicinity of the target from those of its consorts by a timing device, automatically adjusted to range, which buzzes in the control tower when the shells are due to strike. The star-shell, which contains a parachute flare and is fired from the secondary armament, much enhances the effectiveness of night fire, though it is often possible under modern conditions to dispense with illumination of targets.

A curious incident relative to the timing of shells in flight occurred at the Battle of the River Plate (or Montevideo). The British cruisers dropped depth charges overboard at the time the shells of the *Graf Spee* were due to strike, which much confused the latter's fire since the depth charge explosions were indistinguishable from shell splashes. The German gunnery officer did not know he had been thus deceived until some time after the battle.

It is difficult to conceive of gunfire at thirteen miles—the distance at which the *Hood* was destroyed by the *Bismarck*—being more accurate than aerial bombing from only 2,000 feet elevation, but gunfire is in fact the more accurate.[3] Two things are chiefly responsible. First, two ships in combat tend to change position relative to each other at a comparatively slow rate, even when both are in rapid motion. They frequently move along nearly parallel courses and at almost identical speeds. If one maneuvers rapidly to dodge the fire of the other, it thereby diminishes its own chances for accurate fire (or pursuit or flight), and it will therefore refrain from too

[3] The *Hood* was destroyed by the second or third salvo fired by the *Bismarck*, which opened fire at 23,000 yards. This performance was bettered in November 1942 by one of our new battleships, which at 26,000 yards hit the *Jean Bart* with her first salvo and put her out of action with a second.

33

much dodging unless greatly inferior in strength to the enemy. Besides, dodging gunfire can be little but guesswork, as there is no way of estimating the fall of the next salvo. Against bombing, however, the ship can be intelligently maneuvered. It is far more important to avoid dropped bombs than to score hits with anti-aircraft guns—which, incidentally, are not so much affected by the movements of the ship as the larger guns. Various weather conditions may, of course, favor either gunfire or bombing; but certain new devices are permitting ships to fire at totally unseen targets.

Secondly, the bearing of guns can be constantly and finely readjusted according to the results of shots already registered, while the airplane, which has only one or two large bombs to drop anyway, must make an entirely new run for each attack. Dive-bombers have attempted to remedy this disadvantage by diving in formation, with the last pilot taking his bearing from the results achieved by the pilots ahead of him, but that is a rough rule-of-thumb method compared to the fine corrections used in gunfire. On the other hand, a large formation of bombers can in level flight drop its bombs in such a pattern that evasion becomes very difficult.

Even more significant than the matter of accuracy, the gun is greatly superior to the bomber in the power of penetration of its shell. Against battleships, at any rate, the projectile that counts is the one that can pierce heavy armor, and perforation depends mainly on two things: total kinetic energy of impact and velocity of impact. The two are distinct, even though velocity enters conspicuously into the equation for kinetic energy, which is $KE = \dfrac{MV^2}{2}$, where M is the mass or weight of the projectile and V the velocity. Since the velocity is squared, an increase in velocity does much more to raise the total kinetic energy of impact than a corresponding increase in mass. Besides, raising the total kinetic energy by increasing the weight of the projectile will not suffice unless a certain minimum velocity is reached, because of the peculiarities of steel as a resister of shot. When a shell hits at high velocity, there is no opportunity for the portion of armor against which it strikes to transmit the shock to surrounding portions, owing to the inertia of the molecules in the armor. At low velocities, however, the armor around the area of direct impact helps to take up the burden of the shock. Moreover, high velocity of impact reduces strain on the projectile during penetration and prevents it from breaking up (unless the hit be at very oblique angles, in which case high velocity favors disintegration of the projectile).

A bomb is at present propelled only by the force of gravity, and acceleration proceeds only to the point where gravity is equalized by air resistance. In other words, as the bomb falls its velocity approaches a limit. That "terminal velocity" has in fact never been attained, because it would require a drop from a higher altitude than any yet reached by aircraft; but for heavy bombs it has been computed to be about 1,000 feet per second. To be sure, a drop from 16,000 feet will give a 1,600-pound armor-piercing bomb impact velocity enough (about 860 ft. sec.) to penetrate almost 8 inches of armor, but hits at such altitudes against maneuvering ships are extremely unlikely. The same bomb dropped at 2,000 feet from a rapidly diving bomber has an impact velocity of only 450 feet per second and will be totally stopped by 4 inches of armor.

A large shell, on the other hand, is ejected from the muzzle of the gun at about 2,800 feet per second. Of course, air resistance immediately begins to slow it down—although at long range a great part of the arched trajectory of the shell passes through rarefied atmosphere—but it nevertheless retains upon impact against the target a far greater velocity than the bomb—about 1,500 feet per second even at extreme ranges.

The final advantage of the battleship's guns over the bomber is that each gun when fired needs only to be reloaded to fire again—for a brief period a large gun can fire at the rate of three shells per minute—while the bomber is essentially a weapon of but a few shots. Upon dropping its meager load the airplane has to return to its base for more. The battleship with its eight to twelve large guns is thus capable of a tremendous volume of accurate, powerful fire. Fifteen battleships of the *North Carolina* class could fire in one hour their entire load of 13,500 large shells of over a ton each, or above four times the load of bombs dropped in the great R.A.F. raid on Cologne in May 1942. During rapid fire such a fleet could be hurling huge shells at a rate of 400 per minute. What this means in volume of explosives can be seen from the fact that in the worst raid on the city of London during the period 1940–1941, about 600 tons of bombs were dropped in a twenty-four-hour period.

When the British bombarded Genoa on February 9, 1941, the two capital ships that took part hurled, with devastating accuracy, 270 one-ton shells in less than half an hour, though one of those ships was the battle cruiser *Renown*, whose primary armament comprised only six guns. The British suffered no loss to their surface craft in the operation. The large air fleet that would have been necessary to carry out a similar task during daylight would very likely have suffered substantial losses. In their action against the *Bismarck* on May 27, 1941, the *King George V* and the *Rodney* fired approximately 700 large shells in about an hour and a half of fighting. That shelling was described in some newspapers as "perfunctory," but the fact is that before it began the *Bismarck* was a floating fortress capable of striking the same kind of blows that made such short shrift of the *Hood*, while at its close she was a helpless, battered hulk, incapable of defending herself even against the cruiser which closed in for the *coup de grâce*.

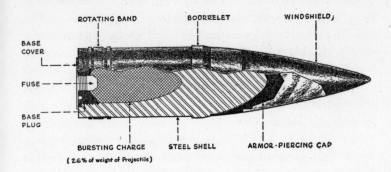

14" ARMOR-PIERCING PROJECTILE

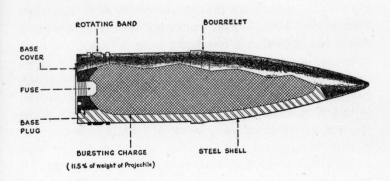

14" BOMBARDMENT PROJECTILE

When fired against enemy battleships, the shell used by the larger guns will always be of the armor-piercing type. Such shells must be of hard, tough steel throughout and must have a blunt head and exceptionally thick walls. To keep down air resistance a thin, easily breakable pointed tip called the windshield is placed over the blunt head. But the diminished length and thick walls of the inner body greatly reduce the amount of explosive contained in the shell, which is one of the reasons ships carry armor even though that armor is penetrable under certain conditions by existing ordnance. The shell that has to push its way through armor will not have nearly the blasting effect of a non-armor-piercing shell or bomb.

The several navies have differed greatly in their attitude toward the relative advantages of thick armor as against high speed. The Italian Navy has notoriously favored sacrificing armor for speed. The United States Navy, on the other hand, has always gone all out for the heaviest protection possible without sacrifice of armament, which means that mobility must suffer. The American battle line is the slowest among the great powers, some U. S. battleships having speeds of less than 21 knots. Even the new *North Carolina's* are somewhat slower than foreign contemporaries. The American theory has been that a few knots more or less make little difference in combat, especially since torpedo hits by destroyers and aircraft are likely to slow down both sides considerably anyway. However, slowness may have strategic as well as tactical disadvantages. The speedier side usually has the choice of giving or accepting battle, and while engaged it can dictate the range.

Battleships take a long time to build, and the facilities for their construction cannot be rapidly expanded. That means that the basic naval position of a nation at war is likely to stand or fall upon its peacetime accumulation of capital ships, unless there is a high wartime mortality among that class. Vessels already on the building ways when war begins may be completed during the war, but it is unlikely that any substantial disparity in capital ship strength between the belligerents will be reversed during the course of the conflict by the building efforts of the inferior power.

Because of this building-time factor, the great significance which some journalists professed to see in the fact that the naval appropriations made by Congress in May and June 1942 did not include provision for battleships has no real basis. Battleships authorized in 1942 would not be ready before the probable conclusion of the war at least in Europe, and the large number of battleships already under construction was sufficient, when added to existing strength, to assure us of overwhelming superiority in this class over our enemies. That superiority being assured, we could afford to concentrate on other types, for which our needs were more pressing at the moment. Ships for the post-war period could wait. In the latter stages of the first World War the British gave up the construction of battleships for the same reasons.

A final characteristic of the battleship that deserves to be stressed, particularly in view of the arguments that it might be replaced by cheaper weapons, is its longevity—in peacetime, at any rate. The life span of a battleship is defined by international treaties and by the domestic law of the United States to be twenty-six years. In 1942, several battleships of the various belligerents were of that age and even older. Of the twelve battleships with which Britain began the Second World War (the remaining three of her capital ships were battle cruisers), six were veterans of Jutland, and four others were sisters of ships that fought at Jutland. Only two battleships and one battle cruiser had been completed after the first World War. The old ships had been largely reconstructed and modernized, but modernization by no means equals the cost of a new ship. The battleship is an expensive but also a long-term investment in sea power.

Other Capital Ships

THE term "capital ship" has only recently appeared in naval literature, being used officially for the first time in the Washington Treaty of 1922. Apparently it grew out of the development of the "battle cruiser" type, which was distinct from the battleship and yet merited a rank comparable to it. Recent naval treaties have defined "capital ships" as being surface vessels of war, other than aircraft carriers, mounting guns of a caliber exceeding eight inches and displacing more than 10,000 tons.

The battle cruiser type was developed in the British Navy in the years preceding the first World War, and copied by other navies, in order to provide a powerful scouting force, one that could "press home a reconnaissance." It was not built primarily to fight in the line, yet its displacement was as great as or greater than the largest battleships of the time and its guns equal to theirs in caliber. But in order to attain high speed it sacrificed some guns and a good deal of armor. The *Queen Mary*, for example, the greatest of the British battle cruisers at Jutland, displaced 4,000 tons more than the contemporary battleships of the *King George V* class, but carried only eight 13.5-inch guns as against the ten of the latter ships and an armor belt with a maximum thickness of 9 inches as against the 12 inches of the *King George V's*.

The brilliant performance of two battle cruisers in moving swiftly from England to the Falkland Islands and destroying Admiral von Spee's squadron there in a pursuing action on December 8, 1914, made this type extremely popular, and all navies, including our own, immediately planned a large battle cruiser program. The Battle of Jutland on May 31, 1916, however, gave some pause to this trend, for the only dreadnought-type capital ships destroyed among the fifty-eight engaged were four of the fifteen battle cruisers. The British lost three of their nine, the *Indefatigable, Queen Mary,* and *Invincible,* and in each case the vessel blew up after receiving only a very few hits. The Germans lost the *Lützow,* but that vessel had taken a good deal more punishment than any of the British battle cruisers, which can be explained primarily by the fact that the German battle cruisers were much more heavily armored than the British.

The destruction of the British ships was undoubtedly facilitated by the exposed condition of the British powder charges—in at least two cases flashes are supposed to have passed down a turret to the magazine. But the fact remains that the lightly armored ships perished quickly while the four heavily armored *Queen Elizabeth* battleships came under extremely heavy fire without suffering serious damage. And if this be not sufficient evidence, the quick destruction at the hands of the *Bismarck* twenty-five years later of the greatest of the battle cruisers, the *Hood,* should make clear the importance of protection, since the British had long since corrected the faulty arrangements of Jutland. The *Hood* was the most heavily armored of the battle cruisers and at the time of her destruction probably the largest warship in the world, yet she was more thinly protected than any contemporary British battleship.

By 1942 the sole survivor among the British battle cruisers was the *Renown,* originally a sister ship to the *Repulse* but subsequently modernized into a somewhat different ship. Before her modernization in 1938, the *Renown* had an armor belt of a maximum of 9 inches thickness, which contrasts strikingly with the 13-inch belt of the older *Queen Elizabeth's.* Moreover, the *Queen Elizabeth's* carry eight 15-inch guns, while the *Renown* carries only six such guns. The only compensation for this relative weakness is four or five knots better top speed in the battle cruiser.

The battle cruiser type is now relatively obsolete, inasmuch as the most heavily protected modern battleships can be given speeds as great as or exceeding that of the battle cruisers built a quarter-century ago. On the other hand, the battle cruisers have been the only old capital ships which have been able to share missions with the newest battleships. The *Hood* at the time of her destruction was operating with the *Prince of Wales*, and the *Repulse* was also with the *Prince of Wales* at the time both were sunk off Malaya. The *Hood* and *Repulse* were 31-knot and 29-knot ships respectively, which made them good companions for the 30-knot *Prince of Wales*.

It is sometimes difficult to tell where the battle cruiser type ends and the battleship begins. The four older Italian battleships of the *Cavour* class were given light armor and made capable of 27 knots. This made them more comparable to the battle cruisers than to the battleships among their British contemporaries. And the new fashion is to call any fast battleship of less than average size (e.g. *Gneisenau* or *Dunkerque*) a "battle cruiser," while our *Alaskas* now building are officially designated as such.

The most atypical among modern capital ships, if they may be called such, are the German "pocket battleships," originally three in number, the *Admiral Graf Spee*, the *Admiral Scheer*, and the *Lützow* (formerly *Deutschland*). The German Navy does not regard them as battleships at all, but classifies them simply as *Panzerschiffe* or "armored ships." These vessels are generally agreed to be abortions, the result of building according to treaty limitations rather than tactical or strategic considerations. The Treaty of Versailles limited Germany to vessels of no more than 10,000 tons. By using Diesel engines, electrical welding instead of rivets, and by keeping side armor down to a maximum of 4 inches thickness, the Germans were able to build vessels within the 10,000-ton displacement figure which were yet capable of mounting six 11-inch guns and of making a speed of 26 knots. Ton for ton,

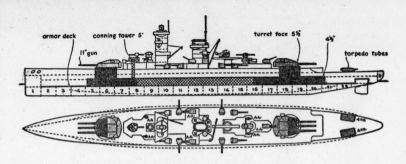

German armored ship "Admiral Scheer"

armor deck
conning tower 5"
11" gun
turret face 5½
4½"
torpedo tubes

GERMAN ARMORED SHIP "ADMIRAL SCHEER"

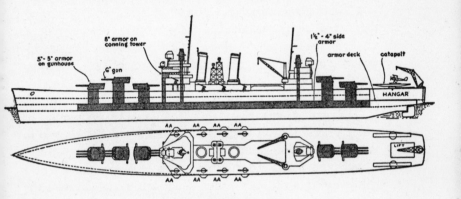

8" armor on conning tower
5"- 5" armor on gunhouse
6" gun
1½" - 4" side armor
armor deck
catapult
HANGAR

U.S. LIGHT CRUISER BROOKLYN

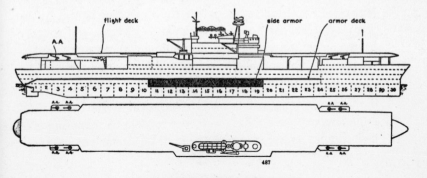

flight deck
A.A
side armor
armor deck

487

U. S. AIRCRAFT CARRIER "ENTERPRISE"
Complement 83 Aircraft (capacity over 100)

however, these ships were clearly the costliest of their time.

The British and French feared that the pocket battleships would be extremely dangerous as commerce raiders, since at the time of their completion it was thought that only the three battle cruisers in the British Navy were capable both of overtaking and of outfighting them. The Battle of the River Plate, however, proved that three lighter vessels, if well handled, are capable of dealing with a pocket battleship, even though two of the three cruisers concerned were of the "light" or 6-inch gun type, and in fact carried only eight such guns each. The great weakness of the *Admiral Graf Spee* was its light protection, which hardly exceeded that of some cruisers.

Upon the appearance of the pocket battleships, France proceeded to build an "answer" in the form of two moderate-sized battleships (or battle cruisers), the *Dunkerque* and the *Strasbourg*, each of 26,500 tons displacement, 30 knots speed, 11-inch armor, and eight 13-inch guns. The completion of these vessels as well as of the *Gneisenau* and *Scharnhorst* in 1935–1936 demonstrates that many factors other than treaty stipulations may limit the dimensions of capital ships. These vessels were about 9,000 tons under the treaty limits of the time. But two ships, each of which is big enough, are much better than one ship which is more than big enough. The French did not expect to fight the British. They built two vessels capable of dealing with the German pocket battleships and light battleships. The Germans, on the other hand, knew they could not stand up to either the French or British battle line, and certainly not to a combination of both, and concentrated on building vessels of maximum nuisance value. Shortly afterwards, however, both France and Germany proceeded to construct battleships comparable to the best of any other power.

The Cruiser

THE object of naval warfare is to control maritime communications. In order to exercise that control effectively there must be a numerous class of vessels specially adapted for patrol. These must be fast, of long range, at least powerfully enough armed to cope easily with any armed merchantman, and yet inexpensive, since costliness conflicts directly with the requirement of large numbers. It so happens that the better of the vessels with these qualifications are also admirably adapted to service with the battle fleet as scouts and as a defense against destroyer-torpedo attack. There has therefore always been a demand on the part of the battle fleet for more vessels of the cruiser type, of which there are never enough to fill all needs.

But whether used as a scout for the battle fleet or on detached missions in the commerce lanes, the cruiser is designed under the burden of a dilemma. Regardless of how strong a battle fleet cover may be, it cannot absolutely protect cruisers from disturbance by sporadic attack. There is always a danger that even a closely blockaded enemy will be able to get one or more powerful vessels onto the shipping lanes. A cruiser is therefore not sufficiently armed if it is designed to cope merely with armed merchantmen. It must be able to fight enemy warships. But what are to be the limits of its power? This dilemma can hardly be solved by any mathematical formula.

The cruiser is the type of vessel which above all others has pressed against the upper limits of size. It is tending always to develop into an intermediate type approaching the battleship in fighting power, but as it does so it begins to lose its whole reason for being. The history of the cruiser type is a history of constant tendency upward in power punctuated by periodic and drastic adjustments downward.

Some years before the first World War, a type of warship

common in all navies was the "armored cruiser." These displaced from 9,000 to over 12,000 tons, carried armor belts as much as 8 inches thick and guns as large as 10-inch caliber. The Italian Navy had one of this type, the *San Giorgio*, completed in 1908, until January 22, 1941, when it was destroyed at Tobruk. Some armored cruisers actually had a greater displacement than contemporary battleships and almost as much armor, and in the Sino-Japanese War of 1894–1895, the Spanish-American War, and the Russo-Japanese War they were used in the battle line along with battleships. They differed from the later battle cruisers mainly in that their primary armament was of lesser caliber than the battleships of their time, while battle cruisers always carried the same guns as contemporary battleships. The armored cruisers were, however, too weak to make good battleships and too expensive as cruisers.

The modern cruiser is a compromise between the small, light cruiser of World War days and the old armored cruiser. It is a vessel of from 5,000 to 10,000 tons, armed with from six to as many as fifteen identical medium-caliber guns, besides anti-aircraft armament and torpedo tubes. It is classed as a "light" or "heavy" cruiser, depending not on displacement but on the caliber of its primary armament. By treaty definition, light cruisers are those which carry guns of under 6.1-inch caliber, and heavy cruisers are those which carry guns of from 6.1-inch caliber to 8-inch caliber. Almost all existing "heavy" cruisers are armed with the 8-inch gun.

The naval limitation treaties of the inter-war period limited the cruiser's size to 10,000 tons and its gun caliber to 8 inches. The immediate result was that every nation raced to build up to that displacement and gun power regardless of strategic requirements or experience. Great Britain, particularly, was dissatisfied with the outcome, finding herself with a number of large and expensive but unduly vulnerable vessels, and shortly returned to smaller vessels and to the 6-inch gun type exclusively. She retained the 6-inch gun even in the few 10,000-ton cruisers which she continued to build. This change in policy is simply an additional evidence of the unsatisfactoriness of intermediate types.

The United States, needing fewer cruisers than Great Britain, has in general elected to build somewhat larger types. While the British have a good number of 5,200 and 5,400 tons, the American Navy until recently had none under 7,000 tons. New construction includes the 8-inch gun *Baltimore* class, to displace 13,000 tons each. These will be even more heavily armored than the *Wichita*, and will cost $24,000,000 each without armament. The new, speedy *Atlanta* class of cruisers, however, are of 6,000 tons. Until recently, also, the United States had more heavy cruisers than light cruisers, but most of the recent building has been in the 6-inch gun type.

The newer light cruisers of the American Navy swarm with guns. Each of the numerous *Brooklyn* class carries fifteen 6-inch guns (in five triple turrets) and eight 5-inch anti-aircraft guns, besides smaller weapons. The recent and much more numerous *Cleveland* class have three fewer 6-inch guns but carry twelve 5-inch dual purpose guns of a type much superior to those of the *Brooklyn's* plus a large number of 40 mm. and 20 mm. automatic guns. The peculiarly square stern of the *Brooklyn's* provides for a hangar in which as many as eight aircraft can be stored. This is a radical departure in warship design, since the three aircraft ordinarily carried on cruisers or battleships have hitherto been carried in exposed positions above deck.

The 6-inch gun may seem a light piece compared to the primary armament of a battleship, but it should be remembered that in land warfare a 6-inch rifle is deemed a very large field piece indeed, and hence is relatively uncommon. Most field artillery weapons of comparable caliber are of the

47

howitzer type. A 6-inch shell weighs 100 pounds and can be used quite effectively at ten miles, the distance at which the *Sydney* opened fire on the *Bartolomeo Colleoni* in the action of July 19, 1940, in which the Italian ship was destroyed. The 8-inch gun hurls a shell of about 250 pounds and has greater range and far greater hitting power than the 6-inch weapon, but the 6-inch size can be carried in greater quantity on a vessel of given size and can be fired more rapidly. The volume of fire of the larger light cruisers is tremendous; they are capable of hurling over 150 aimed shells per minute. The French have a 5.5-inch gun on their *Mogador* class light cruisers which has a range of fifteen miles and can be fired at a rate of 16 rounds per minute. These extreme rates of fire, however, can be maintained only for very brief periods.

Although some modern cruisers, particularly a few French and Italian types, are virtually unarmored or have very restricted armor coverage, most of the newer ones have a considerable amount of protection. The American heavy cruiser *Wichita*, the most heavily armored cruiser existing in 1941, has a 5-inch armor belt at the waterline and carries 6-inch armor on the turret faces and 8-inch armor on the conning tower. She also has two armor decks totalling 5 inches in thickness. American cruisers, like American battleships, are rather more heavily protected than those of most other navies, but again as in the case of our battleships we pay for it in speed. Our four new *Atlanta* class cruisers are capable of 38 knots, but most of our others can do only about 32.5 knots. The Italian cruisers, on the other hand, are generally five knots faster than our cruisers or those of the British, and the *Alberico da Barbiano*, completed in 1930, reached 42 knots on its trials. But the high cost of additional speed at top levels is reflected in the fact that our two *Pensacolas* can do 30 knots with but 60 per cent of their power and only 32.7 knots at full power. Besides, ship for ship, our cruisers are more than a match in fighting strength for vessels of corresponding tonnage in most foreign navies, and their strong armor decks stand them in good stead in aerial bombing attack. The *Houston* demonstrated her sturdiness under a heavy barrage of Japanese bombs off Java, though she was later lost in mysterious fashion.

The cruiser has, in general, the longest cruising radius of any surface warship. Our *Brooklyn*'s have a radius at economical speeds of 14,500 sea miles, which is about twice that of the usual battleship. Such endurance, coupled with high speed and reasonably powerful armament, makes the cruiser the ideal vessel for independent missions far from home. She can usually pull away from a more powerful ship and can give a good account of herself with an equal. If she is lost, she does not represent any indispensable element of security.

The cruiser has therefore played a conspicuous part among the "task forces" whose operations figured so prominently in the war in the Pacific during 1942. Because of the paucity of United Nations capital ships in that area, our heavy cruisers often performed missions which would normally have been left to battleships. The *San Francisco* accomplished one of the most brilliant feats in cruiser history when she defeated an old Japanese battleship of the *Kongo* class in the night action off Guadalcanal on November 13, 1942.

CHAPTER III

The Tools of Sea Power (*Continued*)

Aircraft

THE introduction and development of the airplane is one of the two great naval revolutions of the twentieth century, the other being the perfection of submarine warfare. The airplane resembles the diving boat in that it has carried military operations into the third dimension. It is similar also in its capacity for evading the superior enemy, for when warfare enters the third dimension the space of the battlefield is so immense that absolute command is hardly ever possible. Mere superiority in numbers does not give "control" of the air in the same manner in which superiority in surface squadrons can give control of a sea. Only the well-nigh complete destruction of the enemy air arm as an operating force can give command of the air, as the German Luftwaffe discovered over England in the autumn of 1940.

The airplane differs from the submarine, however, in the purpose of its three-dimensional movement. The latter submerges solely for concealment. The airplane may also achieve concealment—in a cloud, in the rays of the sun, in altitude, or in the blackness of night—but this is always incidental to its main purposes in flight, which are elevation for its own sake and extreme rapidity of motion. But the airplane differs most from the submarine and other naval vessels in that its sphere of operation is not limited by coastlines. It moves in an ocean of its own which covers land and sea and which knows no barriers save weather and distance. The land plane can be used at sea and the seaplane over land. This fact gives the air arm great elasticity and makes it difficult to distinguish between naval aviation and other forms of military aviation save by the criterion of purpose.

Whether based on land, on sheltered waters, or on carriers, aircraft must be considered as naval weapons so long as their influence is felt at sea, that is, so long as they affect sea-borne communications. Their numerous activities include attacks on merchant shipping and on harbor installations, on warships and on naval bases. They are an indispensable adjunct to the battle fleet; they scout for it, spot its fire, defend it against enemy air attack, shroud it in smoke screens, and furnish added firepower with their bombs and torpedoes. They also operate on many important naval missions entirely independently of warships.

Aircraft are marked by inconceivable variety and specialization. One might be tempted to classify them according to whether they are land planes or seaplanes, but both may be naval craft. In general, seaplanes have a somewhat poorer flying performance than land planes of comparable size and power, but they can often be used where it is impossible to use land planes. They can be catapulted from cruisers and battleships and operated from small tenders. As a rule, however, seaplanes require relatively smooth water even to alight safely, and need it especially if they must take off from the water. They cannot usually be operated from tenders unless the tender stations itself in some sheltered body of water. But it is sometimes easier to find sheltered water than large airdromes—in the lagoons of the numerous Pacific atolls, for instance.

The particular purpose of an aircraft determines its entire design, especially since every pound of weight has an importance out of all proportion to its importance in surface craft. Most of the qualities desired in an airplane, such as high speed, maneuverability, long range, weight-carrying capacity, rapid climb, quick take-off, and high ceiling, are inherently incompatible in the same design. High speed, for example, is attained by designing a plane with high wing loading—that is, with a small wing surface relative to the weight carried—and with a low power loading; but both are incompatible with long range, and high wing loading is incompatible with all the other qualities mentioned. Long range means weight devoted to fuel load which might otherwise be devoted to additional armament and power, and a fighter designed for long-range operation would therefore always be handicapped in combat with planes designed for operating close to home. Similarly, other things being equal, a plane lightly loaded will always be able to climb more rapidly and to reach greater heights than a heavily loaded one, and an aircraft which does not have to carry bombs but which devotes half the weight saved to additional armament (fighter type) will always be able to out-climb, out-maneuver, and out-fight the bomber.

Though almost any military plane can shoot, drop bombs, and carry out reconnaissance, and though conditions will sometimes demand the use of multi-purpose planes, the best airplane for any job is the one specifically designed for that job. Especially among fighter planes, slight marginal differences in performance among the various models will determine the success or failure of each. Some fighters are designed primarily for speed and range, while others are designed with an eye particularly on rate of climb. As a result one finds on the one hand an extraordinarily high rate of obsolescence among all military planes and particularly among fighters, and on the other hand a tendency toward ever-increasing specialization which is in constant conflict with the desirability of standardization. The British have even set aside a certain type of plane, which is painted black, for night fighting alone.

In general, the smaller the plane the more maneuverable it is, and the larger the model the greater its range and capacity for military load. There is no necessary correlation between size and speed, but since the larger types are generally designed primarily for heavy bomb loads and sometimes for extreme range, they are usually considerably slower than the small fighters. On the other hand, except for carrier-based types, the larger planes are the only kind that are capable of extensive reconnaissance or of making attacks far out at sea.

The small size of airplanes as compared with other naval craft makes it possible to produce them in great numbers, though ton for ton there is unquestionably no vehicle of war as costly as an airplane. It is a mistake to regard aircraft as being generally a cheaper means of doing the same thing which a warship can do, especially since the latter is usually equal in hitting power to a very considerable number of air- craft. The airplane or the warship must stand on its abilities to do things which the other can do either less well or not at all, and the fact is that the margin of utility for each is very great. The results of two and one-half years of the Second World War have proved beyond question that aircraft and warships have functions which are much more complementary than competitive.

The most marked deficiency of the airplane for naval use is its short endurance. A very small number of planes of the larger bomber type have ranges with small bomb loads of several thousand miles, but range does not mean the same thing as ability to keep the sea. The range of a plane must be divided by its high cruising speed to indicate its sea-keeping endurance, and the result is inevitably a matter not of weeks or days but of hours. For a craft which must keep station with a convoy or carry on a patrol in an area considerably removed from its base, high cruising speed is of far less consequence than ability to remain at sea. The escorting of convoys by big flying boats is possible only when those convoys are near their terminals, and even then it requires relays of aircraft. When it comes to fighter planes, a constant patrol escort even of ships close to shore is usually out of the question. During 1940–1941 the British usually did not keep constant fighter patrols even over the convoys moving up the English Channel. The fact that the Germans maintained such a defensive patrol over the *Gneisenau* and *Scharnhorst* in their dash up the Channel in February 1942 reflects only the unusual importance of those vessels, which incidentally can move at more than twice the speed of the fastest convoys.

No other type of craft is so much at the mercy of the weather as the airplane. Bad visibility, low ceiling, and icing conditions not only may reduce the effectiveness of aircraft to zero, but also may endanger any already in the air. At various critical times planes have been prevented because of adverse weather from exploiting great opportunities. On the day following their initial successes against the *Bismarck*, the planes of the *Ark Royal* were unable to repeat their exploits and to finish the task they had begun so brilliantly because heavy seas prevented them from taking off. The story of the British Bomber Command's efforts to stay the German invasion of Norway is a running account of battle not with Germans, whom indeed they could hardly find, but with adverse weather, which obliterated the targets. The same has been true of innumerable other bombing and reconnaissance missions over the North Sea. The huge bomber force which the British had built up by the late autumn of 1941, and which they had eagerly expected to use to the fullest during the long winter nights, was kept on the ground by the unusually bad weather of that season. On one occasion the British defied the weather, and twenty-seven bombers were lost over Germany in a single night due to icing conditions alone.

Finally, of all naval craft the airplane is far the most fragile. An explosive shell of the smallest caliber and even machine gun bullets may destroy it with direct hits, and a medium caliber shell can frequently destroy it by bursting in

the vicinity. Planes caught on the ground or on the decks of
carriers are easily destroyed by other aircraft. The significance
of this is two-fold. First, during war the wastage of aircraft
and of the elite personnel that form their crews is terrific. For
every successful assault by aircraft against warships or merchant shipping one must count into the score the far more
numerous failures which result only in the dead loss of planes.

Secondly, and more important, an airplane superiority is a
relatively unreliable means of seeking a decision in naval battle. If attack planes are unopposed by other planes or by sufficient anti-aircraft fire, they are capable of the most devastating results, particularly with torpedoes. On the other hand,
anti-aircraft guns and a few fighters may frequently neutralize many bombers or torpedo planes. The results of different battles or even different phases of the same battle may
lead to the most conflicting conclusions. In the Battle of the
Coral Sea of May 1942, for example, each of the two American carriers engaged was set upon by about fifty-two Japanese
planes. Although the two attacks were carried out simultaneously and apparently pressed home with equal determination, one American carrier was destroyed while the other
escaped destruction, though how much damage it received,
if any, is not known. Of the 103 Japanese planes which took
part in the combined effort, forty-three were shot down, nineteen by anti-aircraft fire and twenty-four by fighters. By any
standards, this is a terrific rate of slaughter. Upon paying
this cost the Japanese were able to hit the *Lexington* with two
bombs and two torpedoes,[1] and those hits need not have been

---

[1] According to the official U. S. Navy communique of June 12, 1942.
Stanley Johnston, *Chicago Tribune* correspondent who was aboard the
Lexington at the time, reported in his dispatches to the press that the vessel
received five torpedo hits. The official report may be considered as clearly
the more accurate, not only because of its source but also because there
would be no reason to minimize the extent of damage received by a vessel
acknowledged as lost.

fatal except for the accidental ignition many hours later of leaking gasoline vapors.

In the Mediterranean battle of June 13–15, 1942, the bombers and torpedo planes of each side apparently inflicted heavy destruction; yet the British official communique reported one occasion during the fighting when British fighters intercepted a raiding party of forty Junkers-87's and Junkers-88's escorted by more than twenty Messerschmitt-109's and not only forced it to jettison its bombs far from British ships but inflicted heavy losses upon it. On the day before it suffered its heaviest losses during the Battle of Crete, the British Mediterranean Fleet had undergone a thirteen-hour air attack without receiving significant damage. The same kind of attack which is fantastically successful on one occasion will be a total failure on another. Unfortunately for a balanced public opinion, it is only the successful one which makes the headlines.

It is clear, however, that the airplane is essentially the weapon of surprise. Its tremendous speed often enables it to appear on the scene and drive home its blows before effective opposition can be mustered, even when the means of opposition are at hand. The Japanese carrier *Ryukaku* and a heavy cruiser were sunk in the Coral Sea battle when they were attacked by American aircraft while the Japanese carrier was turning into the wind to launch her own fighter aircraft. By that very maneuver she made herself a perfect target, and received fifteen bomb and ten torpedo hits and sank in a few minutes. Had the Japanese planes been launched two or three minutes sooner, the outcome of the attack might have been very different. The same kind of story can be told over and over again, with luck favoring now the attacker and at another time the defender.

Naturally, a superiority in aircraft is a great advantage, but unless the superiority is overwhelming and unless it involves

THE TOOLS OF SEA POWER

a large total number, it is not likely to be decisive in a big fleet action save by the most extravagant intervention of Fortune. When the American battle fleet was temporarily put out of action at Pearl Harbor, our admirals rightly decided that a small margin of American superiority over the Japanese in carrier-borne aircraft was not at all sufficient to redress the balance in fighting power. They insisted upon waiting until damaged battleships had been restored to service and new ones added before assuming an all-out offensive.

The far-reaching strategic implications of the airplane in naval warfare are reserved to later chapters. These observations on the function of the airplane as a tool of sea power are of necessity brief. If they seem to stress unduly the limitations of the airplane the reason is simply that there is now no danger of air power being underestimated in the public mind. On the contrary, the real danger is that enthusiasm over a comparatively new instrument of war which has performed the most brilliant exploits and which has undeniable imaginative and even aesthetic appeal may cause a powerful public opinion to deny the continuing utility of older tools.

The Aircraft Carrier

THE aircraft carrier is the vessel in which the mobility peculiar to surface fleets and the mobility peculiar to aircraft are combined. Aircraft, while extremely mobile within range of their base, are tied to their base by a relatively short tether, and the base is not easily moved. Moreover, the endurance of the plane and the amount of military work it can do in a single sortie are both markedly limited. Warships, on the other hand, though much slower moving than aircraft, have a far greater cruising radius—especially when accompanied by a tanker or two—and are immeasurably more self-contained

57

during their stay at sea. The carrier is a floating airdrome possessing all the advantages in mobility and seakeeping power of the large warship and all the advantages inherent in the use of aircraft. Strategically the carrier is merely a warship which strikes its blows not through guns or torpedo tubes but through relatively autonomous instruments capable of great range.

Although ships called "aircraft carriers" made their appearance during the First World War, none had flight decks large enough to permit planes to alight as well as to take off. Planes which took off from their decks usually landed upon the water, where they floated upon air bags until hoisted to the mother vessel. There were also seaplane carriers which functioned simply as tenders, using derricks to lower and hoist the planes to the water. The first vessel designed with a clear deck which could be used both for taking off and alighting was the British ship *Argus*, completed in September 1918, too late to be of use in the war.

The modern aircraft carrier is already one of the most important units of the fleet, and some observers expect it eventually to replace the battleship itself. A great many journalists after the battles of the Coral Sea and of the Midway Islands threw caution to the winds and proclaimed that it had already replaced the battleship as the "dominant arm" or "backbone" of the fleet. This is arriving at far-reaching conclusions on the basis of scanty evidence indeed. It is a very common but dangerous kind of error to form convictions as to what would happen in large-scale fleet actions on the basis of a few engagements of small task forces, particularly where one or both of the task forces involved had a specific mission such as that of effecting a landing. This will be discussed more fully, however, in a later place.

The aircraft carrier is unquestionably a ship of considerable striking force with a hitting power extending as far as the range of the torpedo and bombing planes that take off from it. It must be remembered, however, that its volume of fire is very low, particularly at extended ranges. Naturally, if its aircraft attack with torpedoes, its effectiveness must be weighed in terms other than those implying comparison with gunfire; but, on the other hand, it is too often forgotten that the present effectiveness of the torpedo against large warships may from the long-term point of view be a transitory phenomenon in naval development. There is no doubt that future navies will have far greater numbers of aircraft carriers than they have today, but there is no reason to suppose that this type of ship will drive other types out of existence any more than did the destroyer or submarine.

If the aircraft carrier were going to drive any type of ship out of existence it would probably not be the battleship but the large cruiser—on the one hand because of the relatively poor protection of the cruiser against aerial attack and on the other because of the great utility of the aircraft carrier in reconnaissance, which has always been one of the chief functions of the cruiser. In favorable weather a single carrier can keep a very large portion of the sea under constant surveillance. It can scout for the battle fleet, and when action is joined supply aircraft not only for direct attack but also for artillery spotting service, which enormously enhances the fighting value of other warships. But the limitation to favorable weather for the carrier's successful operation means that the cruiser remains necessary even for reconnaissance. Not only are there a great many days in large and important maritime areas when planes simply cannot fly, but there are many additional days when visibility is actually much better from the deck of a ship than from a position 1,000 feet aloft.

There are several serious and apparently ineradicable weaknesses in the carrier type of vessel. It is a huge and extraordinarily vulnerable target, whether to gunfire, torpedo attack or aerial bombs. The gasoline stores and the aircraft which it carries create a considerable fire hazard, as was proved by the fate of the *Lexington*. The fact that it must keep a steady course in a direction determined by the wind while aircraft are taking off or alighting upon its deck does not reduce the perils it faces in action, which was demonstrated more fortunately in the destruction of the *Ryukaku*. The *Courageous* too was steaming into the wind to receive her planes when a U-boat torpedo struck and sent her to the bottom.

Most modern carriers have a patch of side armor and a heavy armored deck low in the ship to protect their vitals, but in each case the greater part of the immense vessel is exposed. The flight deck, too high above the water to carry heavy armor, is a particularly inviting target for aerial bombs. Hits upon it even with lighter bombs will sometimes make short work of flying operations. The determined air attack upon the *Illustrious* on January 10, 1941 forced all the planes which had already taken off her deck to land at nearby Malta. In the naval actions during the Battle of Crete, a 1,000-pound bomb destroyed all but a few of the planes aboard the *Formidable* and put a huge hole in the carrier's side. It was at that point that Admiral Cunningham decided to withdraw his fleet to the south of Crete. In the Battle of Midway, the American carrier *Yorktown* received a torpedo hit which created such a list that she was unable, long before she sank, to receive or send off planes.

In general, the aircraft carrier must rely for defense mainly on escorting warships, high speed, and on her own planes and armament. The British carriers of the *Illustrious* class were equipped with sixteen 4.5-inch dual purpose guns from the beginning, while the eight 5-inch dual purpose guns of our *Enterprise* and *Wasp* classes has been raised to twelve in the *Essex* class, and all our carriers enjoy a plentiful array of

40 mm. and 20 mm. automatic cannon and lesser armament.

After less than three years of war, the British had lost five of the six carriers they possessed in September 1939—the *Courageous, Ark Royal,* and *Eagle* to U-boat attack, the *Glorious* to the guns of the *Scharnhorst* (an incident too quickly forgotten), and the *Hermes* to Japanese bombers. Various surviving carriers, including several completed after the beginning of the war, were at one time or another laid up for repairs. The Japanese in exactly six months of war with the United States had lost the majority of the first-line carriers with which they began the conflict. The United States by the end of 1942 had lost four of the seven with which she started the war.

It is an odd commentary on the tendency toward polarized opinions among commentators of the press and radio that while most of them after the battles of the Coral Sea and the Midway Islands were exalting the carrier as the dominant ship of war, a few took pleasure in referring to the same type of vessel as the "clay pigeon of the Navy." Unquestionably there has never before in the history of warfare been a type of vessel that was so large for its time, and so important tactically and strategically, and yet at the same time so vulnerable. Traditionally the "dominant ship" of the fleet has always been one that was able to take more punishment than any other as well as to deliver it, but the carrier certainly does not fall into this category. The losses suffered by all the belligerents prove that a nation carrying on spirited offensive warfare is not likely to be able to replace losses in this type except by conversion of other vessels.

But usefulness, not invulnerability, determines the value of a warship, and no type could show a more brilliant record of accomplishment in the Second World War than the aircraft carrier. Its participation had been vital in the attack at Taranto and in the destruction of the *Bismarck.* It had performed inestimable service in the defense of shipping. Its decks had served as bases for aerial patrols of the broad seas in search of all types of raiders—submarine, surface, and aerial. The considerable control of the Mediterranean which the British were able to exercise with forces scarcely superior and at times inferior to the Italians would have been impossible without the help of reconnaissance planes based on carriers. Carriers served our own fleet well in numerous task force operations in the Pacific. Unfortunately, the aircraft carrier also proved valuable to the enemy. The catastrophic blow at Pearl Harbor, as well as many Japanese aerial sorties in the western Pacific, would have been unthinkable without that type of ship.

Almost any large, fast vessel can be converted into an aircraft carrier of sorts. The best model, of course, is the ship originally designed as such, but vessels under construction as large cruisers, battle cruisers, and even battleships have been altered during building into successful aircraft carriers. The United States Navy's experiment with the *Mormacmail* in the spring of 1941 indicated how a considerable number of carriers might be made available on short notice. The *Mormacmail*, a 7,900-ton merchant vessel, was successfully converted at Newport News into a carrier—the *Long Island*—capable of operating about thirty fighter planes, and the conversion was accomplished in about forty-five days. The success of this experiment naturally resulted in a substantial conversion program.

The largest and fastest aircraft carriers in the world are those in the American and British navies. The new American *Enterprise* class have a normal complement of eighty-three aircraft each and space for well over one hundred. In view of the high cost and vulnerability of the type, however, it is a question whether the Japanese were not wiser than ourselves in resorting to smaller, cheaper models. Besides saving themselves excessive loss in the sinking of one such ship, the dispersion of aircraft among more numerous carriers would probably speed up the flying operations of a fleet. On the other hand, the large *Lexington,* a converted battle cruiser, took two torpedo hits without even suffering a substantial loss of speed prior to the explosions which led to her destruction. A smaller vessel could hardly have taken the blows so well. The survival of the British *Formidable* and *Illustrious* under heavy punishment from the air also indicates that large size has its compensations. Naturally a larger ship will also provide a longer and roomier flight deck.

The Germans have at least one aircraft carrier, the *Graf Zeppelin,* which up to the middle of 1942 had figured scarcely at all in naval operations. It was hardly necessary in the Baltic, but the Germans were wary of using it in the North Sea, not to mention the North Atlantic where it would almost certainly be intercepted in the same manner as the *Bismarck.* The Italian Navy never provided itself with aircraft carriers, due not to a lack of air-mindedness in Italy but to an excess. Italian military airmen derided the aircraft carrier as being excessively vulnerable to aerial attack, an attitude common to the extremely air-minded in all countries, including our own. But even in the narrow Mediterranean, lack of aircraft carriers proved a signal disadvantage to Italy in her fight with Britain, particularly before the Axis conquest of Crete. The land-based aircraft which the air extremists usually prefer were simply not on the spot when needed.

Planes which operate from carriers can never be quite the equal of the best land-based aircraft, and they should not be pitted against the latter if it can be avoided. The design of the carrier-based plane is rather rigidly circumscribed. It must be of exceptionally sturdy construction, it must fit into a small space—hence the usual folding wings—and it must be able to take off and alight with a short run. Neither large

63

bombers, which require too much space for take-off, nor the fastest fighters, which have too high a landing speed, can be used. The British have found it useful to provide fighters for carriers which are two-seaters, even though the pilot does all the fighting, in order to have a navigator along who is unoccupied during the fighting and who keeps track of the position of the aircraft and its mother ship. The carrier must also be provided with planes that have all-round rather than specialized uses. Usually only three general types are carried: fighters, scout-bombers, and torpedo-bombers. The British have combined the latter two functions in one design which they call "T.S.R." planes (i.e. torpedo-bombing, spotting, and reconnaissance).

The Destroyer

In the autumn of 1940 Great Britain was short of all the means of self-preservation. She had no battleships to spare, and was critically lacking in cruisers and aircraft. But what she needed most desperately, what she pleaded for above all from her friends across the Atlantic, was destroyers and more destroyers. "Give us destroyers to save ourselves," was her plea, "and in return we will sign away territories which you will need as naval bases if we go down." It was the cry of a nation that had been rescued once before by destroyers, for in World War I they had been the chief antidote to the German submarine.

Destroyers are multiple-duty vessels. They screen the battle fleet against torpedo attack and shroud it with smoke to protect it against enemy guns. With their torpedoes they attack the mightiest battleships of the enemy fleet. They protect convoys against the U-boat menace, and by that fact become the mainstay of a nation which must carry on a vast shipping in order to survive.

For vessels whose role is so largely defensive they bear a

curious name. "Destroyer" is a short form of the original name, which showed the defensive conception. In the latter nineteenth century, the torpedo-boat had become a frightening menace to the battle fleet. The small caliber quick-firer gun, developed to provide defense against it, was not sufficient. The solution was the "torpedo-boat destroyer," a light swift vessel mounting several quick-firer guns which could destroy the torpedo-boat before it approached close enough to the fleet for effective torpedo attack. The new vessel proved so effective that the true torpedo-boat almost disappeared from all navies, whereupon the "destroyer"—the prefix having become meaningless—perversely adopted torpedo tubes and took on the characteristics of the ship it had been created to destroy. The basic difference, however, was that in its guns, and later its depth charges, it had the means to block as well as deliver torpedo attack.

The modern destroyer is an unarmored vessel of from 1,050 to 2,000 tons, carrying four to eight guns of 4-inch to 5-inch caliber and from four to as many as sixteen torpedo tubes. The so-called "flotilla leaders" are usually the larger of the destroyers. As a class destroyers are the swiftest of the vessels thus far considered, all the newer ones being capable of over 35 knots. However, top speed is possible for any small vessel only in relatively smooth seas. In rough weather a fast cruiser or battleship may outdistance a destroyer.

Because of its small size, high speed, and maneuverability, the destroyer is a difficult target for enemy guns when it is pressing home a torpedo attack. It presents an even more elusive target for a torpedo, especially since its modest draft sometimes permits the underwater missiles to run completely under it. These qualities fit it ideally for the anti-submarine hunt. It can turn swiftly, bear down at top speed to a spot where a submarine has just been detected, and drop a pattern of depth charges before the submerged craft can change its position appreciably. The one objection to use of the destroyer in anti-submarine work is that probably it is too good a ship for that purpose, inasmuch as it is designed to meet the more exacting requirements of battle fleet maneuvers. A much cheaper and more swiftly constructed vessel might prove almost as effective against submarines.

Although the destroyer is not easy to hit from the air, its unarmored character makes it susceptible to injury even from the lighter type of bombs. After the battles of Norway and France in 1940, seventy British destroyers were retired from service for repairs; most of them had sustained their damage in air attack. A good number of others had been sunk outright.

One weakness of the small destroyer of World War I was its limited endurance. The range of the destroyer determined the range of the whole fleet, particularly in combat theaters. Admiral Scheer complained that he could not send the German High Seas Fleet against the British-French communications between Portsmouth and Le Havre because his destroyers were incapable of so long a journey. That factor could hardly have been the chief dissuasion from such an attack, but Scheer's statement illustrates the impediment to extended action which the destroyer imposed upon the battle fleet. The newer American destroyers, however, have an endurance of 6,000 sea miles at economical speeds, which is comparable to the range of the battleship itself. By increasing its range, the destroyer has in effect become a small cruiser. In fact, there are vessels in several navies which can be classified either as destroyers or light cruisers; the French *Mogador* class of 2,884 tons are examples.

The Submarine

THE great strategic value of the submarine lies in the fact that it is the only warship which can operate independently for extended periods in seas which are dominated by the enemy. If it has the help of strong surface squadrons to counter the anti-submarine blows of the enemy, so much the better, but it can get along without such aid. The ordinary type of surface blockade means little to the submarine, for it can pass under it just as the airplane passes over. Though not strong in resistance, it can secure quick concealment almost anywhere on the seas by the simple expedient of slipping beneath the waves.

The submarine is much older in the history of naval warfare than is generally supposed. The American Revolution saw the use of one-man submarine boats designed by the young American David Bushnell. The American Civil War saw the first sinking of a warship by a submarine. By the end of the nineteenth century the French Navy had a respectable fleet of electrically driven undersea boats. The gasoline engine, introduced on submarines about the turn of the century, made possible considerable range. But the final fruition of the submarine's offensive powers had to await the development of the periscope, the gyroscopic compass, and the Diesel engine, all of which were perfected only shortly before the first World War.

Submarines vary enormously in size and in tactical and strategic potentialities. In World War I they ranged from 127 to 1,930 tons surface displacement; they carried from four to nineteen torpedoes and one or two deck guns of from 3-inch to 6-inch caliber. One out of every three German U-boats (the term comes from the German word for submarine: *Unterseeboot*) was outfitted primarily as a mine-layer and usually stowed about thirty mines. Toward the close of the war the British built a class of three submarines, the "M-class," each of which was fitted with a 12-inch gun in a turret. The gun could be loaded under water and aimed through the periscope, and could be fired six seconds after the submarine appeared on the surface. At short ranges the trajectory would be flat and gunnery calculations simple. These vessels were tested after the war and some of the personnel concerned were much impressed with the results, but the British Navy dropped the experiment and took good care to broadcast reports that big-gun submarines were a failure.

Modern submarines range from the two-man baby submarine of about ten tons tried by the Japanese at Pearl Harbor to the 2,880-ton (surface displacement) *Surcouf* recently of the Free French Navy and lost in action early in 1942. The *Surcouf*, named after a great French commerce raiding captain of the Napoleonic Wars, was the largest submarine ever built and carried on its deck two turret-housed 8-inch rifles, anti-aircraft armament, and a hangar containing one airplane. However, it is generally conceded to have been a failure, chiefly because the great weight on the decks required such a flooding and blowing of tanks in submerging and emerging as dangerously to slow down these vital maneuvers. The safety of a submarine, particularly since there are bound to be hostile aircraft to contend with, often depends on the alacrity with which it can dive. The *Surcouf* might have been a success had its designers been content to make it either a heavy-gun submersible cruiser or a submersible aircraft carrier, but their effort to make it both doomed it to failure.

A common classification distinguishes between the "coastal" type, comprising vessels of about 600 tons, and the "seagoing" type, ranging from 1,000 to almost 2,000 tons. The United States and Japan have shown a particular predilection for the larger classes, since such vessels may have cruising ranges of over 15,000 miles and may, therefore, be used across the whole width of the Pacific. That the submarine is unique among small naval craft for its great range is due chiefly to the fact that it does not have to rely upon high speed to protect it from attack by ships of superior strength. Moreover, its construction, with an inner "pressure" hull and outer ship-shape hull, leaves a large space between the hulls for fuel storage.

Most modern submarines have top surface speeds of less than 18 knots, though a few of the larger types reach 20 to 22 knots. Submerged top speed is usually 8 or 9 knots, and no existing type, except for the freak Japanese baby submarines, is known to exceed 12 knots. Moreover, top speed submerged can be maintained for only a short time, probably less than an hour. It is noteworthy that while modern submarines are on the whole faster at surface than those of the first World War, the maximum speed records both surface and submerged established by craft used in that war have not been exceeded. The British "R" class of World War I, designed to stalk enemy U-boats, had a submerged top speed of 14 knots, and the steam-driven "K" class were capable of 23 knots on the surface. The modern British *Severn* class of two vessels, however, were the first Diesel-driven submarines to exceed 21 knots, and with their 22.25-knot surface speed they are probably the fastest submarines of World War II. These and their American counterparts are sometimes known as "fleet type" submarines, since it was hoped that their high surface speed would enable them to keep up with a battle fleet and cooperate with it in action.

The submarine is beset, however, by several inherent disadvantages. Its slow speed, especially when submerged, often prevents an effective attack on its own part and reduces its ability to dodge depth charge attacks. The limited space available in the submarine for propulsive machinery must be given over to a completely dual system—Diesel engines for surface cruising and storage batteries with electric motors for submerged cruising. The low power which enhances its range is less a matter of choice than of necessity.

The submarine is also handicapped by a low cruising radius when submerged, for the bulky storage batteries are of markedly limited capacity. Submerged endurance may be extended by proceeding at very low speeds, but this is ill-gained economy if a destroyer is in the neighborhood. The submarine must remain in motion submerged or it tends to lose longitudinal control, unless it is in water shallow enough to permit its resting on the bottom. In some regions, however, the water will have layers of varying density due to temperature differences, and by delicately adjusting its buoyancy a submarine can sometimes lie on a dense layer as though it were on the bottom.

Vulnerability is the submarine's cardinal weakness, for even in the largest types armor is not feasible except in very light plating on the conning tower. A single well-placed hit which perforates the inner hull will usually prevent diving. Moreover, since the submarine has so little reserve buoyancy, one shell from a medium caliber gun may even sink the vessel. While submerged, the submarine is vulnerable to the deadly hammer blows of depth charges, which may destroy it though they explode as much as fifteen yards from its hull. Of course, its three-dimensional movement makes it a difficult target for depth charges, which not only must be dropped in the proper place but must also be set to explode at the proper depth.

Another handicap to the submarine is its poor vision. When under water it has only a periscope with a very restricted view, and since the periscope leaves a "feather" as it moves through the water, which is often easily seen, the submarine must be wary of showing it in the presence of the enemy— precisely when it needs it most. Even when awash the submersible has no elevated position for observation. True, like any other vessel it may call upon the scouting services of aircraft, but unless it carries its own—which it rarely does—the aircraft are available to it only within flying range of the air bases, and, of course, only under favorable weather conditions.

A further limitation on the use of the submarine is its requirement of deep water. The larger ones may need as much as 100 feet for submerged operations. Along coasts, in some straits and channels—precisely where the submarine is most valuable—and even in some portions of the open sea, this requirement is not easily met. At the height of the U-boat campaign of 1917, the convoyed traffic between the Thames and Rotterdam passed unmolested under the noses of the U-boat flotilla based on Zeebrugge and Ostend, because that route was too shallow for submarine maneuvers, especially if counterattack with depth charges was to be expected.

Finally, the submarine is liable to detection even when submerged, which tends to undermine its whole reason for being —although present means of detection leave much to be desired. The search for the U-boat detector has been one of the dramas of underwater warfare. In the early days it was almost comic opera. During 1915 the British took some sea lions from the London stage and tried to train them to find U-boats. The sea lions, however, shrewdly appraised U-boats as inedible, or at any rate unsavory, and declined to waste effort upon them. And since the Germans refused to coat their submarines with fish oil, there was nothing to do but return the animals to vaudeville. By the middle of the following year, however, the hydrophone was in use, and before the war was over, it had been made amazingly sensitive. Even when a submarine was lying on the bottom, the slight sound made by the motor of its gyroscopic compass could sometimes be heard by listening craft above.

The chief disadvantage of the hydrophone was that it picked up other noises besides that of the submarine's propellers, and when the hunter was churning its own propellers or was in the company of a convoy, detection of hostile U-boats became well-nigh impossible. After the war, however, the British developed a device which they named the "Asdic" (after Anti-Submarine Defense Investigation Committee), and which employed an old and well-known principle in physics. Plates of quartz crystal can be caused to vibrate electrically at very high frequencies, thus producing "supersonic" or ultra-audible sound waves, which can be transmitted under water in any desired direction. These waves will rebound upon striking surfaces of various objects, and the echo can be detected upon the same crystals.

Early tests with the Asdic revealed that supersonic waves are reflected not only by the walls of submarines but by shoals of fish as well, and by various other natural phenomena. The spectacle of great battleships fleeing from schools of little fish during naval maneuvers was by no means infrequent. Such indignities were trying to the spirit of the Royal Navy, but the Asdic survived and reached a high state of development by the beginning of the Second World War. Its range, however, was inherently limited—about 2,000 yards.

Unfortunately for the British, the chief result of the development of this fine instrument was to lull them into a sense of false security respecting the submarine. The Chamberlain government forgot that a detecting device, however good, requires numerous destroyers and other small craft to carry it, and to carry also the depth charges by which the attack must be delivered. The outbreak of war in September of 1939 found Great Britain with only 185 destroyers in her navy, whereas she had 500 available in the last stages of the First World War. This weakness almost proved her undoing in 1940 and 1941, when it cost her shipping losses so terrific as materially to affect the course of the war.

The record of the submarine in the Second World War

indicates that it still has a distinguished future as a naval weapon. The loss to U-boats by the middle of 1942 of perhaps 10,000,000 tons of British and Allied shipping and of numerous warships including the battleships *Royal Oak* and *Barham* and the aircraft carriers *Courageous* and *Ark Royal* is no mean toll for any category of craft. And when that toll is compared with the amount of money and war materials expended by the Germans in achieving it, the disparity is astounding. A happier example can be found in the similarly impressive achievements of United Nations submarines in the Far East and in the Mediterranean. By July 1942 the submarines of the several belligerents had sunk about as many warships and certainly far more merchant vessels than any other type of combat craft including the airplane.

Even if the submarine is defeated in its primary purpose, the destruction of enemy shipping on a large scale, the efforts required to overcome it must be of such magnitude that the submarine retains an important nuisance value. The necessity of sending ships in convoys, which reduces the effectiveness of available shipping by at least 25 per cent, the wearisome, unending efforts of innumerable small naval craft and airplanes, the constant anxiety of the battle fleet commander and the marked restrictions upon his movements, all add to the achievements of the enemy submarine fleet. The submarine makes the enemy disperse his force and causes a strain upon his naval resources that may endanger his whole strategic position.

On the other hand, events up to the present have indicated that the submarine can be countered. Convoy and patrol are remarkably effective in reducing losses if carried out with sufficient escorts and aided by aircraft, which can search broad areas of the ocean and sometimes even detect submarines lurking below the surface. Guns on merchant ships and escorting warships can force the submarine to remain submerged when attacking and thereby use up its slender supply of torpedoes.

More telling still is the progressive elimination of the more valorous of the U-boat personnel. The commander of the submarine at his periscope is the sole witness of his own acts. Whether he goes close in to the target for effective torpedo fire or discharges his missile from a good safe distance is entirely his own choice, and one which he can make without fear of criticism or contempt. As a result, a disproportionately large amount of enemy shipping will be sunk by a handful of the most courageous submarine commanders. In the first World War, twenty-five German U-boat aces out of about 300 commanders of attack-type submarines accounted for almost 40 per cent of British losses. But the bolder commanders are the first to be eliminated.

During the later stages of the first World War the fighting spirit of the German U-boat crews cracked badly; the continual depth charge attacks from escort vessels, the fear of annihilation at any moment from mines, the countless hairbreadth escapes, and finally the knowledge that a submarine could hope for only six voyages before meeting its doom, blunted the valor of men and commanders both. To defeat the submarine it is not necessary to sink more than are being built. If destruction becomes as high as 50 per cent of new construction, the number of submarines will increase, but their effectiveness will diminish.

But the submarine has probably not had its last word. Innumerable mutations are possible to it. It can evolve into many specialized forms and adopt new weapons and techniques of attack. If the long-range submarine, because of its great size, is unduly liable to detection and vulnerable to attack, perhaps it can become a tender of baby submarines which will push home the thrust while the mother submarine

74

remains at a distance. The last twenty years have seen remarkable advances in pressure hull strength, and early British experience with big-gun submarines indicates that in the future destroyers may have to cope with heavy shells, which are much less easily dodged than torpedoes.

Other Combat Vessels

THE development of underwater warfare has called into existence numerous types of small vessels whose primary function it is to supplement the always-too-scarce destroyers in escort duty and in patrol operations against submarines. The most notable of these today is the "corvette," named after a light warship of the days of sail which was used primarily as a dispatch vessel. The modern corvette, which bears little relation in function to its older namesake, has been developed by the British in order to provide an escort vessel much more quickly produced and not requiring as large a crew as the destroyer. It is usually of about 900 tons displacement, carries one 4-inch gun, one anti-aircraft pom-pom gun, and a store of depth charges. The corvettes of 1939–1940 were not too successful because of their slow speed—about 17 knots—which was not even equal to the surface speed of many submarines, but recent types are appreciably faster. The American counterpart is the new "D.E." boat (destroyer escort) with a larger complement and considerably greater fire power.

Numerous smaller vessels, frequently called "sub-chasers," are used for off-shore patrol and escort. Many of these are specifically designed and built for their military function, but a large number of pleasure yachts have been inducted into service in the anti-submarine campaigns in both world wars.

The old torpedo-boat which the destroyer once forced out of existence has returned in the form of the small, speedy, motor torpedo boat, called by the Italians the "M.A.S. boat,"

by the British the "E-boat," and by our own navy the "P.T. boat" or simply the "M.T.B." They are weapons of surprise and opportunity, like the torpedo plane which they resemble in function. They have in general not fulfilled the hopes—or fears—held out for them. A few American boats of this type accomplished some startling successes against Japanese cruisers and other vessels in the bays of the Philippines and later off Guadalcanal, but no notable successes can be credited to them thus far in European waters. They are fairly vulnerable to the automatic anti-aircraft guns with which warships are now so generously armed.

The menace from the air has created an all-antiaircraft-gun ship for use as an escort to convoys or naval squadrons in zones near enemy air bases. Thus far no ships have been built specifically for this purpose, existing models being mostly old cruisers with converted armament; but all our newer cruisers carry so profuse an anti-aircraft armament as to be in effect dual purpose cruisers.

The British have an interesting type of ship, built during the first World War, which they call "coast defense monitors," though they have always been used offensively against the coasts of the enemy. Carrying two 15-inch guns and lesser armament on a displacement of about 7,000 tons, they provided a means of delivering a powerful artillery fire against coastal objectives without unduly risking valuable battleships. One vessel of the type made history on May 12, 1917, by using aircraft to spot at extreme range a totally invisible target. It bombarded the locks of the canal at Zeebrugge at a range of 26,200 yards during a time when the visibility was never more than 4,000 yards. One of the three monitors surviving into the Second World War was used quite effectively against Italian positions on the Libyan coast during Wavell's offensive of December 1940, but it was subsequently destroyed.

Though offensive mine laying is now carried on mostly by submarines, aircraft, and occasionally cruisers, every large navy has a few specially designed minelayers which must be classified as combat ships. The characteristics of the type are usually high speed plus very large mine capacity; the older British *Adventure*, for example, is capable of 28 knots and can carry 340 mines. It is armed with four 4.7-inch anti-aircraft guns besides smaller armament. Minelayers of this type can be used in fleet actions, just as Jellicoe did at Jutland when he sent one ahead during the night to mine one of the three avenues of German escape. This class of vessel is of course not to be confused with the craft used to lay mines defensively along one's own coast. Any tug will do for that kind of operation.

Auxiliary Naval Vessels

EVERY navy has an entourage of auxiliary craft which have military uses or which are normally manned by naval personnel. Ships not used directly in combat but which have great military importance include coastal minelayers, mine-sweepers, net-layers, tenders of various kinds, repair ships, store ships, and tankers. Navies will also maintain fleet tugs, transports, cargo ships, and hospital ships. Although these vessels are frequently designed specifically for naval uses, the outbreak of war finds any belligerent pressing great numbers of merchant ships and tugs into service as fleet auxiliaries. During each of the two world wars Great Britain has used upwards of 1,000 small craft, including drifters and trawlers, for combatting the German mine menace alone. Fortunately, a great many private or commercial vessels prove admirably fitted for the tasks assigned them. A fishing vessel may make an excellent mine-sweeper, a yacht may provide a good escort vessel, and any fast tanker can be pressed into service with the fleet.

The Torpedo

THE mightiest of warships may be vitally jeopardized by this underwater missile, which the smallest of vessels is capable of launching. Without the torpedo the submarine boat would be of minor significance, and even the airplane would be robbed of much of its deadliness over the seas. The torpedo has revolutionized not only tactics but naval strategy as well. The battleship, which used to be a self-contained unit needing no other vessels for its defense, now requires the protection of a screen of lesser craft and airplanes against the torpedo-launching craft of the enemy. And since the availability of such craft to the respective adversaries will vary greatly with distance and especially with proximity to bases, the whole geography of naval war is affected. Moreover, a ship which has taken a torpedo hit must, if it floats at all, be lifted out of the water for repairs. Such repairs may take months, and will in any case require establishments such as are not too plentifully distributed over the globe.

The torpedo has steadily pushed wider the range of gun-fire in fleet actions. A bold threat with torpedoes may enable an inferior fleet to escape its enemy, as was the case in the Battle of Jutland. On the other hand, a few effective torpedo hits upon an escaping fleet may force it to turn and fight. It is therefore difficult to say whether the torpedo has made fleet actions more conclusive or less so. What is certain is that the torpedo is likely to figure tremendously in any battle. Its effect is not to be measured in actual hits alone, but also in the extent to which it influences the tactics of the opposing admirals.

The modern automotive torpedo was invented about 1860 by an Englishman named Whitehead. His particular contribution was the hydrostatic-valve-and-pendulum-balance device by which the torpedo could be set to run at any desired depth.

Later a gyroscope was attached to the vertical rudder to give directional accuracy. From that moment the torpedo became one of the deadliest missiles in the arsenal of naval weapons. Subsequent improvements increased the weight of the explosive charge and the range and speed of propulsion. The air for operating the machinery was stored under ever-increasing pressures. An alcohol flame was added to warm and expand the stream of air. Then a spray of water was introduced to keep the flame from melting the mechanism. The result is that the modern torpedo is run by steam and the products of combustion as well as by compressed air. The range and speed of modern torpedoes are kept secret by most navies, but it is safe to say that several types have ranges up to 20,000 yards and speeds of well over 40 knots, though the higher speeds are possible only at short ranges.

The increase in the proportion of steam and hot combustion gases in the exhaust of the torpedo has greatly reduced the amount of wake which the "tin fish" leaves in its progress, since the steam condenses and the hot gases contract as they meet the cold water. In the first World War, the broad, white wake often made it easy for ships to spy the torpedo coming and to dodge it. The wake betrayed the position of the attacking submarine almost as clearly as did the compressed air which ejected the torpedo from its tube and which caused a great boiling of water at the point of origin of the torpedo track. The boiling has now been completely eliminated, and the torpedo wake, while not invisible, is less easily seen. Certain electrically driven torpedoes used by the Germans are also eliminating wake.

The enormous destructive power of the torpedo owes nothing to the force with which it collides against the ship's hull —which is insignificant compared with the impact energy of a gun projectile—but is due entirely to the peculiar nature of underwater explosion. Incompressible water of great inertia

THE TOOLS OF SEA POWER

surrounds the explosion on all sides but one, that one being the yielding hull of the ship. It is as if the explosion were taking place in the breech of a gun, with the water acting like the walls of the gun and the ship's side taking the place of the movable projectile. A significant difference, however, between the mining effect of an underwater explosion and the kind of explosion which occurs inside the gun is that the latter, because of the slow-burning nature of the powder, gives the projectile a thrust-like impetus, while the torpedo explosion is instantaneous and shattering.

Like any other weapon, the torpedo has inherent limitations. It is a complicated precision mechanism, and therefore costly. Of greater military significance, however, is its considerable size and weight; American torpedoes range from 2,100 to 3,600 pounds in weight and from 13.5 to 23 feet in length. A submarine boat can carry but a limited number, and the usual torpedo-dropping airplane can carry only one. Despite its phenomenal accuracy, range and speed, the torpedo bears no comparison in these respects with the gun projectile. To sink its victim, the torpedo-launching craft must make a close-in attack. The torpedo must run its course at proper depth; if it is too near the surface it will break waves and be deflected, and when it explodes there will be too little burden of water above it to vent the explosive force into the ship rather than into the air. It must thus run at least six feet and preferably ten or twelve feet below the surface. But if it runs too deep, it will go entirely under the target. Many small warships and merchant ships have too shallow a draft to permit effective torpedo attack against them.

The various types of torpedoes used on surface warships, aircraft, and submarines are generally of 21-inch caliber, and carry war heads of 550 to over 1,000 pounds of TNT. The British Navy has also an 18-inch torpedo weighing 1,750 pounds and carrying a charge of under 400 pounds for use by lighter aircraft. The largest known size in use is the 24.5-inch caliber on the British battleships *Rodney* and *Nelson*. A battleship, however, is likely to have few opportunities to use its torpedo tubes, and most recent designs have dispensed with torpedo armament altogether. But in her fight with the *Bismarck*, the *Rodney* apparently discharged one of her huge torpedoes after the German ship was completely disabled and it is thought to have struck. Since the *Bismarck* absorbed perhaps ten torpedo hits before sinking, it is impossible to tell what damage was involved in the *Rodney's* particular contribution.

Mines

THE mine is simply a non-mobile torpedo. There are too many kinds to warrant detailed description of each. The most common type is the anchored mine, but this has many variants, including several different types of contact mine, antenna mines, mines which rise to effective position at a predetermined time after being laid, and mines attached to anchored nets. There are floating mines, which may be dropped by a ship fleeing from an enemy, and magnetic and acoustic types, which lie on the sea floor. But all these differ from torpedoes not only in that they are stationary, waiting for their prey to come to them, but also in that they are tactically effective in the absence of the craft which laid them. The mine therefore functions strategically as an independent weapon, and a mine barrage is akin to a line of invisible fixed fortresses in land warfare, or to some natural obstacle.

Each type has special uses and peculiar limitations. Anchored mines may usually be swept up by the simple expedient of catching and cutting the cables holding them to their anchors. Ships proceeding in unswept channels use paravane sweeps for protection. These are simply underwater kites attached by cables to the prow of the ship; as the vessel moves forward they draw their connecting cables out sidewise. These outspread cables form a sweep to catch the cables of anchored mines that would otherwise strike the vessel. The mine cables thus snared are drawn out to the paravane where a cutting device severs them.

Since the cable of the anchored mine is of constant length, any movement of the mine away from a position directly over its anchor will tend to depress it below effective position. For that reason this type cannot be used where there are strong currents or where the water is very deep, since the mine moves more freely with a long cable. A large fluctuation in tide levels also reduces its dangerousness. During the first World War, German U-boats frequently passed over the mine barrage in Dover Strait by surfacing at night during a high tide. The British finally stopped this easy exit by floodlighting the Strait.

Magnetic and acoustic mines are generally made to lie on the ocean bottom where they cannot easily be swept up. They must, however, be laid in water which is neither too shallow for shipping to pass over nor too deep for the detonating mechanism to be activated. Magnetic mines have been rather effectively countered by the use of the "degaussing belt," which is simply a system of electric cables girdling the vessel. The magnetic field set up by the current flowing through these cables neutralizes the magnetic attraction of the ship's steel hull.

In both world wars, mines have been responsible for a good proportion of the shipping losses and for a sizable number of casualties among warships. Even if they are satisfactorily countered by protective devices and sweeping, their nuisance value is tremendous. Warships could scarcely leave port without being preceded by the snail-paced sweepers for a considerable distance. Fear of hidden mines restricted tactical and strategic movements on both sides. The British, for example, decided early in World War I that they would not send their fleet into the southeastern portion of the North Sea near Heligoland Bight, primarily because of the mine danger. By this decision they sacrificed at the outset much of their chance to bring the German fleet to battle. Allied mine barrages were notably successful in containing German U-boats within the North Sea. With the capture of Norway and the fall of France in the Second World War, however, the British lost the chance to repeat their former success. No mine barrage could barricade the whole coast of western Europe.

Among the unsung heroes of both world wars have been the few thousand men who have daily taken small boats to sea, in fair weather and foul, to sweep the traffic lanes clear of the diabolical deposits of the enemy. And their work would be halted were it not for the handful of officers and men whose job it is to salvage live mines of every variety in order to examine their detonating mechanisms and thereby to devise appropriate means of dealing with them. The countermeasures of one month may not be suitable to the month which follows, and the process of keeping abreast of unconscionable times may involve working at forty feet of depth with a huge black monster filled with booby traps and containing 1,600 pounds of TNT activated by an ultra-sensitive magnetic-acoustic detonator.

CHAPTER IV

Command of the Sea

IN WAR at sea there are no "fronts," no lines which are held by one side and besieged or attacked by the other. A large body of water cannot be occupied in the sense in which land areas are occupied. Yet surprisingly enough, one finds during most great wars that certain important maritime areas have a considerable ocean traffic from which one of the opposed sides is almost entirely excluded. The side which is able to carry on its own commerce and stop that of the enemy is said to be in "command of the sea" in the region where it enjoys that marked advantage.

Command has never meant a control which was either complete in degree or unbounded in maritime space. It has meant only that the efforts of one of the belligerents to control sea-borne communications over certain areas have been on the whole successful. Historically, nations carrying on a great sea-borne commerce during war have always suffered severe (though not decisive) losses from raiders in those seas which they claimed to command, and there have often been important seas lying outside the commanded area. In both world wars, for example, Germany has inflicted huge losses on Great Britain and her allies in the Atlantic, despite British command in that ocean, and has also enjoyed control in the Baltic. In neither war was the whole North Sea really commanded by either side, and the same has been true of the Mediterranean in the Second World War. Japan's command of the western Pacific in the months following her entry into the war did not save her from considerable losses there in merchant shipping and warships.

In fact, command has usually been subject to so many limitations and qualifications that some modern writers have balked at use of the term and have preferred to speak only of "control of communications." There is nothing objectionable in that except that it is a needless rejection of a useful concept. So long as one bears in mind that "command" is always relative and means simply a marked ascendancy in the contest for control, one might as well continue to use a phrase which has so ancient and honorable a tradition. One must remember, too, that command includes both the positive advantage of using the sea for oneself and the negative advantage of denying its use to the enemy. Where neither side can use the sea without excessive cost, or where both sides can use it even though at some peril, the sea is not commanded but in dispute. It might be said at the outset that disputed rather than commanded seas are normal in war, and that the first aim of the naval offensive is to establish command in the areas of chief importance.

If rejection of the word "command" were confined merely to terminology, there would be no point in mentioning the matter at all, but the repudiation of a symbol too often results in the repudiation also of the idea with which it is associated. The opinion has become current of late that command is not only an old-fashioned term but also an old-fashioned principle. A surprisingly large number of naval men have apparently decided that since the ultimate purpose of a navy is to control communications, its entire strength should be applied directly to that end without diverting it through an intermediate stage of "purely military" operations designed to secure command. Based upon that idea is the current doctrine that whole-fleet actions can no longer have a place in naval operations, which will henceforth be restricted on the defensive side to convoy and on the offensive side to the operations of "task forces" or cruising patrols.

This supposedly revolutionary idea is nothing other than a repudiation of what has been learned the hard way in more than three centuries of war. It brings naval strategy back to its prenatal days of the sixteenth century—when operations were largely confined to mere cross-raiding—and without any acceptable justification whatever. To the inferior power it may represent the only way out of a hopeless situation, though the *Bismarck* episode must have convinced the Germans that it was not a happy alternative, but a superior power which forfeited the chance for securing command in order to follow such a policy would simply be throwing away most of the advantages of superiority.

Obviously some nations are much more vitally affected by losses in shipping than others. Great Britain could be defeated in war by the destruction of a major part of her shipping regardless of what naval defeats she inflicted on her enemy. But Britain's command of the Atlantic during the first World War enabled her to win that war despite her considerable losses—losses which she proved capable of sustaining—and Japan's command of the western Pacific has been extremely effective in enabling her to execute her designs. To the United Nations in 1942 it was clear that Anglo-American maintenance of command of the North Atlantic was a prerequisite to the defeat of Germany—though it would not by itself guarantee that defeat—and similarly, that Japan could not be defeated until the United Nations achieved command of the western Pacific.

It is useful to distinguish between acquiring command of the sea and exercising that command. A fleet acquires or asserts command in a given area by offering to beat the strongest force which the enemy can place there. It exercises its command by using its fighting supremacy to keep its own shipping moving and to stop that of the enemy. The enemy may not be disposed to challenge one's battle fleet, but that does not stop him from attempting to wreak havoc upon one's shipping by a vigorous use of raiders of all kinds and by trying to slip his own shipping past one's patrol forces. To assert command may require only a modest margin of superiority to the enemy in fighting power—and no superiority at all if the enemy's bases are distant from the area which one wishes to command —but to protect a vast shipping even after command is established may require a great number of additional warships and aircraft beyond that margin of superiority. From the beginning of the war in 1939 to the end of 1941, Great Britain was superior to her enemies in naval fighting power, yet her tremendous losses in shipping during that period reflected a woeful insufficiency of fighting craft for convoy escort and patrol.

The number of warships available to a belligerent is always limited, and the problem is one of disposing them in such a manner as to secure and exercise command. How is this done? Obviously not by mere convoying, because convoy neither denies the sea to the enemy nor offers *by itself* any real safeguard to one's own shipping. A fleet dispersed into numerous convoy escorts is nowhere strong. Even a much weaker enemy fleet would, if concentrated, be superior to any of the numerous parcels of convoy-escorting warships it might encounter. The dispersed fleet would then suffer a series of losses which would shortly reverse the whole naval situation to its disadvantage. Similarly, enemy shipping is not stopped merely by dispersed patrol craft.

The first step in gaining command of a given maritime area is to keep concentrated in that area, or available for quick concentration, a force capable of dealing with the greatest concentrated force which the enemy can bring to bear. This idea is sometimes spoken of as the "principle of concentration," and the force which is retained for this purpose is usually known as the "battle fleet." Of course in some areas large land-based air forces will establish command or aid a fleet in doing so.

The battle fleet can secure command of the sea either by destroying the enemy fleet in battle or by denying it access to the seas which one wishes to control. The first of these alternatives is obviously preferable. It settles the matter completely and permanently; its effects may extend to areas hitherto controlled by the fleet which has been destroyed; and it releases one's own warships for other forms of service or for service in a distant theater in which control was previously relinquished. For example, destruction of all the German and Italian battleships in December of 1941 would have neutralized immediately the consequences of Pearl Harbor. British and American battleships otherwise necessary in the Atlantic could then have been shifted to the Pacific. A subsequent destruction of the Japanese Fleet would have opened the way for simultaneous assaults against many Japanese-held territories, and in such assaults even battleships could have been risked for the use of their heavy artillery. When the enemy has few or no battleships, one's own capital ships become an expendable commodity; but if the enemy has a considerable force in that category, one's own heavy ships must be jealously hoarded.

Unfortunately for the superior navy, however, the fleet which knows itself to be inferior in fighting power will usually refuse to offer itself for destruction. Within the shelter of its defended ports it is safe against attack, save perhaps from airplanes. It will present the adversary with an empty sea. That is one great difference between naval and land warfare, since in the latter a great superiority in strength is almost always capable of forcing a decision. It also explains why a too-overwhelming concentration of strength in a battle fleet may be a wasteful disposition of force, particularly if some of that force is needed elsewhere.

Yet a fleet which elects to refuse battle does not by that fact cease to be a threat. It is likely at any time to leave its base for destructive sorties. That kind of strategy on the part of the inferior fleet—of avoiding battle but retaining the maximum possible threat value—has been known since Admiral Torrington's time as the strategy of the "fleet in being," a term often erroneously used to connote other things. Such a fleet requires watching; its menace can be countered only by keeping a superior force constantly ready to intercept and engage it should it advance too far from its base. In other words, if one has not been able to destroy the enemy fleet, one must always be on guard to deny it access to those seas where it can do significant damage.

In the old wars, the inferior enemy fleet which avoided battle was usually neutralized by what was called "close blockade." The British upon the outbreak of war would, in theory at least, make immediately for the enemy coasts, where they would keep the hostile fleet locked within its ports. The menace of the enemy fleet was thus stopped at its source. Storms or adverse winds might blow the blockaders temporarily off their stations, or send them back to nearby bases, but often the very same weather conditions took up the role of blockader.

Close blockade was the next best thing to destroying the hostile fleet. The amount of sea left to the enemy's control was practically nil—no more than the water within his harbors. Since the fighting spirit and seamanship of the blockaders steadily improved as a result of their continuing activity and effort while that of the blockaded personnel steadily deteriorated, the British often contented themselves with a blockading squadron that was inferior in material strength to the squadron within a port, just as Nelson was inferior to Villeneuve at Toulon and Cadiz. On one famous occasion in 1797, two British warships blockaded a whole Dutch squadron by standing out to sea and signalling to what the Dutch took to be a strong English fleet over the horizon but which for quite a time was merely empty space. Ships on blockade would be battered by the weather, and their crews sustained by the foulest of food and sometimes racked by scurvy, but that only made them the more ready and eager to fight in order to terminate their vigil.

However, several inventions, and particularly the development of the various machines of underwater warfare—the mine, torpedo, and submarine—finally made close blockade impossible. The Russo-Japanese War of 1904–1905 was the last major war in which one side carried on a successful close blockade of the opposing fleet, and even in that instance the Japanese blockaders of Port Arthur suffered severely from anchored mines, losing two of their six battleships in a single day. Two years before the outbreak of the World War of 1914, the British cancelled their strategic plan of a close blockade of Germany. The submarine, underestimated as it then was, had become too potent a weapon. To be sure, if the submarine weapons of warfare had not made close blockade obsolete, the torpedo-bomber airplane would undoubtedly have done so.

The modern form of "containing" an enemy fleet consists of what is sometimes called distant blockade. This method is bound to be less effective than the old, because the moment the superior fleet retires to a distance, it concedes to the inferior a certain freedom of movement. The inferior fleet thus undergoes much less of the humiliation and deterioration which result from being locked within a harbor. It is able largely to control shipping within the seas left to it, just as the German fleet has controlled the Baltic in both world wars and has had pretty free use of the eastern portion of the North Sea at least in the latter of these wars. In 1940–1941 the British battle forces based on Alexandria and Gibraltar could impede but not stop Italian communications with North Africa, and they scarcely even impeded Italian coastwise trade. A blockade of Japan maintained from a distance could scarcely affect Japanese communications with Japanese-held territory in China and Malaysia, and would not begin to affect the Sea of Japan unless Russia were also in the war.

Distant blockade also makes greater demands upon naval strength, because the enemy may strike in any of several widely separated areas and it may be necessary to keep strong forces in more than one of those areas. In the first World War the British had to keep capital ships not only at Scapa Flow to the north of Scotland but also in the south of England. And in the Second World War the British have kept a battleship force at Gibraltar as well as at Alexandria and Scapa Flow.

In fact the process of containing an enemy fleet from a distance is not blockade at all. It does not keep the enemy within his base, it only threatens him with interception and punishment, possibly destruction, if he slips too far away from it. The battle fleet which does this is providing cover—the extent of which depends upon the specific circumstances—to the convoys and patrolling cruisers which operate independently of it. This kind of protection may be termed "general cover" to distinguish it from the "close cover" given by escorting warships to the convoys they are attending.

One writer on naval strategy, Captain Russell Grenfell of the Royal Navy, makes a distinction not between general cover and close cover, but between "general" and "full" cover, the latter being the cover which brings the enemy to action *before* he can attack the object of cover, and general cover being that which merely threatens him with interception following such an attack. Captain Grenfell's distinction really differs little from the one presented above, because ordinarily the only way in which a force can be certain of engaging an enemy before he attacks a convoy is to provide an escort for that convoy—that is, close cover.

In narrow waters, however, a force may, without being

near the object of cover, be in a position to interpose itself before the enemy attacks. That was the fashion in which the forces in Dover Strait protected the great traffic between Portsmouth and Havre during World War I and during the first year of World War II, and somewhat the same thing apparently occurred during the British evacuation from Dunkirk in June 1940. Smaller British warships took part in the evacuation itself, but the heavier warships which guarded the movement against attack by German battleships and heavy cruisers seem to have been stationed somewhere to northeastward. It should be noticed, however, that during the first World War the force that really protected the Channel against the full strength of the German High Seas Fleet was not the Dover Patrol but the British Grand Fleet at Scapa Flow, as will shortly be explained.

Naturally, whether a system of general cover really provides protection depends entirely on the degree of likelihood that interception will take place if the enemy makes an attack. It also depends to some extent on the relative military importance of the object of cover and the forces which the enemy might have to sacrifice in order to destroy that object. The enemy might be willing to risk important warships to get in a telling blow against unusually valuable convoys, just as the Germans had risked the *Bismarck* in the Atlantic and seemed willing several times in 1942 to risk the *Tirpitz* to get at a Russian convoy from Great Britain. For that reason such convoys often require a powerful escort, perhaps of capital ship strength, as well as satisfactory general cover.

A superior battle force can provide adequate general cover to friendly shipping and patrolling cruisers only if it occupies a favorable geographic position relative to the enemy and to the area it is attempting to dominate. A fleet based on North America would have a difficult time denying the North Atlantic to a powerful Continental European enemy, but one based on the British Isles is able to do so with relative ease. This fact, incidentally, reveals something of the importance to America of British maritime power quite apart from quantitative considerations. Britain protects the American Atlantic seaboard not only by her strength but also by her position, and because of that position Germany has been far less likely than she otherwise would be to hazard aircraft carriers in the Atlantic for the purpose of bombing American objectives. A fleet based on Pearl Harbor, regardless of its strength, could never afford satisfactory cover to convoys bound to Australasia, but one based somewhere closer to the sources of Japanese naval power would be in a much handier position to do so.

In order really to control a maritime area and to provide general cover for its own shipping, a superior navy must be able to base strong forces, or at least reconnaissance units, on the side of that area which is nearest the enemy. In other words, a forward position must be established; and if only reconnaissance aircraft or warships are kept at that forward position, the main force of the fleet must not be too far away to intervene decisively when important enemy activity is observed. But another requirement for full control is that enemy ships be forced to approach or leave their ports by lanes which pass within easy reach of the dominant fleet. Or, to use more technical language, the forward position ought to be astride some focal area or terminal area which is important to the enemy. Ships upon the trackless seas have great latitude in the choice of a route, which means they are hard to discover and intercept, but if they pass through a narrow sea on their way to or from their ports their routes will necessarily converge. Such a point of convergence, usually a channel or strait, is called a "focal area." But even if enemy ships do not have to pass through a focal area, they will have to converge as they approach their ports of destination, which therefore are known as "terminal areas."

The manner in which the British Grand Fleet secured command of all the oceans and most of the North Sea during the first World War provides a classic example of a fleet providing general cover to its own shipping and stopping that of the enemy by its domination of certain focal and terminal areas. The Grand Fleet, containing practically all the British

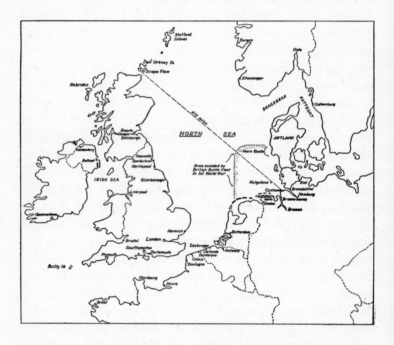

dreadnought strength, was concentrated at Scapa Flow in the Orkney Islands to the north of Scotland. An advanced battle cruiser force was based on Rosyth somewhat further south. Rosyth would have been a more favorable position for the whole Grand Fleet as well, but the anchorage there was not at first as suitable as Scapa Flow, particularly in the matter of providing defense against submarine attack.

The Grand Fleet was overwhelmingly superior to the German High Seas Fleet, which was based mainly on Cuxhaven and Wilhelmshaven, and generally concentrated for action in the bay called the Jade. All the German bases available to the High Seas Fleet lay along the narrow strip of coast between Emden and the Kiel Canal, which connected the North Sea with the Baltic. For the most part, strong German forces known to be in the North Sea could be expected to return homeward by direct route to a certain small patch of German coastline.

The German Fleet was safe anywhere within the Heligoland Bight and in fact for some distance beyond it, because the British had made up their minds not to risk their capital ships upon the great German mine fields south of the Horn Reefs and east of the 5th Meridian, except under unusual circumstances such as a hot pursuit. However, the distance between the German bases and Scapa Flow, which was about 575 miles, represented the maximum of the cruising radius of the High Seas Fleet, either northward or through the English Channel. If it was discovered beyond that distance from its bases, it was almost certain to be intercepted.

The actual radius of safety was in fact considerably less than that, for several reasons. First of all, the Grand Fleet might at any time be at sea and thus be much closer than 575 miles from the German bases, particularly since the British had a way of knowing when the High Seas Fleet was preparing to leave its harbors. Secondly, with many British cruisers and submarines on reconnaissance patrol in the North Sea, some submarines being stationed inside of Heligoland, there was no guarantee that the sally of the German fleet from its base would not be observed and reported to the British long before the High Seas Fleet had reached its appointed destination. Thirdly, a British fleet hastening to intercept would be steaming at top speed, while a German fleet unaware that it was being stalked would be proceeding at a more normal pace.

Thus, an effort to reach the Atlantic by either of the two exits from the North Sea would have carried the High Seas Fleet beyond the radius of comparative safety and was therefore out of the question, unless the Germans were prepared to give the British the opportunity which the latter so eagerly desired. Command of the two exits of the North Sea under the circumstances peculiar to the first World War gave the British command of all the oceans of the world. Within the radius of action of the German Fleet, however, the British exercise of command was much more precarious, and had to be furthered by special means.

One of these was the advanced striking force at Rosyth already mentioned. Here were gathered not only the fast, heavily armed battle cruisers but occasionally also a division of what were, during the first half of the war, the fastest and most powerful battleships in the world—the *Queen Elizabeths*. These could deal with any task force and were fast enough to "have the legs" of any superior force. The chance that the whole High Seas Fleet would overtake or intercept them on the seas before they gained the support of the Grand Fleet was almost nil, though the Germans longed to do it.

Another special means was the force guarding the narrow defile of Dover Strait, beyond which lay the important trans-Channel communications between Portsmouth and Havre. Dover Strait was heavily mined, patrolled by numerous destroyers based on Harwich, and these destroyer flotillas were supported by about seventeen predreadnought battleships based on Portsmouth. These obsolete battleships were not needed with the Grand Fleet and would have been almost useless with it, but they were excellent for defending narrow seas where their slow speed did not count unduly against them. Their job was to make it necessary for the Germans, if they wished to raid the Portsmouth-Havre line, to come in considerable strength—not merely with cruisers or battle cruisers but with battleships. Such a raid would then justify the intervention of the Grand Fleet, and would probably result in an interception after the German fleet had been exposed to gunfire, torpedo attack, and mine hazards.

The Germans had to content themselves with cruiser and destroyer raids on the Harwich destroyer flotillas. It so happened that a raid promised little prospects of success anyway, because the shipping between Portsmouth and Havre would have had ample warning of the approaching force and would have found shelter in either of those ports, the two being only about 100 miles apart.

The German Fleet was thus a prisoner within the North Sea, although it remained a considerable menace within that area. The longest cruise it made throughout the war was its voyage to the vicinity of Stavanger on the Norwegian coast on April 24, 1918, in a vain search for the Bergen convoy, which had twice fallen victim to raids of lighter German forces and was then being strongly escorted. All movements of the High Seas Fleet were dominated by the fear of interception. In the few raids that were made on the English coast, the Fleet itself advanced only half-way across the North Sea and sent the battle cruisers on alone to carry out the actual bombardment.

The Grand Fleet, it should be noticed, played its great role throughout the war without firing very many shells against the enemy. There was only one meeting of the two fleets, off Jutland, and since it occurred late in the afternoon of a hazy day the results were inconclusive. But the dreadnoughts of the Grand Fleet were an impenetrable barrier to German operations in force in the Atlantic, and they thereby enabled the Allies to win the war. The Grand Fleet was an enormous organization to send to sea, and its incalculable value to the Allied cause prohibited its being risked on mines and torpedoes except to achieve the one purpose for which it existed—the neutralization or destruction of the German High Seas Fleet. It was therefore rarely called upon to intervene except when the main German Fleet was thought to be at sea.

As a result of this relative inactivity, the end of the war saw a considerable diminution of popular regard for the value of the battleship. This costly instrument seemed to have no place in the war at all. Yet there were several times during the conflict when a transfer of four dreadnoughts from the Grand Fleet to the High Seas Fleet would have made Britain's blockade of Germany and her defense of her own shipping highly precarious at best, and might have enabled Germany to win the war. Such might be the value of a battleship when wars are decided at sea.

It is worth noting that while modern inventions made close blockade impossible, they also enabled a superior fleet to dominate a large sea from a relatively remote area. Steam made the battle fleet independent of wind and therefore enabled it to reach any desired point in a time that could always be predetermined. The requirement of fuel brought in by steam circumscribed the movements of both sides and made them more predictable, which also favored interception. Submarines on reconnaissance patrol could report the movements of each side to the other (which happened, because of geographical circumstances, to favor the British more than the Germans). Lastly and above all, the radio made it possible instantly to report enemy movements wherever observed.

Although these instruments and improvements were available equally to both sides, anything which reduces the opportunity for concealing movements at sea usually redounds to the advantage of the superior fleet. The threat value of the enemy force as a "fleet in being" is much diminished if it cannot proceed to sea without great risk of interception. Furthermore, the phenomenal growth in the size of warships, their dependence upon large supplies of fuel, and the constant risk of underwater damage made the fleet dependent upon huge shore establishments, of which there could be but few, and from which the fleet could depart but for limited periods. During the first World War the British knew that when the German Fleet was at sea it would within a relatively short space of time have to make for a certain spot on the map. Contrast this situation with an incident occurring in 1804–1805, when a French squadron of five line-of-battle ships left Rochefort and ranged the seas off Europe for five months without encountering an English squadron.

The further development after the First World War of another instrument, the reconnaissance airplane, enabled the British to control the Atlantic in World War II even after June 1940, when the entire Atlantic and North Sea coasts of Continental Europe from Spain to the Arctic had fallen to the enemy. England could no longer contain the German naval forces merely by controlling the exits from the North Sea. But the constant long-range observation flights of the Coastal Command of the Royal Air Force, supplemented by reconnaissance flights of the Fleet Air Arm operating from aircraft carriers, enabled Britain to dominate the Atlantic approaches to Europe in a manner essentially similar to the control she exercised in the first World War.

The *Bismarck* episode is an excellent case in point. The presence of this most powerful of existing warships in Bergen and later her departure from that port were both observed by observation craft of the British Coastal Command. She was shortly thereafter picked up in the waters between Iceland and Greenland by cruisers and was engaged by capital ships and later by torpedo planes of the carrier *Victorious*.

After she had destroyed the *Hood* and been lost again, she

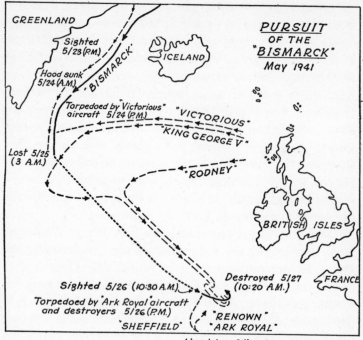

PURSUIT
OF THE
"BISMARCK"
May 1941

GREENLAND

Sighted
5/23 (P.M.)

Hood sunk
5/24 (A.M.)

"BISMARCK"

ICELAND

Torpedoed by "Victorious"
aircraft 5/24 (P.M.)

"VICTORIOUS"

"KING GEORGE V"

Lost 5/25
(3 A.M.)

"RODNEY"

BRITISH ISLES

Destroyed 5/27
(10:20 A.M.)

FRANCE

Sighted 5/26 (10:30 A.M.)

Torpedoed by "Ark Royal" aircraft
and destroyers 5/26 (P.M.)

"RENOWN"
"ARK ROYAL"

"SHEFFIELD"

*Adapted from Gilbert Cant's The War at Sea,
courtesy of the John Day Company*

was sighted 400 miles from Brest by a Catalina flying boat of
the Coastal Command. She was then attacked by aircraft
(launched by the carrier *Ark Royal*, which had rushed up
from Gibraltar to join in the hunt), destroyers, and later battleships, and a combination of torpedo hits and gun-fire sent
her to her doom. But the most impressive feature of the
whole event is the quick manner in which the *Bismarck* was
tracked down on the broad Atlantic and brought to account.
Important as they were in the actual attack, aircraft were even
more vital in finding this vessel when she otherwise would
have eluded pursuit.

The attack airplane, particularly the torpedo plane, has also played a large role in the struggle for command. In narrow seas there has been some trend toward the use of the land-based air arm as a covering force comparable to that formerly provided only by a concentrated battle fleet, with battleships serving more and more as escorts to important convoys. Such a trend might proceed to its ultimate conclusion, particularly if aircraft became more indifferent to weather and visibility than they are now, or, on the other hand, it might be completely reversed by battleships becoming as immune to torpedoes as they now are to bombs. It would be rash to insist that either development is improbable. We do know from a host of incidents, such as the successful passage of the *Scharnhorst* and *Gneisenau* up the English Channel in February 1942, that at least in some important areas planes are not yet by themselves a sufficiently reliable means either of establishing or challenging command.

But they certainly play a large part in supplementing the power of the battle fleet, and it might be observed that Britain's geographical position in the struggle for command of the North Atlantic is almost as favorable in the use of aircraft as in warships. German airplanes, it is true, have kept Britain from basing any of her few and vital capital ships on the south of England—which is the chief reason the *Scharnhorst* and *Gneisenau* got through the Channel—but British attack aircraft in that area can in part carry on the same function, as they did in damaging those same ships. The fact that no British capital ship had by October 1942 been torpedoed or seriously bombed by German aircraft in the North Atlantic, despite the considerable convoying activity in which that class of British ships was engaged, indicates how overwhelmingly the geographical factor operates to Britain's advantage.

The solution to the problem of keeping German shipping off the seas was also aided by aircraft. Germany's extensive coastwise shipping was much more exposed to hostile aircraft than most British coastwise shipping, and certainly more so than British commerce with the Western Hemisphere. The successful return of the *Bremen* to Germany at the outset of war in 1939 showed that even under conditions similar to those of the first World War, isolated ships could not always be kept from crossing the Atlantic and reaching German ports, although it must be remembered that the *Bremen* was unusually fast and made its celebrated trip during a season of lengthening nights. It certainly did not attempt to repeat the feat. But Britain kept shipping out of German-held ports after the fall of Norway and France not by having cruisers patrol terminal areas off Europe, where they would have been unduly exposed to danger, but by supplementing cruiser patrols on the broad seas with reconnaissance aircraft. In large part, however, the blockade was carried on by keeping cruisers off the ports of the Western Hemisphere and by closing such focal areas as Gibraltar and Suez. When most of the nations of the Western Hemisphere finally entered the war or broke off diplomatic relations with the Axis, their terminals no longer had to be patrolled. Commerce blockade need not be a matter of stopping ships; embargo is far more effective.

On the other hand, the situation facing the British in the Mediterranean after June 1940 showed the obstacles confronting a navy which does not have an advantageously placed base from which to control an area. After the extraordinary British success at Taranto with air-borne torpedoes, the British Mediterranean Fleet was easily superior to the Italian. Had it been able to base itself at Malta, it could in very large measure have controlled the entire Middle Sea. But Malta was too exposed to air attack to warrant use as a permanent base, although it remained available as a fueling station for convoys and warships passing down the Mediterranean, and as a base for submarines, airplanes, and other

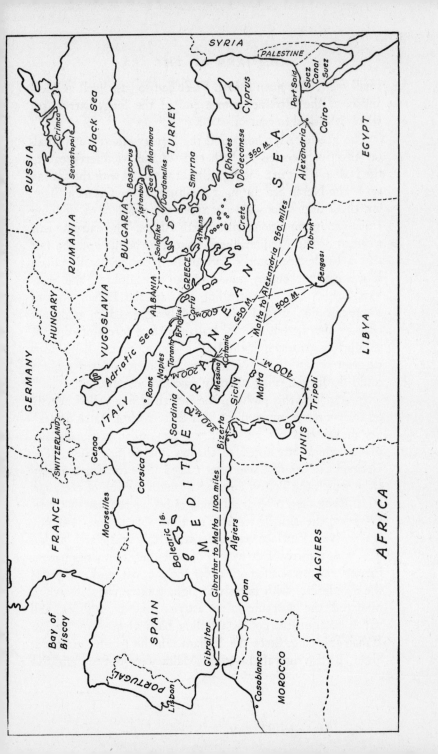

COMMAND OF THE SEA

small craft. The main British Fleet had to base itself at Alexandria at the extreme eastern end of the long, narrow sea which it wished to control.

The fleet at Alexandria and the forces gathered at Gibraltar effectively sealed up both ends of the Mediterranean to the Italian Fleet in a manner almost identical with the sealing up of the North Sea during 1914–1918 to the German Fleet, but these dispositions did not solve the problem of stopping Italian communications with North Africa. The extreme narrowness of the Mediterranean at several points and the fact that a battle fleet cannot spread itself out and still remain superior to the enemy added to the difficulties of the problem. British cruisers patrolling athwart the Italian lines of communication with Libya would be exposed to raids not only by aircraft but also by Italian surface forces of superior strength, particularly if the Italians knew that the British battle fleet was well out of the way. Besides, isolated cruisers could do little against strongly escorted convoys.

In attacking this problem the British at first relied heavily on their aircraft carriers, not only to keep close watch on Italian movements but also to drive off Italian reconnaissance planes which attempted to shadow the British Fleet. The German capture of Crete later ruined the exceptional advantages which the British enjoyed through the use of their carriers. Even despite their advantages before the loss of Crete, however, the British were at no time able to interpose any real cordon of surface vessels between Italy and North Africa. The most they could do by way of providing a semi-permanent barrier was to use submarines for the purpose, and to support the submarines with patrols of light surface warships which hindered the anti-submarine activity of the Italians, and which occasionally got in a telling blow themselves against Italian shipping. Since the Italians ran the gantlet mostly at night, British aircraft based on Malta were not too effective in direct attack, though their long-range reconnaissance greatly aided British submarines and surface craft.

A "blockade" by submarines can never be more than partial at best, and the Axis built up considerable forces in Libya first under Graziani and later under Rommel. At crucial instants the communications of those armies with Italy proved precarious and costly to maintain, but only rarely and for short periods were they completely severed. The terrific aerial pounding of Malta during the spring of 1942 tended further to neutralize that base, and the British were even less able to interfere with Axis communications.

In presenting general cover for its own shipping, the Italian Fleet was far more favorably situated than the British. The few British convoys that passed from time to time to Malta or down the whole length of the Sea had to have the close cover either of the Gibraltar force or of the Eastern Mediterranean Fleet. In those narrow waters the covering force did not necessarily have to attend the convoy directly during the whole trip, but it had to be somewhere between the convoy and the Italian Fleet.

The extensive use of aircraft on both sides further tended to confuse the contest for command. In the several narrow constrictions of that sea, the land-based aircraft available to both sides in great numbers were bound to play a large part in controlling communications. The British convoys were of course far more exposed to air attack than those of the Axis. The events of June 13–15, 1942 show the confusion of the issue in boldest relief. The British convoy moving eastward from Gibraltar to Malta pushed through to its destination but apparently suffered large losses among both the transports and the naval escort. The convoy moving westward from Alexandria was confronted by an Italian naval squadron which included two battleships, and turned back. It is noteworthy that the convoy which faced only air attack pushed through while the one which faced superior surface strength did not. On the other hand, the Italian squadron was subsequently attacked by British and American aircraft and forced to retire, not without suffering the loss of one of the few heavy cruisers remaining to the Italian Navy and a torpedo hit on one of the battleships. British losses in warships in these operations were five destroyers and one light cruiser, and probably damage to the heavier ships.

The only conclusion that can be drawn from these events is that while the aircraft of neither side were able to achieve real command, they certainly prevented the naval forces of their respective opponents from doing so, at least in the middle of that sea. However, events occurring during the very same period in another area show that one must be cautious about making generalizations from the peculiar circumstances of the Mediterranean. During June 1942 the large German air forces on the Crimea were quite unable to challenge effectively the command of the Black Sea maintained by the rather weak Red Fleet. The Germans admitted as much in their communiques, and they proclaimed it even more in the terrifically bloody effort made against Sevastopol during that month. Had the Russians not commanded the Black Sea, that base would have been much easier to take and it would also have been a much less valuable prize.

The Mediterranean naval war is exceptional in many respects. It is not unusual to find a maritime theater in which neither side enjoys command, but what is singular here is that both sides should maintain communications, however precariously, along lines which bisect each other. The British lines were of course far less frequently traveled than those of the Axis, due not to superior Axis strength in the decisive area but simply to the fact that the British lines were so much longer and more exposed. The Mediterranean was to the British what

COMMAND OF THE SEA

Macassar Strait was to the Japanese during January 1942.

The absence of command is particularly likely to be the rule where the areas in dispute are vast and the bases of the opposing forces widely removed from each other. Such a situation is almost inevitable in the broad reaches of the Pacific. After the Pearl Harbor attack of December 1941, the chief factor which kept the Japanese Fleet from controlling the whole Pacific including the eastern portion was the tremendous span of that ocean. Though greatly reduced in strength, the American Pacific Fleet was still more than able to deal with any Japanese cruiser patrols or "task forces" that might invade the eastern Pacific, and the Japanese certainly could not maintain their battle fleet in that region. To be sure, the immediate objectives of the Japanese were all on the other side of that ocean anyway. But the middle portion of the North Pacific was clearly in dispute, and even the western portion was not fully under Japanese control until she had used her fleet supremacy to capture new bases in Malaysia.

Numerous writers have emphasized the Japanese use of naval vessels other than battleships in their many descents on United Nations' coasts, but such an attitude merely betrays a lack of understanding of the strategic function of the Japanese Battle Fleet in those campaigns. That fleet was the covering force, invisible but dominant, under which all the Japanese invasions proceeded. It did not attack hostile coasts but it prevented the American Pacific Fleet, much inferior after the Pearl Harbor disaster, from intervening to prevent the invasions. So long as it held sway the Japanese had the run of the western Pacific. It is reasonable to suppose that Japanese battleships were kept out of reach of enemy coastal guns and strong air forces not because they were less able to do what the lighter warships did but because they were too valuable militarily to be risked for such purposes, particularly as long as the American battle fleet remained a threat for the future.

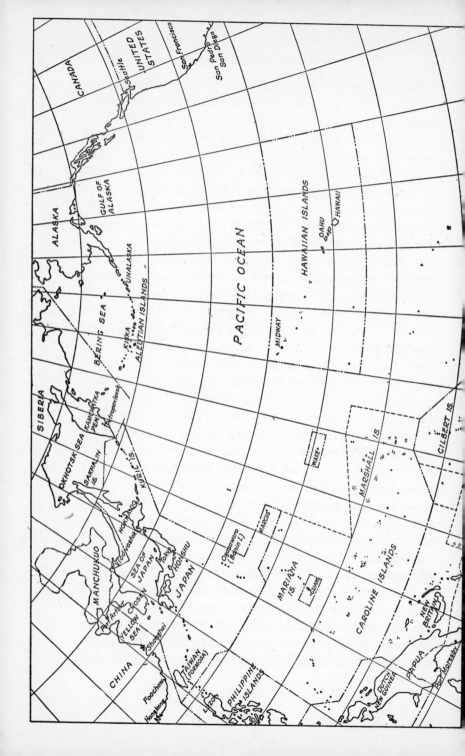

The Japanese could send their powerfully escorted convoys throughout Malaysia and the East Indies and land their armies without fear of being hindered by a strong naval force. Their battle fleet stood poised to intervene against any such menace, and we were powerless to defeat that fleet. Light surface forces could inflict some injury against the advancing enemy but usually had to be sacrificed in the process, as the battles off the coast of Java soon proved. Had our battle line not been so severely crippled, our Pacific Fleet could have been reinforced within three weeks by the most powerful of our ships then in the Atlantic, and the whole body could have sailed for the Far Eastern bases of our Allies—which were then still in our hands—where it could have barred all further Japanese sea-borne penetration southward. Naturally, it would have been necessary also to increase the defenses of those bases against air raids, but that would not have required nearly the number of planes and anti-aircraft guns that would have been necessary if air power alone were relied on for defense.

But once the bases had been lost to us, we could no longer challenge Japanese ascendancy in the Far East except with a fleet whose superiority to the enemy was overwhelming. With such a superiority we could wrest bases from him just as he had used his superior strength to wrest bases from us.

As the Japanese launched their attack southward against Singapore and the East Indies in the opening months of 1942, their naval supremacy, and the air superiority which was in large part derived from it, made it possible for them to move their convoys wherever they wished, albeit in some instances at bitter cost. Sea-borne invasion against territories upon which hostile air forces, submarine fleets, and light surface forces are based is bound to be expensive in shipping, but the Japanese were willing to pay the price and they succeeded. As they advanced their conquests they automatically ex-

tended their area of command, and their shipping losses in maintaining their communications fell off drastically.

On the other hand, the Japanese were unable to cut off from the outside world many of the islands upon which they were advancing until they had actually conquered them. Their seizure of bases on New Britain and New Guinea could do little to stop the flow of troops and materials to the important harbors on the south of the great sub-continent of Australia. Port Darwin could be reached from the east only through narrow Torres Strait, but the approaches to Sydney and especially to Melbourne had no such constrictions and left almost unlimited opportunity for "evasive routing" over the broad Pacific. The American convoys which entered those ports had to be protected with escorts against roving Japanese cruisers and submarines, but the chances that the Japanese battle fleet or any substantial portion of it would be able to intervene at such great distances from its bases were extremely remote. If the Japanese had captured New Caledonia they would have caused us to make a much wider detour to Australian ports, but it is doubtful whether even that move could have severed our communications. Sea-borne traffic to southern Australian ports could be really strangled by the Japanese only by capture of the terminals themselves.

The pattern of Japanese conquest was an eccentric one, a moving outward from a center toward a periphery. This gave Japan the advantage known as "interior lines," with Japanese forces always disposed between the major concentrations of the forces opposing her and thereby able to threaten two or more widely removed points simultaneously while concentrating mainly against one. After the fall of Java, for example, the United Nations were in doubt as to whether the next full-scale Japanese effort would be against India or Australia. Provision against the possibility of major attack had to be made in both places, even though they were separated by thousands of miles and could do little to support each other. The American troops sent to Australia were useless in the defense of Burma. Moreover, Japanese lines of communication to the different fronts were much shorter than those which her enemies were forced to use.

But this eccentric movement, this advantage of interior position, had also a marked inherent disadvantage. However far the surge of Nipponese conquest might reach, always beyond its periphery were uncommanded seas over which Japan's enemies were bound ultimately to bring the full pressure of their superior strength. Because of the many islands of the

East Indies, Japanese communications ran through narrow seas permitting great opportunities to enemy submarines, but the lines of the United Nations ran across the broad Indian Ocean and the immense Pacific. Japan might push wide the walls of her cage, but she was isolated from her allies and surrounded by a hostile world.

The preceding pages have emphasized the value of concentration of force in winning command of the sea, but it is necessary to express some qualifications of the doctrine. In the first place, there is a difference between tactical and strategic concentration. A tactically concentrated fleet is one which is operating as a unit. But forces which are considerably dispersed in space may be concentrated strategically so long as they can readily coordinate or combine their efforts. Because of their great mobility, naval forces are especially adapted to coordinated action though operating from widely separated bases. A spectacular and perhaps extreme example occurred in the *Bismarck* hunt, when naval forces based on Scapa Flow cooperated not only with air forces based on the south of England but with a naval force which rushed up from Gibraltar, about 1,500 miles away from Scapa Flow. The Gibraltar force included the cruiser *Sheffield,* which made contact with the *Bismarck* and kept her in sight until she was destroyed, the aircraft carrier *Ark Royal* whose planes wounded and slowed down the great ship and permitted the *Rodney* and *King George V* to catch up with her, and the *Renown* which served as a strong escort to the *Ark Royal.* The *Rodney,* incidentally, had left a convoy to join the *King George V* which had come from Scapa Flow. The radio is, of course, the agent which permits such coordination.

The naval officer is so accustomed to preaching the value of strategic concentration to an uncomprehending public which seems always to be demanding the opposite that he frequently

becomes dogmatic about it. He is of course thoroughly familiar with the idea of exercising with dispersed forces that command of the sea which is gained by a concentrated main body
of battleships, but he balks at the idea that the battle fleet itself may have to be divided. In the American Navy, faced always with the possibility of a crisis in the Atlantic and Pacific
simultaneously, there has developed an axiom of "Don't divide the Fleet!" This commandment sometimes results in a
thoroughly unrealistic view of the strategic problems facing
the country.

After the Pearl Harbor disaster, bitterness was manifested
on some hands at the fact that the Pacific Fleet had already
been reduced to a state of inferiority to the Japanese Fleet
before the attack. Several American battleships, including the
powerful *North Carolina's*, were operating in the Atlantic at
the time. It would have taken about three weeks for those
ships to be ready to cooperate with the Pacific Fleet. It might
be said that the *North Carolina's* would have been the first
victims of the Japanese attack if they had been at Pearl Harbor on December 7, but that argument does not excuse a disposition of force which is inherently faulty. Although we may
be glad they were not there, one should not depend on mistakes to have fortunate consequences. The question remains,
why were those valuable ships in the Atlantic when the major
part of our battle fleet was stationed in the Pacific?

All through 1941 the situation in the Atlantic was one of
utmost seriousness. The submarine menace required the attention of larger destroyer forces than Britain had at her disposal, and it was not at all clear that the British had even in
capital ships a strength equal to the many demands that were
being made and might be made upon them. The status of the
French Fleet was in doubt, the Italian Fleet had largely recovered from the Taranto disaster, and in the *Tirpitz* the
Germans had, among other heavy vessels, a ship which had

been proved by her sister, the *Bismarck*, to be disturbingly powerful. Britain could not at all be sure that our Congress would see fit to declare war against Japan if the latter attacked Britain in the Pacific without directly striking at us. In any case, it was imperative that she make a show of strength of her own in that area. Moreover, it would have been impolitic for President Roosevelt to send American battleships to Singapore. From the purely military point of view it might seem silly for us to keep battleships in the Atlantic in order to permit Britain to send the *Prince of Wales* and *Repulse* to the Far East, but politically it was not so absurd. As a matter of fact, it was not absurd from the military standpoint either, because each of our 16-inch gun *North Carolina's* was a much better match for the *Tirpitz* than any one British ship and also because the supply depot at Singapore was provisioned for British rather than American ships.

The dilemma of war in two oceans is not solved by reiteration of the axiom that the Fleet must not be divided. Even the soundest strategic principles must be considered as flexible, and in any case they must be governed by necessity. The problem is one of determining, first, the area of chief importance, and second, the minimum amount of strength necessary to achieve one's objectives in that area. Any remaining strength can be spared for service elsewhere if it be badly needed elsewhere. That is the real meaning of the principle that has been corrupted into the doctrine of "Don't divide the Fleet."

The British, who have fought their naval wars quite successfully on the whole, have frequently divided their fleet even when it meant that one of the portions was inferior, at least in material strength, to the fleet opposing it. The strategy familiar in land warfare of concentrating overwhelmingly against one enemy at a time and defeating him in turn is not feasible on the seas, where it may be blocked by the simple refusal of the inferior enemy fleet to offer itself for destruction.

Following the Japanese conquests in Malaysia, it was impossible for a fleet based on Pearl Harbor to conduct a real, all-out offensive against Japan unless it enjoyed overwhelming superiority. That superiority, and especially the vast fund of shipping which would also be needed, was not in the cards until the defeat of Germany should be accomplished. For a strategically defensive policy, there was no need for superiority at all. In the immense spaces of the Pacific, an inferior fleet could accomplish much if aggressively handled.

Events in the Mediterranean toward the close of 1942 completely reversed the strategic situation in that area. The brilliant pursuit of Rommel's defeated forces by the British Eighth Army—made possible by the support of the Royal Navy, which enabled Montgomery to supply his advancing forces by sea—and the adhesion to our cause of French North Africa (following the landing of the American Army) placed all the southern Mediterranean coast with the temporary exception of Tunisia in United Nations hands. Axis air power could now be largely neutralized by British and American aircraft based on Africa. This fact plus the acquisition of valuable new naval bases permitted our combined naval forces to reassert a large measure of control in the hitherto bitterly disputed Middle Sea.

In the Solomon Islands campaign, an important phase of which terminated with the Japanese abandonment of Guadalcanal in February 1943, the importance of decisive concentrations was again demonstrated. After a campaign into which each side kept pouring larger and larger task forces, with resulting naval battles which failed to be conclusive, the issue was finally decided by our gathering in that area a fleet so powerful that the Japanese were persuaded to acknowledge defeat without attempting to engage it with surface forces.

CHAPTER V

The Defense of Shipping

IF ONE touched the point of a blunt pencil to the chart of a large maritime region like the North Atlantic or Eastern Pacific, one would have darkened an area large enough to contain in cruising formation the battleships of the largest fleet in existence today. It is phenomenal enough that a battle fleet occupying at any one time so tiny an area should exert as great an influence over vast seas as it does. One cannot expect it also to account for every ship, friendly or enemy, which attempts to cross those seas. The battle fleet which gains command must ordinarily be concentrated for that purpose, and a concentrated fleet cannot be everywhere at once. Though essential to control of communications, command is but a prerequisite to those many operations which are necessary to keep one's ships moving across the ocean and not plunging into its depths.

Command of the sea by no means excludes the likelihood that the enemy will have substantial means of inflicting damage upon one's commerce—not even that command which is gained by the annihilation of the enemy battle fleet. The word "annihilation" has a loose meaning in military usage anyway, but it is hardly conceivable in modern times that the victory of one large fleet over another will be so thoroughgoing that none of the engaged vessels of the defeated side escapes destruction. Morover, the fleet which takes part in a battle will never represent the entire naval strength of any great power. Not all of even the capital ships possessed by either side were present at the Battle of Jutland, and great numbers of cruisers and destroyers were absent. When it comes to the mass of submarines, converted merchant cruisers, and various small torpedo-boats possessed by any strong belligerent, there is scarcely any thought of their taking part in a fleet action, and these, along with land-based aircraft, will certainly be available for raiding.

As a matter of fact, it is not inconceivable that a battle at sea could result in a somewhat enhanced immediate danger to the shipping of the victorious side. A navy which had husbanded its battleships in the hope that it might someday beat the enemy and thus win command of the sea would be likely to abandon such a plan after a decisive defeat, and it would thereafter be more willing to use its heavy ships in the direct assault on commerce. The Battle of Jutland, though not tactically a defeat for the Germans, brought home to the German naval command the realization that their so-called "equalizing campaign" by which they hoped ultimately to win command —a policy of wearing down the British fleet by degrees to equality with the German fleet—was doomed to failure, and the High Seas Fleet was thereafter used chiefly to support the U-boats in their great onslaught against British and Allied shipping. One might point also to the almost reckless use against shipping of the few German battleships existing in 1940–1941, which contrasts strongly with German hesitancy in risking the great High Seas Fleet during most of the first World War.

When command is attained by containing or neutralizing the enemy fleet through distant blockade rather than by crushing it in battle, it is hopeless to expect that raiders will not be able to operate on a large scale. Even in the old wars when close blockade was practicable, raiders frequently stole out of presumably blockaded ports, just as numerous French ships did in the Anglo-French wars, as American privateers and frigates did in the War of 1812, and as the *Sumter* did in the American Civil War. When the blockading ships are hundreds of miles from enemy bases, the chances for escape of the raider are much increased. The airplane and the submarine, of course, have little respect for any surface blockade.

The *guerre de course* (war of the chase), as strategists call the technique of commerce raiding, is ordinarily the recourse of the belligerent who is inferior generally, or at least inferior in the particular area where he practices it, and his own commerce as a rule has been entirely swept from that area. It represents an attempt to deny in part to the enemy what that enemy has already succeeded in denying completely to oneself. It thus differs from blockade, which indicates command and which aims at totality. Blockade is carried on by the entire naval strength of the superior force; commerce raiding is conducted only by aircraft and submersibles and by the few surface vessels that manage to elude the blockade.

Before the outbreak of the first World War in 1914, it had become axiomatic among naval strategists that the *guerre de course* could never be decisive. They insisted that it could only postpone an unfavorable decision, not alter it. Command of the seas would determine the naval issue in any struggle, and the depredations of a few cruisers were not likely to have much effect on the outcome. And indeed, the accomplishments of the great sea raiders of the past, while often spectacular, were rarely decisive. They sometimes influenced by their costly exactions the enemy's will to fight, but rarely his ability to do so.

That is not to say that the losses inflicted by raiders were trifling. American privateers and cruisers during the War of 1812 made hundreds of captures. Yet it was American commerce, not British, that was destroyed by the war. The British made up their losses by captures and by new building, and their commerce, far from declining, flourished increasingly. The ports of the United States, on the other hand, particularly in the latter phase of the conflict when we alone were at war with England, were subjected to a tight blockade which brought American commerce and industry to the point of collapse. Similarly, for all their successes during our Civil War, the Confederate *Alabama* and her sister raiders reduced in no appreciable degree the military strength of the North. Northern shipping as an industry declined catastrophically, but it was permitted to do so only because most of the trade it carried was not vital to the war effort—if it had been, it would have been maintained by convoy. On the other hand, the Federal blockade of the Southern ports played a vital part in bringing about the Confederate collapse.

The naval lessons of the nineteenth century thus seemed to warrant Mahan's dictum that the *guerre de course* "could not be by itself alone decisive of great issues," and the Russo-Japanese War of 1904–1905 offered no evidence to the contrary. But the World War of 1914–1918 proved that when practiced on the scale and with the persistence possible to large numbers of submarines operating in focal areas of maritime traffic, this form of strategy could reach such a magnitude of success as to bring to its users at least the negative benefits ordinarily associated with command of the sea. It was clear that a surface blockade, however complete, could now be met with something approaching a counter-blockade, and that the decision on the seas might go not to the belligerent with a stronger navy, but to the one least vulnerable to interrupted communications. What had been meant by the term "command" in the old language of strategy had become in a sense divisible, and naval authorities began to distinguish between surface command and sub-surface command.

The German U-boat campaign of 1916–1918 was defeated by the timely development of special techniques, but the margin of British victory was harrowingly slender, and the effort required to accomplish it was out of all proportion to the effort that the Germans put into their assault. And while Britain was reeling under the great submarine attack, surface raiders like the *Wolf, Möwe,* and *Seeadler* added their grievous tolls to the terrific total of losses, as did the thousands of German mines sown by U-boats and surface vessels alike. Moreover, there was no guarantee that the U-boat would be defeated again in any future attack if the campaign were waged under circumstances more favorable to the attacker.

The period between the two world wars saw the development of still another threat to shipping—the bombing airplane. Particularly to Great Britain, whose terminal areas lay within bombing range of the Continent, the bomber and torpedo-plane constituted a menace the proportions of which defied all prediction. Airplanes had been used against shipping in the first World War, but on a small scale and with meager results. Moreover, the enormous technological advances in aircraft during the inter-war period vitiated the worth of the experience gained. Unlike the submarine, which did not change remarkably between the wars, the airplane in 1939 was an almost wholly untried factor in naval warfare, and upon its unknown potentialities hinged the life of the British nation.

The war that followed brought England face to face not merely with defeat but with extinction. Winning the Battle of the Atlantic was for her only the first lap in a long hard race to victory, but if she lost that battle she was finished. Cut off Britain's sea-borne communications and all the tanks and planes in the world could not save her from subjugation. The entry of the United States into the conflict relieved the anxiety for England's life, for we at once began the most gigantic shipbuilding program in history, but the shipping situation remained a heavy curb upon our offensive effort. After the terrific losses of three years of war, losses that continued on a dangerous level well into the period of our participation, it was abundantly clear that a shortage of bottoms was bound to remain for the rest of the war a distressing limitation upon the total of blows that could be rained upon the enemy.

On the industrial front the foremost problem facing the United Nations was the production of new ships, and the urgent necessity of keeping afloat and in service those ships already in existence was plainly the most pressing problem facing their navies. The problem of shipbuilding lies outside the field of naval strategy, falling rather under the economics of war. But naval strategy as a field of study can have no meaning if it neglects the various techniques of defending the squat, ugly cargo carrier steaming its way over oceans filled with menace and under unfriendly skies.

It is now a commonplace that technological advances in the tools of war affect not only the tactics but the whole strategy of war. But in no kind of struggle is this more true than in the waging of the *guerre de course*. The reason for this is that the tactics of commerce raiding ordinarily involve the clash of wholly diverse kinds of weapons. The target is always the slow, vulnerable freighter, and that militarily unimpressive object must, with the aid of its escorts, be ready to repel or evade attacks from submarine, airplane, torpedo-boat, cruiser, and mine. Thus, the development of particular devices, such as those which permit the more perfect detection of submarines or which notably improve the accuracy of anti-aircraft fire, may mean all the difference between victory and defeat in the defense of shipping. The situation is different in the battles of naval squadrons (*guerre d'escadres*), where like tends to meet like, even though the participants have lost all resemblance to their predecessors of a century earlier, and where the advantage which change has brought to one side usually accrues also to the other.

The techniques adopted for the direct defense of shipping naturally depend upon the type of enemy attack which is most feared, the resources available for meeting it, and the character of the shipping defended. The kind of protection necessary against submarines is different from that required against surface raiders, and both may differ markedly from that most useful against aircraft. Measures taken against one menace are not necessarily incompatible with precautions taken against another, but some incompatibility is inevitable, and one must in any case balance means with ends. The enemy will not announce in advance how he intends to attack, or where. Even at best, resources for defense are bound to be limited, and one must make the proper distribution of those resources to secure their maximum effectiveness.

One type of cover for shipping has been examined in the preceding chapter, namely general cover, which is involved in the concept of command of the seas. The power to afford general cover is not, however, restricted to the force capable of commanding a sea. Any naval force placed in a favorable position affords general cover for shipping against all enemy forces inferior to itself. The Germans prefaced their invasion of Norway by sending their heavy ships, led by the *Gneisenau* and *Scharnhorst*, into Norwegian waters to cover German ship movements against British cruiser squadrons. To be sure, the covering forces were taking the risk of being intercepted by British capital ships, and the *Scharnhorst* was in fact briefly engaged by the British battle cruiser *Renown*. It was a risk well worth taking, and considering that the British at that time had no capital ships other than their lightly armored battle cruisers which were capable of matching the speed of the German heavy units, it was not an excessive risk. Similarly, the Italian Fleet has been able to afford a large measure of general cover to Italian ship movements to North Africa against the intervention of light British surface forces. In both Norwegian and Mediterranean waters, the powerful air forces of the Axis Powers were also an effective means of general cover.

General cover represents the most economical use of a limited number of powerful ships. True, it is effective only against the enemy's surface forces, and is therefore easy to dismiss as unimportant in an era when the major part of shipping losses are due not to surface warships but to submarines, aircraft, and mines. But the fact that losses to one kind of menace are low means not that the menace is trifling but that it is well under control. The surface warship is potentially far more effective against shipping than any other type of craft. Submarines and aircraft may take large tolls, but only surface forces destroy whole large convoys or strangle enemy commerce altogether. And it must not be forgotten that it is the cover provided by the battle fleet which makes possible convoying operations and anti-submarine measures in a region like the North Atlantic.

On the other hand, general cover is not by itself sufficient protection even against surface raiders, and it is no protection at all against marauders of the air or of the deep. Other techniques must be employed as well.

One such technique, the most elementary of all, is evasive routing. Although the approaches from the east to Sydney and Melbourne are distant from the bases of substantial Japanese naval forces, the Japanese were not unable in 1942 to send powerful squadrons to stop American ship movements to those ports if they knew the approximate time of passage and especially the route followed by the American ships. But it is one thing to send a battle squadron to a distant point and quite another to keep it cruising far from home in a search for ships which may elude it by hundreds of miles. Roving cruisers that might carry on such a search would be no match for the escort squadrons attending the American convoys. The defenses of such an escort would also be adequate to deal with any submarines that might be lurking in the terminal areas and with the few long-range bombing planes that might dispute passage, especially if the escort included an aircraft carrier with fighter planes. American supply routes to Australia illustrate how evasive routing may be used to get convoys through an area in which the enemy is in a position to place superior strength, but obviously this device is also indispensable in passing shipping through areas over which one has achieved command. The immensity of the sea is thus the first element in the protection of shipping.

It should be pointed out that the term "evasive routing" is here applied to any deviation from the normal peacetime route, whether by escorted convoys or by individual ships, but some writers on strategy speak of evasive routing as an alternative to convoy. They imply a scattering out of individual vessels in their journey across the ocean, so that if a raider is at large he will not succeed in catching more than one or two. During peacetime, shipping generally follows certain well known and narrow lanes across the seas, lanes which tend to conform to the great circle path between the terminals involved. In wartime, enemy raiders would need only to place themselves astride those lanes in order to pick off ships one by one as they came along. The extraordinary success of the German cruiser *Emden* during its two-month career at the beginning of the first World War was due largely to the fact that its victims had not yet shifted from their peacetime modes of travel. While the great circle route is the shortest distance between two points on the globe, ships on a long voyage may deviate from it by hundreds of miles without proportionately lengthening their journey. This makes feasible a considerable fanning out of vessels plying between the same ports.

The drawback of scattering individual ships is that it tends to sacrifice some vessels in order to get the majority through. If a raider is at large, one or two of the scattered ships are likely to come afoul of him precisely because they are scattered. Winston Churchill pointed out in his history of the first World War that the convoy system adopted against the submarine would have been advantageous even in the absence of escorts, inasmuch as a convoy, while seemingly a large and inviting target, gathered the prey of the raiders into a single area which was after all swallowed up like a mere speck in the ocean's vastness. Of course, Mr. Churchill was writing of a time when submarines operated individually and without aerial reconnaissance, but it is true that a convoy is not a great deal easier to find on the ocean than a single ship. The present procedure is to arrange all shipping on important and much-traveled routes in convoys and to scatter the ships only when a convoy is contacted by a raider which is stronger than the escort.

In general, however, the defense of shipping involves something more than general cover and evasive routing. It requires the attaching of fighting power directly to the merchant ships. The first step in this direction is arming the merchant ships themselves. A 5-inch or 6-inch gun mounted on a freighter is enough to make it highly dangerous for any submarine to expose itself on the surface in daylight within range. That obviously does not protect a vessel from torpedo attack, but it does keep the submarine below the surface. The submarine is thus unable to use its deck gun and is forced to expend its slender supply of torpedoes, and, more important for the intended victim, the submarine must maneuver into a position much closer to the target than would be necessary if it attacked by gunfire. Considering the submarine's low submerged speed, an approach for effective torpedo attack is not always easy. And torpedoes, even when well aimed, are often seen and successfully dodged.

A convoy of a dozen or more vessels each armed with a 5-inch or 6-inch gun represents a considerable concentration of fire, which is valuable against surface raiders as well as submarines. This fact was quickly appreciated by certain British convoy commanders upon the institution of the convoy system during the first World War. Some of them proceeded on their own initiative to drill the vessels under their care in the maneuver of forming a single line ahead from double column in order to be able to concentrate the whole fire of the convoy on either beam. Naturally, the fire of guns dispersed singly among several vessels cannot be well coordinated and controlled, and a battle line of merchant vessels is not easily maneuvered, but the fact remains that even a convoy lacking strong escorts is not so helpless against surface attack as it might appear. A converted merchant cruiser would hardly dare attack such a convoy, and even a light cruiser might regard it as too formidable a quarry. The net result is that the number of vessels available to the enemy for effective surface raiding is vastly reduced.

Because of the new threat from the air, merchant vessels have latterly taken on light anti-aircraft armament as well, which provides a helpful defense at least against low-level bombing. It was thought before war broke out in 1939 that convoying, which was necessary against submarines, increased the vulnerability of shipping to air attack. But the British decided to institute convoying at the beginning of the war and then wait and see the proportion of the air menace, with the understanding that if it became too alarming the convoys would have to be dispersed. Fortunately, the defense against the two diverse forms of attack proved to be not so incompatible as was expected. The concentration of ships in a convoy, with escorting warships in attendance, made it possible for the whole group to throw up a veritable barrage of small-caliber anti-aircraft fire.

But armament on the merchant ships themselves, however valuable, is not usually a sufficient protection against the various types of attackers. The armed escort is indispensable. And the chief naval problem of the United Nations in the Second World War has been that of scraping together a sufficient number of the right kind of warships for the protection of their shipping. Great needs have had to be measured to meager means. It has been too sadly true that the only thing more valuable than a merchant ship is the warship that protects it.

The best defense against the powerful surface raider is naturally a warship of greater power, whether cruiser or capital ship, and in both world wars capital ships and sometimes whole battle fleets have been used as escorts to convoys. Where a convoy with which no chances can be taken is involved, such as one carrying large bodies of troops, escorts must be provided which are capable of dealing with the most formidable squadrons the enemy can feasibly send to sea. For convoys of lesser significance cruisers of varying power will be in attendance. Since the number of heavy ships for escort service is certain to be uncomfortably limited—it has been far more embarrassing for the United States and Great Britain in the second of the two world wars than in the first—the raiding squadron sometimes encounters a convoy escorted by vessels considerably inferior in fighting strength. The results are usually disastrous. Several times in both world wars a whole convoy, including its protecting warships, has been completely annihilated.

The epic of the *Jervis Bay*, on the other hand, is an illustration of the worth of valor and initiative in defending a convoy against overwhelming odds. Just what German vessel attacked the convoy of thirty-eight ships she was protecting is not clear. It was first reported to be one of the pocket battleships, but it is more likely that it was an 8-inch gun cruiser of the *Admiral Hipper* type. At any rate it was a formidable warship, and the *Jervis Bay* was an eighteen-year-old converted merchant liner armed with six 6-inch guns, though unable to fire more than four on either beam or more than two or three ahead. Yet Captain Fegen's suicidal charge toward the German raider resulted in a two-hour battle, during which the raider, intent on avoiding damage, held off from the *Jervis Bay* to take advantage of the longer range of her own guns. But by the time she finished off the hen, the brood had scattered and night had fallen, so that no more than four out of the thirty-eight ships fell to the raider.

Before the outbreak of war in 1939, the British had been much concerned about the raiding potentialities of certain vessels of the German Fleet, notably the three pocket battleships and the three 8-inch gun cruisers of the *Blücher* class. And when the Germans gained control of the Norwegian and French coasts, the opportunities for surface raiders were at a maximum. Yet German surface raiders, while they have kept the British worried, have not done much damage. The *Graf Spee* was destroyed at Montevideo after she had sunk nine British vessels totalling 50,139 tons, a record which compares very poorly with that of the *Emden* and *Karlsruhe* of the first World War, both much smaller warships. The *Deutschland* (later *Lützow*), a sister of the *Graf Spee,* made a cruise in the North Atlantic during 1939 which showed negligible results except for the sinking of the converted merchant cruiser *Rawalpindi*. A year later the *Admiral Scheer* also made a commerce raiding cruise in the Atlantic with poor results.

German merchantmen armed as raiders have had somewhat better luck, but on the whole they have failed to match the results of the *Seeadler, Wolf,* and *Möwe* of the first World War. One, however, which operated under Captain Rogge in the Indian Ocean during the early summer of 1941, achieved outstanding success. Rogge was decorated by the German Government for having destroyed more than 100,000 tons of British shipping, which is probably a record haul for a single surface raider in either of the world wars. One of the most amazing feats of a converted merchant cruiser in modern war was the destruction of the British cruiser *Sydney* by the *Kormoran*, which landed some hits at close range before she was herself destroyed. The *Sydney* left the scene afire, and was never heard of afterward.

In March 1941, the *Gneisenau* and *Scharnhorst*, then the only German battleships actively in commission, made a sortie into the Atlantic in which they destroyed an entire convoy amounting to almost 100,000 tons of shipping, plus a few additional singletons. This was commerce raiding on a majestic scale, the kind the British most feared, but on the return of those two ships to Brest at the end of March they were bombed endlessly and mercilessly by the R.A.F. Although the actual damage inflicted upon them was not vital, they were at least prevented from returning to the Atlantic. During and after their dash up the Channel in February 1942, they were again savagely attacked, and British reconnaissance planes later reported both to be severely damaged. The *Bismarck*, far the mightiest warship ever to start upon a mission of commerce raiding, was sunk on her maiden trip into the Atlantic, though she brought the *Hood* down with her.

On the whole, therefore, we may conclude that despite certain successes, the part of the surface raider in the Second World War has not been brilliant. It has in fact been on the way out since sails disappeared from warships and merchant vessels; it began to go out faster with the coming of the radio, which reported its position; and now with the development of reconnaissance aviation it has been reduced to the role of a fugitive. Nevertheless, the threat of the powerful surface raider is always a concern to the nation which must defend a great shipping and greatly influences the disposition of her warships.

The German air arm, on the other hand, especially after the German occupation of the western coasts of France and Norway, has been a major threat to British shipping. Of the 581 British and Allied ships which the British admitted lost between the beginning of the war and March 27, 1941, the number sunk by air attack was 136 or about 23 per cent. If the shorter period between the fall of France and the end of March 1941 is considered, the proportion of losses from air attack must have been much higher, perhaps as much as 40 per cent. These figures take no account of the use of aircraft as scouts for submarines or as minelayers. They refer only to direct air attack.

The old dispute about whether the airplane could or could not sink a battleship has long since been answered, but the issue was always somewhat beside the point. The warship may still remain essential to the exercise of sea power even if it is relatively vulnerable to air attack. But if the Royal Navy with its air support could not defend British and Allied shipping against enemy air attack, the warship would lose all its reason for being, even if it were itself completely immune to injury from the air. Before the war, discerning observers asked not so much how well the warship would fare under air attack as whether Britain's vast shipping, with its 2,000 ships at sea and its 400 ships in the danger zone daily, could be carried on in the shadow of the Luftwaffe.

During the first two years of the war anti-aircraft armament aboard the merchant vessels and their escorts was extended and much improved. Balloon barrages proved unexpectedly effective. The balloons were kept lowered to the deck of the ships until enemy aircraft were sighted, and then rapidly raised. By keeping the planes above balloon altitude, they prevented low-level bombing and made the job of the anti-aircraft gunners much easier.

But the best solution of the problem of air attack was that of providing on some of the convoyed ships fighter planes which were catapulted into the air at the approach of enemy bombers. The fighter was good for only one flight, since it could not be recovered from the water. But inasmuch as the planes used were older Hurricanes, they could be sacrificed without great loss, provided the pilots were saved. The weight and great landing speed of the modern fighter prevented the use of air bags under the wings to keep the plane afloat—a device used during the first World War—but it seemed reasonable to expect that a similar solution would ultimately be found. Heavy pontoon floats would of course diminish the combat efficiency of fighter planes.

Since the attacking bomber had to descend to relatively low levels in order to deliver its blow, the swift-climbing fighter was easily able to gain sufficient altitude to beat off the attack. As a rule, however, the bomber would make off as soon as he saw the defending fighter taking to the air, with the result that rather few attacking bombers were destroyed; but the shipping was adequately defended. By the autumn of 1941 the number of merchant ships being lost to air attack had shrunk to 8 per cent of losses in the preceding April. This figure includes even shipping lost in the Channel, where enemy air attack was heaviest.

It might be argued that the enemy could overcome such defenses either by escorting his bombers with fighters or by using large concentrations of bombers in each attack. But fighter escort is not possible in attacks far out at sea, and large concentrations are neither easy for the enemy to muster nor as likely to find convoys as are bombers which spread out to operate individually. Even if large concentrations are sent against convoys already discovered by reconnaissance planes, they would be hard put to it to overcome the defenses which could be massed on convoys.

There is no reason why a large convoy could not be provided with such aircraft defenses that it could put 100 fighters into the air in short order, particularly if the convoy is escorted by one or two small aircraft carriers which might be improvised by conversion of merchant ships. In relation to the military and economic value of the shipping defended, the cost would be small indeed. Besides, a really large-scale air attack would under certain conditions expose itself to interception by land-based fighters, which a few isolated aircraft could evade. In that way the land-based interceptors would be giving the same kind of general cover against air attack that the battle fleet offers against heavy surface attack. One of the fortunate things about the usefulness of aircraft in the defense of shipping is that airplane production can be accelerated far more rapidly than warship production.

Whatever may be the future of air attack upon shipping, it was clear by the summer of 1942 at any rate that one of the specters which had been most terrifying to Britain in the previous year had been at least temporarily dissipated.

The menace of the German air arm against British ports was another story, however, and unless that kind of threat could also be countered adequately, Britain could still be blockaded from the air. It makes little difference whether trade is stifled on the open sea or at the water's edge. The full story of the defense of British shipping terminals remains to be told, but it was clear after two and one-half years of war that the Germans had not succeeded in knocking out of action a single one of the major British ports, despite continued efforts. Traffic into the port of London, although not eliminated, was considerably reduced, but this was due more to the exposed position of the shipping lanes leading to London than to damage at the port itself. The port of Liverpool continued to function not only at undiminished level but at greater capacity than in peacetime, although it was one of the most bitterly bombed targets in all Britain. Docks, it should be noted, are not nearly as vulnerable targets as they appear. Only direct hits on dock gates are likely to cripple a port, and such hits are very hard to register, particularly in night bombing.

The history of the mine during the Second World War has

not been very different from the experience of the first. During the early months, especially in October 1939, there was a good deal of destruction from the magnetic mine, but it was quickly countered by the degaussing apparatus. Later, acoustic mines were introduced. Although these types are very exacting in their requirements concerning depth of water, the Germans have had the airplane available as a mine layer to reach areas which are not accessible to submarines. It was reported in the autumn of 1941 that planes based on Crete dropped into the Suez Canal acoustic mines which sank three ships and forced the closing of the Canal for eight days. Because of the danger of repetition the Canal was considered unreliable for important military convoys coming up the Red Sea. Cargoes were unloaded at the south end of the Canal and transferred by rail to Alexandria.

By the summer and autumn of 1941 mines had ceased to take any substantial toll of shipping round the British Isles, but this happy result had been achieved only through a gigantic effort on the part of the British. In September 1941, Mr. Churchill stated in the House of Commons, "We do not hear much about the mine menace now. Yet almost every night thirty or forty enemy aeroplanes are casting these destructive engines, with all their ingenious variations, at the most likely spots to catch our shipping. . . . We do not hear much about all this now because, by the resources of British science and British organisation, it has been largely mastered. We do not hear much about it because 20,000 men and 1,000 ships toil ceaselessly with many strange varieties of apparatus to clear the ports and channels every morning of the deadly deposits of the night."

In both world wars, mines have been laid on the eastern seaboard of the United States, where they were a great nuisance because of the large areas that had to be watched and kept clear. Nevertheless, the mine has been a supplemental rather than a primary menace to United Nations shipping in the Atlantic. It has forced the British and ourselves to divert large resources to combat it, and it has caused some destruction. But it has been clearly exceeded in its frightfulness by another weapon.

That grim, relentless, and unceasing struggle which is called the Battle of the Atlantic has been primarily a struggle against the submarine. It is a struggle shrouded in secrecy, not only to civilians as spectators but to the adversaries as well. The submarine frequently has no chance to observe results after it has discharged a torpedo. It may hear one or two muffled explosions, which indicate strikes, but just what this means in losses to the enemy it often does not know. The destroyer dropping its depth bombs against the submarine knows even less of results achieved. The British have kept reaffirming that the reason they have not been giving out figures of German submarines destroyed is that the mystery is damaging to German morale. Perhaps so, but we know from the first World War that the chief reason for this policy is that they do not themselves know how many have been destroyed.

Occasionally the evidence is unmistakable, but oftener the issue is left in doubt. Although a patch of oil on the surface may be the only trace left by a submarine which is really destroyed, the appearance of oil is no evidence that destruction has occurred. On one occasion during the first World War the entire conning tower of a German U-boat was blown off by a depth charge, and the captain and another officer in the tower came to the surface and were taken prisoner, yet the submarine escaped and limped home. In both world wars the Germans have tried venting chairs and other paraphernalia through torpedo tubes in order to convince the stalkers above that their work was done.

Before war began in 1939, the British were over-confident

that they had mastered the submarine. They remembered too much and forgot too much. They remembered that despite terrible disadvantages they had mastered the U-boat, and felt they could do so again with much greater ease. They forgot that they would never have had the time to develop anti-submarine devices except for the restraining hand which America put upon the German use of the U-boat for two long years; they forgot that the devices which finally overcame the submarine would have failed without a vast flotilla of small warships to carry them. They forgot that the relatively few destroyers they had available in 1939 had a new enemy in the airplane. They forgot the narrow escape from disaster in 1917, and retained only the more comfortable memory that after all disaster had been averted. They forgot that the submarine might also improve its tactics, and that the very detecting devices which enabled the destroyer to find the submarine also helped the submarine to find its target and to communicate with its fellow raiders.

Shortly before the outbreak of war in 1939, when the Parliamentary Secretary for the Admiralty in the Chamberlain Government asserted that science had mastered the submarine, Churchill had warned that "we have this measure of the submarine, this superiority, only if there is an abundance, a super-abundance, of destroyers and other small craft available." But Churchill was playing the role of Cassandra in those days. Nor was another member of Parliament listened to, the son of Lloyd George, incidentally, when he sarcastically remarked, "It is very disquieting to find that . . . countries which ought to know all about submarine warfare have not ceased to build submarines."

As a matter of fact, the results of the Battle of the Atlantic for the first few months of the war were on the whole distinctly favorable to England. It seemed that the tactical trend so adverse to the submarine in the last phase of the first

World War had been a continuing one. The losses sustained by Great Britain were not unduly alarming, and about 10 per cent of the whole German U-boat fleet was destroyed in the first fortnight of hostilities. By the end of 1939 Mr. Churchill confidently exclaimed in Commons, "We should have to go back to the Hundred Years War in order to provide sufficient time and scope for inroads of this degree to make any serious impression upon the scale of our merchant marine. For every 1,000 tons of British shipping sunk, 111,000 tons have entered or left the ports of this threatened island." By that time the Germans had lost about half their original fleet of seventy submarines and had replaced only about ten.

Until April 1940 the Germans were less favorably situated geographically than they had been in the first World War, since they did not have even the Belgian bases of Zeebrugge and Ostend which had served them so well in the earlier conflict. But between April 9, when Hitler began his invasion of Norway, and June 25, when the French armistice went into effect, all that was changed. The Germans had not a mere pair of Belgian bases from which to launch their attack upon British shipping, but the entire coast of Europe from the North Cape to the border of Spain. There could no longer be any thought of enclosing the German U-boats in the North Sea through mine barrages across the English Channel and the northern exit. The French Navy left the war as an ally of England, and the Italian Navy entered it as an enemy—not too formidable an enemy, but troublesome enough. German surface raiders, aircraft, and small motorboats could now play a much larger part in supplementing shipping destruction by U-boats. Moreover, sources in nearby Scandinavia and the Low Countries for various foods and other commodities were now closed to Great Britain. These commodities, if they were to be imported at all, had to be hauled from distant points overseas.

The effect on the naval situation of the German conquests of France and Norway has given the final answer to those Britons who had insisted that England could and should fight a war of limited liability, that she should devote all her efforts to the sea war and let others fight the campaigns on land. It is now clear that what was most necessary to protect Britain's shipping on the seas, not to mention her industrial targets at home, was an army and air force sufficient, when placed alongside those of her allies, to keep the Germans from breaking through to the Atlantic. In modern times no nation can afford to fight a war of limited liability. It must beware of being undone by half efforts.

In June 1940, the losses of shipping useful to Britain reached 397,000 tons, and from that time to the following December averaged over 360,000 tons monthly. The entire shipbuilding resources available to the British, that is, those of the British Commonwealth itself and of the United States, could hardly replace in a year the amount of shipping that was going down every fifteen weeks.

The submarines, which in the first World War had always operated singly, were now operating in packs. The same detecting devices which made it easier for destroyers to find submarines also made it possible for U-boats to communicate with each other while submerged and thus to coordinate their action. The U-boat commanders who had proved their mettle were put in charge of such groups, which meant that the enterprising spirit of the "aces" could dominate whole flotillas instead of individual submarines. And one of the greatest defects of the submarine, poor vision, was overcome. The long-range airplane became the eyes of the submarine pack. The supersensitive hydrophones also were a great aid to the submarines, since they enabled the groups to hear their quarry approaching from distances of over fifty miles.

The British with their new devices and land-based air patrols did succeed in driving the U-boats out of the narrow channels in the approaches to England—and in the first World War such a victory would have been sufficient. But in this war the U-boats with *their* new devices were able to find and attack convoys on the broad seas. The new submarines were faster than the old, and while on the surface could easily keep up with a convoy. They remained beyond the horizon during daylight and closed in for the kill at dark, sometimes following a convoy for days together. By operating on the surface during night attacks they avoided detection by the escort vessels' detecting apparatus, and in the darkness and confusion they did their deadly work and all too often escaped. The shift of activity to westward in the Atlantic further increased the strain on the British convoy system, since anti-submarine escorts had to be sent much farther out to sea.

Britain could not hope to survive, let alone hope to win a war, with any such rate of sinkings as she was sustaining. And then suddenly, at the end of June 1941, the rate of sinkings fell drastically, and remained low, relatively, until the end of the year. It is true that Germany had turned upon Russia, but that hardly entailed a large-scale naval effort. Mr. Churchill asserted in Commons that during July and August the enemy was employing "a greater number of U-boats and a larger number of long-range aircraft than ever before." Why, then, did the rate of sinkings fall?

For one thing, the British had more escort ships. The easily built corvettes, while not entirely satisfactory, were being turned out in appreciable numbers. The seventy destroyers which had been damaged in the Norwegian and French campaigns of 1940 had been repaired and placed back into service. Many new destroyers had been completed, and the fifty transferred by America in October 1940 were no longer functioning as replacements but as additions.

The steadily increasing air fleet of the Coastal Command

of the R.A.F. became an ever more important factor, as did the Fleet Air Arm operating from the new British aircraft carriers. The giant Sunderlands, especially, kept large portions of the vital sea lanes under continuous patrol. The submarines were thereby forced to spend more time submerged, which meant greatly reduced speed, inadequate vision, and a consumption of limited storage battery energy. If the aircraft caught a submarine on the surface it would bomb it, and if the U-boat succeeded in crash diving before being hit, the airplane would hover over the spot and call in destroyers, knowing that the slow submerged speed of the submersible prevented it from removing itself too rapidly. The destroyers with their detecting apparatus and large store of depth charges could usually find and finish off the raider. Aircraft also greatly aided warships in convoy-escorting work by establishing contact between separated units enjoined to radio silence. Escorts could thus meet their convoys on the broad seas, and convoys which had been split apart by attack could be brought together.

And finally, the United States Navy was beginning to have a hand in the business. American cruisers and destroyers did not attack German submarines, but when they found one they followed it and reported its position to Washington by radio. And sometimes it happened that a British warship intercepted that message. The status of "non-belligerency" was, after all, not invented by the United States.

The result was that the Germans were losing a lot of submarines. After April 1940, when the British had claimed the positive destruction of about fifty Axis submarines, they refused to give out further figures. But there were several indications that Axis losses were continuing at a high level. On April 8, 1941, more than 450 officers and enlisted men had been taken prisoner from U-boats, and only seven months later, November 1941, this figure had leaped to 1,276, of

whom 807 were Germans. In World War I, 70 per cent of
the U-boats sunk had given up no survivors at all, and the
remainder gave up an average of thirteen men each. The anti-
submarine campaign has changed in many ways, but if the
1,276 prisoners had been taken under the conditions prevailing in the first World War, they would represent some 326
submarines destroyed.

That is a terrifically high figure—much too high in fact.
It shows that the number of prisoners taken per submarine
sunk has been much greater in the second of the great wars
than in the first, which in part reflects the fact that fewer are
being sunk by mines. On the other hand, that number of
prisoners indicates that the rate of six Axis submarines sunk
per month for the first nine months of the war must certainly
have been continued and probably augmented in the period
following.

Moreover, the British reported that U-boats were surren-
dering more often when subject to attack—a certain sign of
deteriorating morale. In World War I, the peak number of
German U-boats in service, 140, occurred in October 1917,
but the total of shipping sunk in that month was only a third
of the total for the preceding April, when there were about
thirty-five fewer submarines at sea. The crack crews and the
most daring commanders are the first to go. The cream is
quickly skimmed, and the remainder are less enterprising.
The man at the helm and behind the gun is always important
in war, far more important than those who have been swept
away by enthusiasm for technological advances generally suppose, but in submarine warfare he is all-important. By the
autumn of 1941 the German aces who had won fame in the
first year of the war were largely weeded out. Gunther Prien,
who had sunk the *Royal Oak* in Scapa Flow, was dead, as
were also Joachim Schepke and Fritz Lemp. Otto Kretschmer,
whose name had been first in the shipping toll, had been

fished out of a sinking submarine in the North Atlantic and was now a prisoner of war.

Mr. Churchill reported to Parliament in November 1941 that the *net loss* for the preceding four months was only about one-fifth that of the preceding period. That statement has been erroneously construed to mean that sinkings were only a fifth as great—they were really a third as great—but net loss refers to the difference between sinkings and replacement, and the fact that there was a net loss at all indicates that the problem was far from solved. In other words, the quantity of British and Allied shipping afloat was lower than it had ever been during the war and was still going down. And Britain already was fearfully short of shipping.

The British did wonders in alleviating the shipping problems, but they could not accomplish miracles. They could not eradicate the restricting effects of convoy, and they could not abandon convoying. They could not shorten the immense distances involved in their military communications, and they could not raise from the bottom of the sea the 10,000,000 tons which had been sunk by the summer of 1942. The solution of the problem facing Britain and America was two-fold. First, sinkings had to be further reduced by both defensive and offensive measures against raiders. Second, they had to build ships, and more ships, and still more ships—and that quickly.

The advance to full belligerent status on the part of the United States brought some far-reaching changes to the strategic picture in the Atlantic. The respective activities of the British and American navies could be more intimately coordinated, since there was no longer need for carrying on the pretense of independent action. American sailors and merchant seamen who had daily been risking their lives in the ocean fight were now doing so with the knowledge that their country was at war, a change that could not fail to support them in meeting the perils to which they were exposed. Finally and above all, the United States at war could institute a ship-building program which would have been unthinkable in a nation clinging even to the shell of neutrality.

There was, however, a negative side to the picture. With the United States in the war, Axis submarines moved in to attack the insufficiently guarded coastwise shipping of our Atlantic seaboard, and during the spring and summer of 1942 brought shipping losses again to a dangerous level. The shipping situation during the summer was black indeed, with the number of available bottoms at its lowest point since the war began. Russia was being pushed to the wall, but whether we could help her effectively or not depended above all on ships.

To be sure, the fact that Nazi submarines should cross the Atlantic to take up stations was itself an admission of failure elsewhere, and improvement in our coastal defenses in autumn 1942 reduced the rate of sinkings. But the Nazis continued to build substantially more submarines than they were losing, and by February 1943 the leaders of the United Nations were again reminding their peoples that the U-boat was the most serious danger confronting them.

Important in the picture was the great diversion of effort which Japan's power and efforts necessitated. The fact that she was the secondary enemy did not mean she was an insignificant one. Nevertheless, the problems involved were not insuperable, and there was little question but that our resources were ultimately equal to the task.

The convoy system, which has several times been casually mentioned in the preceding pages, deserves special attention because of its extraordinary importance in the defense of shipping, and, on the other hand, because of the numerous drawbacks attending its use. Convoy means simply the herding together of transports in groups, chiefly for the purpose of economizing on escorts. Without such economy, the general escorting of merchant ships by fighting craft would be impossible.

Convoy had been an accepted practice until the end of the Napoleonic Wars, but in the old days the great ship movements across the seas were largely seasonal anyway and hence easily adapted to the system; and with vessels plowing across the oceans under sail at four or five knots, a few extra days spent in gathering them into groups did not seem important. By 1914, however, the whole character of shipping and of the various threats against it in wartime had changed radically, and it seemed that, except for the protection of troop transports, convoy belonged definitely to the past.

Up to 1917 the idea of convoying all or even most of the tremendous sum of British shipping—which normally amounts to 2,000 vessels at sea each day—was regarded by most naval experts as wholly impracticable. But by that spring Britain's position was desperate, and it was clear that unless more effective methods of dealing with the submarine were found, the defeat of Britain and with her of the whole Allied cause was not only inevitable but imminent. British political and naval leaders debated the convoy issue long and bitterly. The controversy is worth remembering as an instance in which amateur civilian opinion as represented by Lloyd George was wholly right, and where expert professional opinion as represented by Jellicoe and most of the Sea Lords of the Admiralty was, at first, wholly wrong. And the substance of the dispute might be briefly reviewed because it throws some interesting sidelights of enduring value on general questions of naval strategy.

The admirals felt that escorts were useless unless placed around individual ships or around two or three at most. They doubted also the ability of merchant vessels to keep station in a convoy, which does in fact require a high order of seamanship, particularly at night when the ships are running without lights. Besides, merchant ships are not equipped with the kind of steam valves which enable warships to adjust their speed quickly and precisely. The merchant marine masters were the most doubtful of all concerning the possibilities. Nevertheless, when convoy was actually instituted, difficulties of station-keeping were found to be not nearly as great as had been expected. The point worth noting here is that a healthy empiricism is as valuable in solving naval problems as in solving any other kind, and that any solution which is not wholly preposterous is worth consideration.

The British naval command also felt unable until the entry of the United States into the war to spare the destroyers, light cruisers, and other armed vessels needed to meet the demands of convoy service. They insisted that to detach a large number of such vessels from the Grand Fleet would so reduce the effectiveness of that fleet that there was a risk of sacrificing surface control in the quest for sub-surface control. In principle, such an argument is entirely valid, but it happened to stem, first, from an exaggerated notion of the number of warships that would be necessary for the convoy service, and second, from a fundamental misconception of the whole purpose of the battle fleet.

The immediate purpose of the Grand Fleet was to defeat or neutralize the German High Seas Fleet, but that purpose was not an end in itself but only a means to an end—the control of shipping. To keep with a battle fleet, beyond a certain minimum, cruisers and destroyers much needed elsewhere may be in the highest degree wasteful. Precisely what constitutes a reasonable minimum of cruisers and destroyers and just how much concentration of battle strength is necessary to secure a reasonable superiority over the enemy are, of course, questions not easy to answer, but admirals in command of battle fleets are usually prone to put the figure much too high.

On the other hand, it is true that the convoy system in practice is subject to certain inherent and far-reaching deficiencies. In the first place, even when completely successful in stopping sinkings, convoy immediately and drastically reduces the fruitfulness of available shipping. Vessels are delayed in their departure in order to form groups, and then the entire group is held down to the speed of the slowest member. This difficulty can be ameliorated somewhat by placing vessels in different categories according to speed, but only at the cost of increasing the difficulties of organization. In any case, the "turn-around" of the individual cargo carrier is slowed up considerably.

The arrival of vessels in large groups at the receiving ports produces an alternate congestion and slackness that further deteriorates the normal handling capacity of the available facilities. In September 1941, after an accumulation of experience with convoy in two world wars, that loss was officially acknowledged by the British to be about 25 per cent. In other words, a quantity of shipping totalling 20,000,000 tons has the carrying capacity of 15,000,000 tons or less if the ships move in convoys.

An additional fault of the system is its predominantly defensive character. It uses craft that might otherwise be engaged in a more offensive manner—hunting submarines near their bases, laying mines for their destruction, or even making direct assaults upon the bases themselves. It may be true that a submarine must come to the convoy to make its attack, but that is not the only place in which destroyers or aircraft can make contact with them. To wait always for the submarine to attack before launching a counter-stroke means that the enemy is bound to get some ships, and he will in fact too frequently make good his escape. Moreover, the numerous ships that cannot be placed in convoys are exposed to greater danger than ever, as the excessive losses suffered by coastwise shipping along the eastern seaboard of the United States in the first half of 1942 clearly proved.

The experience of two world wars has shown beyond doubt that the convoy system cannot by itself control the submarine menace. Such control requires offensive action which actually reduces the number of submarines or which at least makes the life of the submarine crew a nightmare of apprehension from the moment their vessel leaves its base, if not sooner. Certainly the British destroyer *Campbeltown* which blew itself up in the dock gates of St. Nazaire on March 28, 1942 was contributing a good deal more to the control of the U-boat menace than it could have done in any amount of convoy escorting. The aircraft which bombed the submarine-engine factory at Augsburg and the building slips at Hamburg and Bremen during May and June 1942 were contributing to the anti-submarine campaign just as directly as the aircraft which escorted convoys. The campaign at sea needs both convoy and independent patrols, and the problem of finding enough small, fast warships and the necessary types of aircraft to serve adequately both purposes has proved in the Second World War to be a Herculean task.

The gigantic total of British and Allied shipping losses during the first two and a half years of the war was due not to a failure of the convoy system but primarily to the fact that there were too few escorts and aircraft to implement that system properly. With the increasing cunning of U-boat tactics, the problems facing convoy escorts have increased in complexity. But there is no indication that those problems are insuperable or that they are likely to become so, provided only that sufficient fighting craft of the proper type can be made available not only to strengthen each convoy but also to break them up into smaller groups. In the first World War thirty ships was considered excessive, but in 1940–1941 convoys of almost twice that number were not uncommon. Fifty or more ships proceeding across the ocean in four columns abreast present a delectable target for torpedo attack even from a distance—a torpedo which misses one is likely to hit another—and they extend over so much water that submarines can creep into their ranks at night and wreak havoc without being immediately brought to account by the escorts.

On the long coastline of our own Atlantic seaboard and in the Gulf and Caribbean the pattern of shipping is so intricate and involves so many distinct and usually short routes that the handicaps of convoy are multiplied alarmingly. It has been estimated that the convoy system in those regions means a reduction of at least 50 per cent in the utility of shipping. The campaign that puts such a burden upon the adversary does not need a large record of sinkings to argue its weight in the war.

CHAPTER VI

Land-Sea Operations

THE conventional division of the globe into land and marine areas, controlled respectively by land and naval forces, has always been highly arbitrary. The fact that war at sea calls for different techniques from war on land is too often permitted to obscure the more fundamental truth that naval operations are important primarily because of their influence on land campaigns, and conversely, that many great land campaigns are carried through chiefly to secure an advantage in the war at sea. Moreover, there are large and important areas in which operations ashore and afloat are associated in the most intimate manner.

Compared to the great land masses of the earth and the even greater areas of blue water, those zones along the coast which may be controlled by either land or sea forces seem slight in area, but such comparisons are deceptive. For one thing, there are so many islands and continents and they are of such irregular outline that coastal areas, although relatively narrow, may be extremely long. Secondly, on the domains both of land and of water, those zones which fall along coasts are usually of exceptional importance. On land they include naval bases, ports, railroad terminals, and in some instances the only settled and civilized communities to be found on the whole land area which they delimit, as is true, for example, of most of the continent of Africa, particularly the Mediterranean coast. On the sea, coastal zones include all focal and terminal areas of maritime traffic, the importance of which we have already recognized.

The line at which land meets water determines the limits beyond which land forces cannot go without the aid of ships or beyond which naval forces cannot go at all, but coastal batteries mounted on land will have a certain range over the sea, and where concentrated will even dominate the sea, whereas the guns of warships may penetrate twenty to thirty miles inland. Thus the coastal zone may be dominated by either land or sea power depending upon which is concentrated in superior force at the spot in question. Incidentally, the three-mile limit now generally accepted in diplomacy and international law was derived from the maximum range of coastal guns at the time the recognition of territorial waters came into being.

With the airplane the range of influence inland of sea-borne forces or of influence afloat of land-based forces has been phenomenally extended. Land-based aircraft are now capable of ranging easily 1,000 miles to sea and that range is being steadily expanded. On the other hand, as will be explained more fully elsewhere, the maximum range of aircraft is not a measure of the distance over which land-based forces can exercise anything like a consistent control of the sea. Russian control of the Black Sea (while Sevastopol was held) in the face of German air power in the Crimea, and British ability to send shipping through the English Channel while they were still much inferior to Germany in air strength, to send convoys to Russia along a route which runs well within 300 miles of the long Norwegian coast, and to get occasional convoys to Malta and through the entire Mediterranean in 1941 and the first half of 1942 prove that beyond doubt. Although the airplane has greatly extended the overlapping of land and naval warfare, it has not yet by any means obliterated the distinction between them.

One of the greatest differences between naval warfare and land warfare is that in the latter an advance upon the enemy's communications usually tends to expose one's own, but in naval warfare that is not the case. By its control of transportation at sea, a dominant navy can be at once blockading the enemy and defending its own coasts from sea-borne invasion. The offensive and defensive are thus combined in one operation. Seizure of command of the sea, which includes "blockade" of enemy commerce, is the pure form of the naval offensive, but a navy can be used also to initiate a land offensive. This it does by safeguarding the transfer of an invading force to the enemy's coast and by cooperating with it in effecting a landing. Such use of combined land and naval forces to initiate an invasion of hostile territory is known to strategists as an "amphibious" or " combined" operation.

In the hands of Great Britain, sea power historically has been notorious for its ability not only to blockade a continental enemy but also to strike at his overseas possessions and at points on the periphery of his power at home. During the many wars of the eighteenth century, England's favorite occupation was to relieve her enemies of their colonies, which she would either retain or trade back at the peace to remedy losses—usually her own territory or that of her allies—on the continent of Europe. This she was able to do not only with small armies but also with small naval squadrons, since the chief part of her navy, by blockading the enemy's ports, was at once defending the shores of England and preventing the enemy from dispatching reinforcements to his possessions abroad. This explains how England, always a small country with weak armies, gained at the expense of the great military powers opposing her an empire containing some of the most desirable regions of the earth.

The more spectacular strategy of harassing the enemy by raiding along his coasts was particularly manifest in the Napoleonic Wars, when Cochrane in one little frigate kept the Mediterranean coast of France and Spain in a turmoil, and when a succession of raids on a much larger scale culminating in a descent upon Antwerp while Napoleon was heavily engaged in Austria caused the latter to exclaim, "With 30,000 men in transports at the Downs, the English can paralyze 300,000 of my army, and that will reduce us to the rank of a second-class Power!" In that exclamation Napoleon revealed the chief value of those Commando raids of an earlier day, for England's small armies with their advantage of free movement along the sea were able to "contain," that is, keep unavailable for other action, disproportionately large forces of the enemy.

The most famous historical example of combined operations on a large scale was Wellington's Peninsular Campaign, which so greatly contributed to the French dictator's final downfall. Wellington's army was transported to Spain and Portugal and supplied there by the relatively easy road of the sea, while to come to grips with that army Napoleon had to send his forces over France and over the terrible roads of a hostile Spain still living in the Middle Ages. This long-drawn-out campaign in Iberia was the cancer of Napoleon's power and increased his susceptibility to the cold winds of the Russian plains. It was to this campaign that Churchill referred on that April day in 1940 when Hitler invaded Norway, but Churchill proved tragically wrong in his prediction that Norway would fall into the same pattern. Not Norway but Burma was to be the modern counterpart of the Peninsular campaign, with England on the losing side. Once Japan controlled the Bay of Bengal, she was able easily to supply her armies in Burma, while the British and Chinese communications extended over the poor roads of the mountainous Burmese hinterland.

The first World War proved that a blockaded nation was as unable as before to defend its overseas possessions, for Germany lost one colony after another to British and Japanese forces. But the ability to use sea power to strike at the periphery of the enemy's position on the Continent was shown to have suffered a serious decline. The only instance in which it was attempted on a large scale, the Gallipoli-Dardanelles campaign, ended in failure, though it is true that a wiser handling of the effort might have brought success. The only outstandingly successful sea-borne invasion in the war was carried out by the German Navy in 1917 on some Russian-held islands of minor importance in the Baltic.

The deterioration in this peculiar advantage of sea power was attributed to two main causes. The first and most important was the tremendous improvement in overland transportation during the nineteenth and early twentieth centuries. With the railroad and later with the motor truck, the movement and supply of large armies became for the first time faster by land than by sea. The second cause was the development of underwater weapons—the mine and submarine. A German U-boat appearing off Gallipoli near the end of the campaign in 1915 played havoc with British transports, and observers agreed that had submarines been present earlier, no British landing would have been possible at all.

The addition to these developments of the bombing airplane convinced many writers on strategy that the combined operation was a thing of the past—that the usefulness of sea power was now restricted to blockade and to the defense of communications between one's own and friendly territories. Weak island nations like New Zealand and Australia hailed the plane as a "gift from the gods"—to quote an Australian ex-minister—against the threat of an aggressive naval power like Japan.

Yet the Second World War has seen a succession of sea-borne invasions on such a scale as the world has never before witnessed. The earlier Japanese invasion of a weak China could be dismissed as of small strategic significance, and the German sea-borne invasion of Norway caught the Norwegians so completely off guard that it might almost be considered a landing on a friendly coast. Quite another story was the long chain of smashing Japanese victories not only in Malaya, which was an invasion from adjoining Indo-China only partially aided by landings from the sea, but also in the Philippines, Guam, Wake, the Netherlands East Indies, Burma, New Guinea, and New Britain, until finally Australia and India were being directly menaced. On the other side of the picture were the brilliant Commando raids of the British forces, the numerous bombardments by the British Mediterranean Fleet of Axis-held strongholds, both independently and in cooperation with British armies, the British occupation of Madagascar, and the Russian landings behind German lines in the Crimea. Finally, there was the clearly developing plan of a grand invasion by British and American forces of the continent of Europe for the creation of a second front in the west.

Japanese successes were due primarily to the isolation of the defenders—a result of Japanese command of the sea—yet the ability of land forces to defend their coasts proved less than had been expected. It was demonstrated that airplanes and submarines cannot protect coasts against hostile navies unless they exist in great force at or near the threatened point, and it is not easy for nations, particularly those which are already at war, to have large air forces and submarine fleets distributed at all the points which a new enemy might threaten. The submarine is no longer the protection for a coast that it was in 1915 anyway, which was proved off French North Africa in November 1942, when Axis submarines failed to halt the American-British invasion and inflicted some damage only at great cost to themselves. Japanese invasions showed also that it was one thing to move an already massed force overland and quite another to gather scattered forces against a concentrated enemy who has just made a landing, particularly since initial landings are likely to be feints to cover a more serious effort elsewhere. Finally, not all the areas of the world are covered by the same network of railroads and highways as is Europe, and there are many places where it is still easier to move troops by sea than by land.

Where the defender's air forces are small they are likely to be destroyed or beaten off by the carrier-borne aircraft and the anti-aircraft armament of the invading fleet. If the point of landing is within range of the land-based aircraft of the invader, as it was in the case of the Philippines and other points, the task of the invader is of course simpler, but many Japanese landings were carried out without benefit of aircraft, particularly fighter planes, other than those carried with the fleet.

What of the defender's artillery? It has always been axiomatic in naval strategy that land guns are superior in effectiveness to ship-borne guns, and that no fleet should risk itself against powerful coastal batteries while the enemy has a sizable fleet in hand. The American Civil War was one long succession of Federal naval assaults on Confederate fortresses, but in that case the Confederacy had no navy to speak of. Ordinarily the principle of avoiding contests with coastal batteries is rigorously followed by fleet commanders. For many reasons land guns of comparable size have an advantage over those of ships. They have a steady gun platform; they are easily concealed; they can by triangulation from different points along the coast determine very accurately the position of the target ship (an advantage which has been diminished by ships' using aircraft for spotting); above all, they cannot be sunk. The whole of a ship's battery is put out of action by sinking the ship, but each gun of a fort has to be put out of action individually by a direct hit. The fate of the German heavy cruiser *Blücher* in Oslo Fjord in April 1940 and the sinking of several Japanese warships including a cruiser by a handful of American 3- and 5-inch naval guns on Wake Island show how deadly is the effect of even the smaller types of land artillery against ships.

However, the invader has the choice of the point of descent, and the defender will usually be at some disadvantage in surprise. The latter will not be able to bring up a mass of artillery rapidly, and when he does it is not likely that his guns will begin to match those of the attacking fleet either in number or power. The great rifles that guard important bases are fixed. There are in the world a very few rifles of 12-inch and 14-inch caliber mounted on railway carriages, which besides being scarce can be moved only along railroads with firm beds and strong bridges. In the defense of a long coast the only really mobile firepower likely to be available to a defender besides his bombing planes is his field artillery, the largest guns of which will probably be comparable to the 155 mm. (6.01-inch) howitzer of the American Army. Such a gun is equal in caliber but not in range to the guns of a light cruiser. Most field artillery weapons are outranged and outpowered by the 4.5-inch rifle of the usual destroyer. Moreover, the defender's artillery is hardly likely to make its appearance in force at the spot in dispute until after the enemy has effected his landing.

The guns of a large fleet, on the other hand, are unquestionably the greatest and at the same time the most mobile concentration of intense firepower to be found anywhere. The guns of the main batteries alone of fifteen *North Carolina's* could lay down a barrage of fire which it would require at least 3,000 of our newest "flying fortresses" (type B-17F) to match, and many bombers designated as "heavy" carry much less than the bomb load of the B-17E. Moreover, the gunfire would be more accurate and more easily concentrated in time and space. Naturally a whole battle fleet will not be used for a landing where it is not necessary and where the fleet has other duties to perform, but even two 6-inch gun cruisers of the *Brooklyn* class could lay down a volume of fire equivalent to that of several regiments of the heaviest field artillery. Finally, a fleet can lay down such a barrage on a coastal position *some thousands of miles from its base.*

It was largely the great firepower available to him in the Mediterranean Fleet that encouraged General Wavell to launch his Libyan offensive in December 1940 against an enemy outnumbering him three to one in men and equipment. The Alexandria squadron steamed down the coast softening up the Italian positions for the advancing army, the battleships lobbing their 15-inch shells inland with the cruisers tearing up large sections of Marshal Graziani's new coastal road with their 8- and 6-inch guns. Destroyers ran close inshore, despite minefields, and picked off smaller objectives with 4- and 4.7-inch pieces. Sidi Barrani, Solum, Bardia, and Tobruk took their turns of the shelling. Besides contributing its artillery, the Navy undertook the task of supplying the Army as it advanced past Bardia and of transporting prisoners—over 54,000—and captured tanks back to Egypt. Taking a little time out of the Libyan campaign for recreation, Admiral Cunningham took his fleet through the Strait of Otranto into the Adriatic. In passing Valona, the battleships swung their 15-inch guns out to starboard and dropped one hundred tons of shells into the port in a bombardment lasting only four minutes.

It should be noted that Cunningham was aided in his exploits by the offensive spirit of the Royal Air Force, which was all this time administering a severe drubbing to the numerically superior Italian aviation in Libya. The R.A.F. was not used to "defend" the fleet in the narrow sense, that is, by direct attendance upon it, but its vigorous initiative in cooperation with British land forces had very much the same effect. Yet even apart from this offensive, the Italian Air Force at no time seemed able to offer effective opposition to the

British Fleet, a record upon which the German Luftwaffe was able greatly to improve.

The Japanese too did not hesitate to use the firepower of their ships where it was needed. The preoccupation of news reporters with aerial bombardment has obscured the very large part played by naval batteries in the innumerable Japanese landings. In their invasion of the Fukien coast of China in May 1942, for instance, the Japanese hurled on the Chinese defenders of Pingtan and Nanjisu Island the fire of twenty-one warships. To this terrible bombardment the Chinese were able to oppose very little artillery and practically no aviation.

When a small British army was landed north of Trondheim in April 1940, a single German destroyer which had remained undetected in Trondheim Fjord was able to wreak havoc with its communications by shell fire. In the ensuing debate on the Norway fiasco in the House of Commons, no item in the campaign caused more bitterness than the fact that this destroyer had shelled the British land forces with impunity.

The fact that the great gun power of a fleet could be used even against shores upon which large and well-trained enemy air forces were based was indicated not only in the British bombardment of Genoa in February 1941, but also in the Black Sea during May–June 1942, when the Russian Fleet several times aided the defenders of Sevastopol with its gunfire. To be sure, the fleet could not stand off such dangerous shores for very long at a time, but at crucial instances it was able to get in some highly telling blows.

On the other hand, the British failure in Norway in 1940 shows the difficulty of conducting an amphibious operation against a coast well defended by enemy aircraft. The small army which had been assembled managed to get ashore, but the devastating German bombardment of its port facilities prevented the British from bringing their heavy equipment ashore. Landing the massive impedimenta of a modern expeditionary force organized to meet a well-equipped enemy requires substantial facilities. Hundreds of tons of armored vehicles, tanks, and munitions must be methodically hoisted out of ships—a process which large forces of unopposed enemy bombers can pretty effectively hinder. Had the point of disembarkation been somewhat closer to the British Isles and thus within range of R.A.F. fighters, the failure might not have been so complete or so rapid, though that would not have made up for the fact that the British force landed was simply inadequate to deal with the armies which the Germans already had in Norway.

The British failure at Dakar is attributable to errors in political judgment as well as in strategy. The probability of re-sistance was not foreseen, and no plans were formulated in the event of a landing being resisted. Failing to take the advantage of surprise, the British and de Gaullist forces appeared off the base and delivered an ultimatum, forfeiting a strategic gain for political objectives which in fact were not attained. The British-Free French forces were so anxious not to spill French blood that they waited a full hour after the French guns opened fire before replying with their own. In the ensuing fracas their ships took from the coastal guns and the 15-inch pieces of the stranded *Richelieu* blows about as good as those they gave. After two days of desultory exchange of fire, the British and their Free French allies withdrew. A swift, surprise attack, or a landing in force down the coast out of range of the stationary defending guns would almost certainly have resulted in success. Since Dakar later became a refueling base for German U-boats, the British failure there was exceedingly costly.

At Madagascar in May 1942 the British again prefaced their attack with an ultimatum, but in every other respect the situation was wholly different. There the British were prepared for action and after the initial amenities pressed forward with the utmost vigor. The Madagascar episode, incidentally, is also an example of the technique of capturing naval bases by landings outside the zone commanded by their guns, since the base of Diego Suarez was taken by land assault.

The question might be asked, what good is fixed heavy artillery for the defense of bases if the enemy can land forces on another part of the coast outside their range and proceed to attack by land? The answer depends on circumstances. Some bases are on small islands, the entire periphery of which can be effectively defended. In any case, the enemy attack is canalized. Unless his own naval force is overwhelming and willing to engage in a duel, he must put his troops ashore some distance away, usually without benefit of port facilities, and then advance over a terrain which nature may have made difficult and which the defending garrison can make more difficult. A long-established base will have been well organized for defense in every direction. The fleet dares not approach where its artillery would be most useful—on the defenders' stronghold. The 18-inch guns mounted at Singapore did not save that port, but they did, along with their lesser brothers, impose upon the Japanese an arduous, time-consuming invasion from Indo-China down the entire length of the Malay Peninsula. The coast of that peninsula was not suitable for landings because of its reefs—though the threat of landings behind their lines undoubtedly hindered the British defense [1]—and a sufficient army in Malaya would have saved Singapore altogether. Singapore's heavy artillery delayed the

[1] It has been unofficially reported that when the Japanese took the island of Penang off the west coast of Malaya, they found a large number of undamaged British ships and boats, which they subsequently used for landings behind the British lines. The British did not expect to have to counter landings on the west coast of the Peninsula as well as on the east coast.

fall of that base by two months without firing a shot. That delay might have been decisive; it will unquestionably turn out to have been valuable. When the story of the war is told, it may appear that Australia was saved by the unfired monsters mounted at Singapore.

On the whole, therefore, the belligerent who controls the sea that washes the enemy's domain exercises a power which is hardly known in land warfare. He can concentrate an army in his own ports unseen. He can then transport that army to any selected point along hundreds or perhaps thousands of miles of enemy coastline. The approach is not governed by mountains or valleys as on land, except in so far as the terrain behind the coast influences the choice of a place of landing. To confuse the enemy, landings will occur simultaneously at several places. Complete surprise is almost inevitable if the distance from the attacking base is short; if it is long, reconnaissance planes will probably sight the expedition, but discovery may not reveal the exact position of the landing. The expedition will almost certainly be timed to make its final approach by night and to arrive at the enemy coast just before dawn.

It might, incidentally, be observed that land-based planes which strike at enemy coastal objectives by passing over a stretch of water usually have the advantages of surprise that are peculiarly characteristic of attacks from the sea. They are rarely seen by the enemy before they reach their objective, which is not true of raids proceeding over land. The defense of Moscow, for example, proved much easier than it would have if the city had been on or near a coast. Thus, even in aerial warfare, there is something distinctive about raids from the direction of the sea.

To be sure, the unique advantage of the combined operation cannot, except for mere raids, be exploited by the dominant naval power unless that power has the land strength to follow it through. Such an operation is after all merely the use of a navy to initiate and supply a *land offensive*. The navy permits the attacker a wide latitude of choice in place of attack and then assumes responsibility for transporting an army to its place of disembarkation and of supplying it there, of protecting any flanks which rest upon the sea, and perhaps of aiding it with its fire power; but the rest is up to the army.

The reluctance of the British and American armies to invade German-held France or Norway in the middle of 1942 was by no means due to inability to effect a landing. So far as concerned nearby France, British air strength as well as naval power would certainly suffice to establish one or more bridgeheads. But whether the British and Americans could pour into those bridgeheads sufficient forces to cope with the large German armies still in western Europe was another question. A "second front" meant an expeditionary force ready to meet thirty divisions at the outset and perhaps a hundred before many months had passed. Otherwise another and more disastrous Dunkirk would be in the offing.

The problem was to provide first the necessary armies and second sufficient shipping to pour the men and equipment onto the Continent quickly. Norway, though of less decisive value, offered an objective with more limited problems, but most of Norway was beyond the operating range of British fighter planes, and German air strength in that country was still formidable. Armies could be landed, but at a great cost in men and in an already critically limited shipping. In any case the price in ships would be high, and to pay it the Allies would have to be in a better shipping position than they were in the middle of 1942. The British and Americans had to restrain their offensive ardor with the knowledge that while "too little and too late" was always bad strategy, "too little and too soon" might be equally bad, particularly if by waiting, the "too little" could be altered to "enough." To be sure, events on the Russian front were as likely to dictate the timing of the assault as any statistical tables of ships and arms.

The problem was in several respects similar in the Pacific, though there it was naval strength rather than armies which was needed in abundance. But it was clear that territories in Japanese hands in the Pacific and Indian oceans would have to be captured from the Japanese and converted into advanced bases for our own offensive strength before Japan could be defeated. Any effort in the near future to defeat that nation by "less costly" means—air raids based on Alaska for instance —would be looking toward a ten-year war with no guarantee of victory at the end.

It is obvious that the enemy's land-based air forces make a descent upon his coasts more costly and difficult than it otherwise would be. *But it is idle to talk about air forces keeping navies out of coastal waters unless we consider both the air forces and the navies in quantitative terms.* On land the machine gun has made infantry assaults more costly and difficult than formerly, and the anti-tank gun has had the same effect on the armored offensive. But the offensive is still possible, and always has been. In the spring of 1918, when the machine gun was supposed to have stultified completely the unarmored infantry attack, the Germans drove the British and French armies to the wall, and almost won the war, without using tanks and without any marked over-all superiority in numbers. When the defense has a new and effective weapon, it must be countered by new tactics and by exploiting to the fullest the possibilities of suprise and mobility in order to achieve sudden concentrations at unexpected points.

The Japanese failure at Midway in June 1942 was no reason for our not making a similar attempt against Japanese Islands at a later time. We would need more strength than they had on that occasion, particularly in carrier-borne aircraft and anti-aircraft armament. We would have to be more on guard against enemy air approach than they were. Above all, we would have to have such a margin of superiority in naval strength as to be able to accept losses.

Since the first printing of this book, the American invasion of the Solomon Islands has taken place. The long sea-air-land campaign which finally terminated in the Japanese abandonment of Guadalcanal in February 1943 served to remind the public that in the attack and defense of coasts the surface warship could still be the controlling factor. During most of the campaign the scarcity of aircraft carriers on both sides due to losses and the even greater scarcity of airdromes limited the aircraft available to a number which could hardly be decisive against the powerful surface forces operating in the area. Our only sizable airdrome in the immediate vicinity was Henderson Field on Guadalcanal. Australia was too far away to serve as a satisfactory base even for large bombers, and dive-bombers and torpedo-bombers could not fly the round-trip distance with military loads at all. The issue was finally decided by a series of naval battles, culminating in a situation where the Japanese acknowledged our complete superiority in surface strength and retired. One of the features of the campaign was the frequent heavy shelling at night of enemy land positions by warships of both sides.

And on the opposite side of the world there occurred in November 1942 an amphibious operation of a magnitude never before approached in history. The passage from Britain and the United States of an armada comprising 850 transports and warships and the successful landing of the large army it carried on the shores of French North Africa proved conclusively that sea-borne invasion is far from dead. But with the approach of spring 1943 even greater amphibious efforts were in the offing.

CHAPTER VII

Bases

THE majority of amphibious operations are undertaken for the purpose of capturing places already functioning as air or naval bases, or which might be made to serve as such. The intention may be to use such a base for oneself, or to deprive the enemy of its use, or both. The British descent upon Madagascar was obviously motivated primarily by a desire to keep that base out of Japanese hands. The Japanese offensive against Singapore seems also to have been aimed primarily at depriving the United Nations of its use, and only secondarily at making it available for themselves. On the other hand, the German invasion of Norway, the Japanese occupation of some of the Aleutian Islands, and the unsuccessful effort of the Japanese against the Midway Islands in June 1942 were clearly aimed at securing new operating bases for the attackers. In other words, while the combined or amphibious operation always involves an offensive campaign, its ultimate purpose in the strategy of a war may be either offensive or defensive.

A base is precisely what its name implies; it is a point of support, or, as the strategists like to call it, a *point d'appui*. Strategically it is meaningless unless a fleet or air force is either operating or available to operate from it. This point would seem to be self-evident, but recent discussion on the strategic importance of certain bases has tended to confuse the public into believing that a base is itself an instrument of offense or defense. The new American bases in the Atlantic and the Caribbean have been spoken of as defending America, without regard to whether we could in a crisis spare naval forces from other theaters to operate from them.

The glib assertion that "bases mean ships," while in a sense true, is confusing to the layman. The relative value of bases and ships is indicated by the fact that while bases can make one's ships and planes more effective, they cannot produce them, whereas ships and planes can produce bases by capture. That the Japanese were mindful of this distinction was evident by their careful avoidance of strong coastal batteries and by their withholding the main battle fleet from participation in the landings. This fleet might have been able to take Singapore by direct assault, but only at a cost in ships that she could not afford to pay in view of the inherent American naval strength in the Pacific. Despite her desperate need to make the most of her time, Japan preferred the slower method of land assault. The situation was exactly similar to that which faced her in 1904, when she had to take Port Arthur by land assault and destroy the Russian squadron within that port before the Russian Baltic Fleet arrived on the scene, meanwhile sparing her own ships for the coming showdown. But in both cases her temporary command of the sea resulting from superiority in available warships and aircraft enabled her to win important bases.

Naturally, the base which can be wrested from the enemy will not ordinarily possess the advantages of a position which has been carefully selected and developed during peacetime. A really good base will of course be heavily defended, and therefore quite costly or perhaps impossible to capture. The cheap price paid by Japan for Singapore is not a good measure of what the capture of such a base should have cost. Besides, when the base is captured, the conqueror will undoubtedly find most of the installations destroyed or damaged.

But in wartime one who lacks the best must make the most of second best. Any island or littoral territory enjoying a favorable strategic location and possessing an anchorage and enough flat terrain for airdromes can be developed fairly quickly into a usable operating base. To be sure, in some important areas of the world these requirements are not easily met. But it is necessary to distinguish between physical requirements which a navy deems desirable when choosing a site for a base in peacetime and those which it will endure under the pressure of grim necessity. One has to distinguish also between types of bases, which vary from mere refueling stations to vast establishments capable of repairing extensive damage on battleships.

In general, a base performs two functions for a fleet—supply and repair. It has now become fashionable to call a base also a place for "resting personnel"—a very new conception in naval strategy—but casinos and amusement palaces are not indispensable. In the past, the fighting efficiency of navies has always been inversely proportional to the amount of time which the personnel spent ashore. Submarine and destroyer personnel need frequent leave because of the unusually trying conditions of their life afloat, but a fleet with a good fighting morale considers a base a place in which to prepare for sea rather than a refuge from the sea.

The supply or "operating" base may have few or many facilities for the repair of ships. There is a tendency for an operating base developed over a number of years to acquire also repair facilities of some proportions, but ordinarily the operating base and the base for major repairs ("home" or "dockyard" base) are different and sometimes widely separated establishments. During the early part of the first World War, Scapa Flow was hardly more than an anchorage. Later a floating dock was sent to nearby Invergordon, but Rosyth remained throughout the war the chief naval repair base on the east coast of Britain. Pearl Harbor, which is our chief operating base in the Pacific, has only one dock capable of taking the largest battleships, which makes our Pacific Fleet somewhat dependent for repairs on the dockyards of the San Pedro-San Diego area. Each major vessel in our fleet has one or more home bases on our coasts at which is kept a store of parts and refittings (new guns, etc.) designed for that particular vessel. Repair bases are thus highly specialized, and one outfitted for the American Fleet would be of much diminished usefulness to British vessels.

The operating base to be useful should be placed close to the main theater of action. Consider for example the operations of a cruiser which has a fuel capacity giving it the exceptional range of 12,000 miles at economical speed. If its base is 2,000 miles from the theater of operations, it will expend fully one-third of its fuel and thus of its sea-keeping duration merely in the round-trip movement between the base and the area of activity. It will, in fact, lose more than one-third its time, because in an action it will move at top speed and thus consume fuel at a rapid rate, and also because it will wish to return to its base on something more than its last gallon. It should plan to have a fuel reserve on its return amounting to about 10 per cent of its total capacity. The time lost to military effectiveness would therefore be closer to one-half the time in which the cruiser was at sea, and acquisition of a base on the edge of the theater of operations would thus have the effect of doubling the number of cruisers available for patrol service.

But we have considered a class of vessel of unusual range. The modern destroyer will have a cruising radius of only half the radius of the cruiser described, and most of the older types have a range of only three or four thousand miles. For vessels of this type, a base 2,000 miles from the area of operations is practically useless except for hit and run raids. One might, of course, send out tankers to refuel ships, in which case the tanker serves as the advance base, but dependence on such means of keeping the sea is bound to be embarrassing. The American tanker *Neosho* attending our task force in the Coral Sea was one of the first victims of the Japanese in the battle

of May 7-8, 1942. For the shorter-ranged destroyers a few
hundred miles' difference in distance between base and destination is of importance, as the British found after ceding to
Ireland bases like Cobh, Berehaven, and Lough Swilly, which
had been so useful in the first World War. And the airplane,
especially, will depend for its usefulness upon the proximity
of the base to the fighting area. Its range is rigidly limited and
its military load is always inversely proportional to the distance it must travel.

While patrolling cruisers usually operate in independent
units or squadrons, and may thus be rotated, a battle fleet
must remain concentrated if maximum effectiveness as a battle force in the face of the enemy is to be retained. Moreover,
such a fleet is too vast an organization and too valuable strategically to be kept constantly at sea where it can be nibbled at
piecemeal by aerial or submarine raiders. Its full effect is felt
when it holds a position enabling it quickly to intervene in a
given theater, and is felt hardly at all when it can engage only
in occasional cruises in that area. Thus, the proximity of a base
to the theater in dispute makes the difference not between
greater and lesser control but between command and for-
feiture of command.

But fuel is not the only commodity expended on a lavish
scale by a fleet. Active squadrons may consume a large portion
of their munitions in a single action. Several times during the
Second World War, warships have almost exhausted their
anti-aircraft shells in one cruise. Destroyers may quickly expend most of their depth charges, submarines their torpedoes,
and bombers will normally use up their entire load of bombs
in a few minutes over the target area. Thus, the need for a
large supply of munitions of all kinds is the second factor
which makes a base close to the theater of action indispensable,
and in a fleet which experiences heavy fighting at sea it may
even displace the fuel requirement in order of importance.

The need for food, fresh water, medicaments, and other essentials for the personnel of the fleet will not ordinarily press so heavily on the operating limits of a fleet, but the store of these materials aboard each ship must nevertheless be periodically replenished.

The position of a base relative to the war theater will also make a great deal of difference in the consequences of damage received in combat. Whether a torpedoed ship can survive or not often depends on how far it has to travel to an emergency repair station after its injury. Many vessels torpedoed in the North Sea and Mediterranean have survived and been restored to service which would have sunk if they had received the same damage in the middle of the Pacific. Moreover, a damaged ship, especially one damaged below the waterline, usually can proceed only at greatly reduced speed. The farther it has to go the more likely it is to be overtaken and destroyed by strong enemy forces, aerial, surface, or submarine. For these reasons, and also because of the possible intervention of land-based air forces and submarines in a sea action, belligerents are profoundly anxious to have engagements take place in areas of their own choosing, which will always be as close to their own bases and as distant from those of the enemy as possible. The disproportion of risk involved is often great enough to overcome an initial superiority on the part of the opponent.

The base used should be secure. It may be useless or worse than useless if it cannot defend itself for a considerable time in the absence of the fleet. The operations which a fleet will be called upon to conduct are usually such that it covers its own base while engaged in offensive action at sea, but often this is not the case. A base like Pearl Harbor is not favorably situated for offensive action against Japan, and it would become more of a liability than an asset if a fleet originally based upon it could not leave it to take up an offensive position in the Far East. It so happens, however—despite the events of December 7—that Pearl Harbor is ideally situated for its security. It is distant from any springboard of enemy attack; it is among islands large enough to support considerable air and land forces, and yet not so large that a long coastline has to be defended, and it is close enough, relatively, to the United States to be reinforced quickly, especially by air, in any emergency.

A naval base should also be situated not too distant from basic sources of supply. The base is the source of immediate supply to the fleet, but it must itself be supplied with fuel, munitions, food, and whatever else is expended on a large scale by active fleets. If these materials have to be brought from a distance, a good deal of naval strength and shipping will be absorbed merely in maintaining the communications of the base. Bases in the home territories of the various naval powers are of course ideally situated in that respect, but outlying ones vary considerably in access to supplies. Singapore, Surabaya, and Amboina in the Far East had large fuel resources close at hand, and the considerable industrial plant of India was not far distant, but the bases which Australia might be able to furnish for offensive naval action, especially one like Port Darwin on the barren northern coast, would have to have all their supplies brought to them from very considerable distances. This is one reason great naval bases are so often found near centers of population.

The population near a naval base may, however, be a source of danger. This unquestionably proved to be the case at Pearl Harbor, where the polyglot population containing thousands of people of Japanese birth and descent proved a vital factor in the leakage of important information to the enemy. Singapore, too, was handicapped by a militarily unreliable populace. Scapa Flow, by contrast, lies in the sparsely settled Orkneys, the few residents of which are of unquestioned loyalty.

A naval base should above all have a good harbor, and one which lends itself to protection against surprise attack of all kinds, especially by aircraft and submarines. This is unquestionably the hardest requirement of all to fulfil, and explains why good sites for full-scale naval bases are so few. The capital ship has a draft of about thirty feet, and since it may come home damaged and low in the water, its anchorage should be at least forty-five feet deep. Yet excessively deep water will permit the vessels to move too freely at their moorings and will prove difficult to close to hostile submarines. A land-enclosed area, preferably with hills surrounding it to screen the vessels from the sea and to favor anti-aircraft defense, is desirable, and it is now indispensable that there be good airdromes in the near vicinity. There ought preferably to be enough land round the anchorage so that enemy planes approaching it from the sea will be observed and fired at while still at some distance, although outlying ships and radio detector devices do much to alleviate the danger of surprise.

The openings from the anchorage to the sea should be rather narrow to permit their being closed to enemy submarines, and it is better to have more than one exit in case one is blocked by enemy action. A situation in the mouth of a river is ideal, since vessels floating in fresh water not only do not become fouled but actually lose the incrustations which already have attached themselves to their bottoms. This factor, however, is of much less importance in the colder regions of the world than it is in the tropics, because fouling progresses more slowly in cold water than in warm. It must be a hardy barnacle indeed which thrives in the waters of Scapa Flow.

Scapa Flow happens to have two additional advantages which are much desired in a naval base. First, the very powerful tides which sweep past the entrances to the anchorage add to the difficulties of hostile submarines which might seek to enter. This fact makes the feat of Gunther Prien who sank

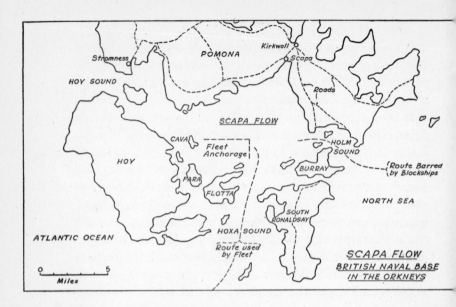

STROMNESS •   POMONA   Kirkwall •

HOY SOUND   Scapa

                                            Roads

                        SCAPA FLOW

          CAVA   Fleet   HOLM

HOY   Anchorage   SOUND

            FARA   BURRAY   Route Barred

              FLOTTA   by Blockships

                                    NORTH SEA

ATLANTIC OCEAN   HOXA SOUND   SOUTH

                                RONALDSAY

                      Route used   *SCAPA FLOW*

    0   5   by Fleet   *BRITISH NAVAL BASE*

    Miles   *IN THE ORKNEYS*

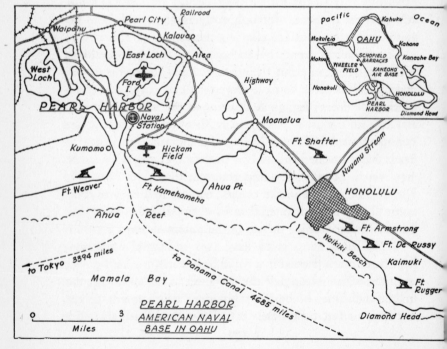

PEARL HARBOR
AMERICAN NAVAL
BASE IN OAHU

the *Royal Oak* within the anchorage all the more remark-able. Secondly, the anchorage is so spacious that ships can engage in artillery and torpedo practice without leaving the defenses of the base.

It is obvious that technological developments in the tools of sea power during the last hundred years have reduced the number of places available for naval bases. The introduction of steam brought in the previously unknown problem of fuel supply, although steam also made it feasible to use refitting bases which are at a considerable distance from the operating base, since the time spent in transit between them is now rela-tively short. The use of iron instead of wood brought in the problem of fouling, since most of the old wooden ships had copper sheathing on their bottoms which prevented the growth of barnacles. Now warships operating from salt-water bases have to be drydocked for periodic cleansings. The great de-velopment of guns has vastly augmented the difficulties of re-pairing ships damaged in action.

The growth in size of the battleship and of the cruiser has cut down the number of available anchorages and made the docking problem serious. In the old days vessels could be heeled over by shifting weights first to one side of the ship and then to the other, and damage or fouling could thus be remedied without docking. The use of the mine and torpedo has brought in the problem of underwater damage, formerly rare, which almost invariably requires resort to a dry dock. The submarine and the airplane have required the construc-tion of elaborate new harbor defense systems. The latter has greatly diminished the usefulness of bases which are too close to enemy territory. Malta is no longer available as a perma-nent base to a battle fleet, and Portsmouth, which had a fleet of predreadnought battleships stationed there throughout the first World War, is not now considered a safe anchorage for important vessels. Formerly a fleet was able to gain well-nigh absolute security by retiring to its defended bases, but since the coming of the airplane this is no longer true.

On the other hand, the use of aircraft in war at sea has meant that various islands which formerly had no strategic significance whatever are now important for their airdromes. Naturally, few bases, certainly no improvised bases, will be desirable in every respect, and the admiral in selecting a site must choose between conflicting ends. He must certainly compromise between considerations of security and of usefulness for offensive action. The security gained by removing the base as far from the enemy as possible is hardly conducive to winning a war. Too great a distance, moreover, may make the keepers of the base careless, and security may thus be jeopardized. It is curious that Scapa Flow, well within range of German bombing planes, had not by October 1942 suffered any serious damage from air raids, while Pearl Harbor, thousands of miles from important enemy territory, was the scene of one of the most damaging air raids in history.

CHAPTER VIII

Must All Our Ships Have Wings?

"IT IS no use thinking of this war in terms of the last war. The power of the air has greatly affected—some believe it has decisively affected—the movements of fleets and armies. We must not exaggerate this new factor—I find myself almost resenting the exaggeration of this new factor—but neither must we refuse to give it its deadly due." So spoke Winston Churchill in the House of Commons shortly after the Royal Navy had suffered its bitterest defeat in three centuries. Norway had fallen, and the fall was in large measure due to the failure of the British to cut the German communications in the Skagerrak. For that the German Luftwaffe was responsible.

In the following twenty months, air forces, operating both from carriers and from land bases, chalked up victories against surface squadrons which were equally impressive and in some respects even more so—Taranto, Crete, Pearl Harbor, and the sinking of the *Prince of Wales* and *Repulse*. Along with these major successes one had to include a good many lesser ones which were nevertheless of great importance in the aggregate. Small wonder, then, that the swift and terrible lance of the attack airplane swept all before it in the popular imagination. It no longer was necessary to talk about refusal to give air power "its deadly due." In the press, on the radio, on lecture platforms, and in the halls of parliaments it was receiving its due in no stinting measure. If Mr. Churchill had confessed himself as "almost resenting" the exaggeration of this new factor in April 1940, how indeed did he feel about it two years later?

Previous to the outbreak of the Second World War, the discussion of the role of the airplane in sea warfare had largely resolved itself into a debate between persons of extreme and equally intolerant attitudes. As is usual in such cases, each side emphasized data which supported its own view and blandly ignored all contrary evidence. But today the side that formerly would have attacked the extreme "air-minded" opinion has been beaten into something like a stupor by the events of a single week in December 1941, when four capital ships were sunk or capsized as a result of attack from the air and perhaps half a dozen others disabled through the same means.

Since then the air enthusiasts have had a field day. The admiral who can be charged with retaining "traditional notions" of naval strategy, by which is meant a disposition still to value the naval gun and the ship which bears it, is the target not only of ridicule but of suspicion. He is accounted as belonging neither to the quick nor the dead. Few press and radio commentators have dared or cared to remain off the band wagon lest they betray themselves as classed among the moribund "brass hats." The result is that all the honors of war have gone to the trim little ship with wings.

In a pursuit as complex as is the waging of war, it might be set down as an axiom that no one factor, and certainly no one weapon, can be exclusively decisive. The propaganda expert is convinced that the psychological front is decisive in modern warfare, the economist is equally certain that the production effort is the most important, and among military men there will be all kinds of divisions of opinion according to the specialties of the disputants. The logistics expert thinks the war will be won with motor trucks, the submarine commander is sure that it will yet be decided underseas, many shrewd strategists, particularly among the Russians, believe that artillery is still the "king of battles," others give preference to tanks, and of course the aviator is completely confident that victory can be achieved only through air power. Each is right in that failure in any of these variously favored factors is likely to mean, and in some instances is certain to mean, military defeat. But each, it will be noticed, attributes prime importance to that item in the whole scheme of things which interests him most.

The hold which the aviator's view has won over the popular imagination is explained above all by performance. But other services with comparable performance—like the field artillery, which has been the mainstay of the Russian armies and which both sides have used so effectively in North Africa—have been almost ignored by the press and practically forgotten by the public. Even the submarine has failed to receive the acknowledgment which is its due. Another factor clearly has some weight. A story goes that an examiner once asked a junior officer in a famous regiment of lancers, "What is the purpose of cavalry in war?" And the young man replied, "To give tone to what would otherwise be a vulgar brawl." Except on the broad plains of Russia cavalry as a shock force has almost vanished in modern war, but its mantle of gallantry has descended to the air force, which wears it very well.

There is something captivating about flight. It is still so new, so beautiful to watch and to contemplate, so swift, that its value in peace and war, however great, is bound to be somewhat magnified. Wheeled vehicles and boats have been with us since the dawn of history; the airplane evolved only yesterday. We have not yet become accustomed to its marvelous characteristics. The result is that we tend to ascribe to it boundless potentialities and to reject other implements of war as outmoded. We are under the sway of a dogma of innovation, just as blind and as dangerous as the dogma that there is nothing essentially new in war.

No one would question for a moment that the airplane has "revolutionized" naval warfare. But just what does that mean? Many inventions in the past have revolutionized naval warfare; we forget too easily how navies have changed in a hundred years. It is necessary to analyze just how and to what extent the airplane has altered campaigns at sea. It is important in discussing the airplane to mention its limitations as well as its advantages, its failures as well as its successes. To do otherwise is simply bad reporting. It might be worse than merely bad reporting; it might be a sinister kind of propaganda.

The inflation of the air arm in the public mind as a result of the most extraordinary and indisputable successes has resulted in a pressure upon political and military authorities which, if it is in error, might have the most unfortunate consequences. When the War Production Board at the end of 1941 placed shipping ahead of bombers on the list of essential commodities, a veritable shriek of indignation rose over the country, and Mr. Nelson was constrained to revise the rating. Yet ships were undeniably more lacking than airplanes. While our army on Bataan Peninsula was carrying on its heroic but hopeless resistance without air support, a general in Washington replied sadly to a questioner, "We have plenty of airplanes all right; all we lack is the means of getting them there." The "means" comprised merchant shipping and the force necessary to command passage, and the latter at that distance from home meant mostly naval forces of the traditional type.

There can be little question but that on December 7, 1941, the United Nations were superior in air power to all the enemy nations including Japan, but they lacked the means of quickly transferring that power where it was most needed. It does no good to say that the aircraft should already have been where it later turned out they were needed. The place of need cannot easily be predicted if the enemy has seized the initiative. Before the Pearl Harbor disaster it would have seemed the height of strategic folly to have kept great air forces apparently immobilized among the East Indies when they were vitally needed in Europe. The United Nations air forces in the Far East were in fact not inconsiderable, but they were dispersed, largely destroyed on the ground by surprise attack, and further whittled away in combat. It was less the weakness of initial numbers than the failure to deliver replacements and reinforcements—and the failure of squadrons on the ground to guard against surprise—that accounted for the deplorable weakness in the air. In any case, the number of aircraft that would have been necessary to defend the whole region indefinitely *without adequate naval support* was probably greater than could have been spared.

Perhaps the most mischievous result of focusing attention exclusively on the air power factor is that defeats are too readily ascribed to inferiority in aircraft when they are in fact due to causes far more fundamental. The American admiral who permitted himself to declare that our reverses in the Pacific were due chiefly to enemy superiority in the air was, probably unconsciously, diverting public attention from the far-reaching consequences of negligence at Pearl Harbor. The British statesmen who allowed the public to understand that defeat in the jungles of Malaya was due to too few airplanes were ignoring the assertion of the generals on the spot, Percival and Bennett, that it was due to their having "too few soldiers," for that might have reflected on the whole colonial policy of Great Britain, especially her failure to arm the natives and give them something to fight for.

The same is true of the Netherlands East Indies. Java had a population of over 40,000,000, and the army which such a population should have been able to put into the field could not easily have been bested by the few airplanes which the Japanese initially sent over that island. They certainly should have been able to prevent the Japanese from seizing airdromes by landings from the sea, just as sufficient numbers of

Malayan and British soldiers would have been able to prevent the Japanese from seizing the airdrome of Kota Bahru in northern Malaya. The Chinese, after all, have fought the Japanese for five long years, during most of which time they had practically no air force whatever.

It has long been considered clever to castigate high military and naval authorities for their allegedly fatuous conservatism. The vehement and bitter kind of indictment in the pages of some writers today can be matched in the literature of a hundred years ago, when a French writer, a soldier to be sure, asserted that with the invention of the shell-gun which could be mounted on a small boat it had become "absurd to construct line-of-battle ships, which not only cost 1,500,000 francs, but which have become useless." Unquestionably professionalism always induces some resistance to change, and that is particularly true in the military profession where the hierarchy of authority is so rigid and all-pervasive. Our military leaders are perhaps too reluctant to profit from the criticism of laymen and junior officers with novel ideas; nevertheless, they have made a life study of the means of waging war, and they have presumably been chosen for their place of authority not only because of their expertness but also because of their intelligence and balance. If our method of selecting military leaders is at fault it should be revised, but having chosen the men, we should be ready to put some trust in their wisdom.

One is justified, therefore, in looking with considerable misgiving upon the persistent editorial campaign of several great American newspapers against what they conceive to be the colossal folly of continuing to build battleships, or for that matter warships of any type. Even more alarming was the uprising in the United States Senate in May and June of 1942 against the considered opinion of the naval chiefs respecting building policy. Mr. Churchill in September 1941 gave the enduring answer to the Liddell Hart species of dogmatism when he said, "I hope, indeed, that some of our ardent critics . . . will reflect a little on their own records in the past, and by searching their hearts and memories will realize the fate which awaits nations and individuals who take an easy and popular course or who are guided in defence matters by the shifting winds of well-meaning public opinion."

To be sure, admirals who are now so bitterly contemned by the air enthusiasts have in some instances deserved the censure. This writer heard an American naval officer of high rank proclaim before a meeting of scholars even after the Second World War was well under way that no airplane had ever sunk a modern battleship or even a cruiser, the implication being that it would never do so. In so far as the bombing of battleships is concerned, by July 1942 he had been proved wrong only in the case of the *Arizona*, which was destroyed while stationary by a bomb passing down its funnel. A ship in motion or a stationary one with a balloon barrage around it would have been far less likely to receive so unlucky a hit, and the dangerous consequences of such a bullseye could be eliminated by the simple architectural device of a sharp cant or crook in the funnel. The Army report that the Japanese *Haruna* was sunk by bombs dropped from a Flying Fortress was totally unwarranted by the available evidence; the Japanese subsequently denied the sinking, and the United States Navy has apparently credited the denial.[1] On the other hand, it should long ago have been apparent that the battleship,

[1] Three "large" bombs, presumably of 1,000-pound weight, were observed to hit, and American airplanes which later flew over the vicinity of the attack could not find the vessel. It was on the basis of such flimsy evidence as this that the Germans several times claimed to have destroyed the *Ark Royal*, which was later sunk by a submarine.

however well armored against bombs, was vulnerable to repeated torpedo hits, and that the airplane was an excellent means of launching torpedoes.

That capital ships could be sunk in the manner of the *Prince of Wales* and *Repulse* had in fact long been predicted by numerous British and American naval officers. They knew also that lesser warships were vulnerable to bombs as well as torpedoes, provided that circumstances permitted an attack of sufficient duration and magnitude. It was an American naval officer, Rear-Admiral B. A. Fiske, who invented the torpedo plane in 1911, and it was British and American naval officers who developed torpedo dropping from aircraft to a fine art. They were responsible also for the development of the aircraft carrier, despite, be it noted, the long and still continuing ridicule of many air enthusiasts. Of course the carrier was bound to be vulnerable—no one denied that. But it has proved itself extraordinarily useful.

When the British cruiser *Southampton* was destroyed and the aircraft carrier *Illustrious* damaged by German air attack in January 1941, Admiral Lord Chatfield, a former First Sea Lord of the Admiralty who had pushed the development of torpedo dropping and of the aircraft carrier, expressed surprise not that the *Southampton* had been sunk but that she was the first vessel of comparable size to be so destroyed after more than a year of war. "Who would have dreamed," he said, "that this was all the German air forces could have accomplished with their innumerable opportunities?" It is totally unfair to assert that the men who now defend the surface warship against its detractors have been blind to the value of the airplane. Churchill, who in 1940 warned against exaggerating the importance of aircraft, was the same man who in 1917 had written to Henry Woodhouse—an early writer on naval aeronautics—that the air forces "at no distant date may be the dominating arm of war."

When has mere liability to loss determined the value of weapons of war? At Sinope in 1854 the Russian Navy destroyed the whole Turkish Fleet in two hours through the use of the shell gun in a surprise attack, but that did not mean the end of the capital ship. In the Russo-Japanese War, three Russian battleships were destroyed or disabled at Port Arthur at the outset of hostilities by Japanese torpedo attack, and later, in the siege of the same port, two out of the six Japanese battleships were lost in a single day to mines. Yet the war was finally decided by a battle fleet action. Mr. Churchill declared on September 9, 1941, that "there is no branch of His Majesty's Forces which in this war has suffered the same proportion of fatal loss as our submarine service," yet British submarines were sinking an average of fifteen supply ships a month out of the enemy's meager store and greatly hampering Axis communications with Africa. It is curious that the air-minded should make so much of the loss of ships to air attack and pay so little attention to the terrific wastage of aircraft in battle. According to British official figures, by December 5, 1941, the total of verified aircraft losses on both sides in British-Axis campaigns alone—i.e. excluding the gigantic German and Russian losses on the Eastern Front—had reached the stupendous sum of 12,520 planes, a substantial portion of which had been lost in attacks on naval objectives.

Of course, such losses carry relatively little weight if the airplane is capable of deciding great issues, as unquestionably it is—but ought not the same criterion apply to other weapons? If battleships should prove so vulnerable to air attack that no substantial force could be kept afloat to perform their function, and if it were impossible to increase the resistance of the battleship to such attack, the day of the naval leviathan would surely be over. That situation is not now at hand.

By July 1942 Great Britain had at least as many battleships afloat and active as at the beginning of the war, despite losses not only to enemy aircraft but, even more, to submarines and surface warships. And no one could deny that the British Navy was deciding the course of events in the Atlantic and to a large extent in the Mediterranean. Yet the British battle fleet was mostly a conglomeration of obsolete battleships designed and built long before the airplane was a major menace at sea.

Such devastation as was wrought at Pearl Harbor would seem to nullify the above argument, but treachery on one side and gross negligence on the other would invalidate any strategical principle. It is clear that American preparedness could have prevented major damage. After the terrible initial attack, which wiped out many of our fighter planes, American anti-aircraft guns and surviving fighters played such havoc with succeeding waves of Japanese bombers that the latter added little to their score of ship damage. The first attacking wave was noted by a detector device when it was still more than 130 miles from the base, and might have been intercepted by fighter craft. Anti-aircraft guns could have been fully manned and ready, balloon barrages (which seem not to have been provided) could have been in place, and important vessels at anchor should certainly have been protected from torpedoes by booms and nets.

Even so, despite all the Japanese advantages and despite the concentration of their major effort against our battleships, only one American battleship was destroyed and one capsized. The others received damages which while serious could nevertheless be repaired. The strategic consequences of those damages happened to be uncommonly great because of the critical meaning of time at that phase of the war, but as a rule there is a tremendous strategic difference between damaging a ship and sinking it. Long before the end of 1942 the Japanese had to be worrying about a Pacific Fleet which was at least as strong as it had been on December 7, 1941.

The British and Germans have been extremely successful in guarding their warships from air attack at such bases as Scapa Flow, Wilhelmshaven, Brunsbüttel, and Trondheim. Even at Brest, where the *Scharnhorst* and *Gneisenau* were for ten months under the very nose of the R.A.F. Bomber Command, 4,000 tons of bombs aimed at them in 3,299 bomber sorties, with the loss of 247 British air force personnel and forty-three aircraft, did not disable the ships sufficiently to keep them from dashing up the Channel to greater security and repair bases in the Baltic. These figures do not include the large losses suffered among the 600 British aircraft which tried to sink them during that dash, and which did succeed in inflicting damage. If warships could be defended at sea or in open harbors as well as they are in adequately equipped bases, they would have little to fear from the air.

The place of the airplane in modern naval warfare has already been discussed elsewhere in this book. Much could be added if space permitted, but certainly the subject of the utility of aircraft hardly needs laboring at this date. If the airplane could not carry a single bomb, mine, or torpedo, it would still have revolutionized naval warfare through its influence on reconnaissance. But since it can carry such missiles far out to sea, its influence has become tremendous. It has been of utmost service to the older instruments of naval power, but has also made notable independent successes against enemy naval forces. Yet a precise analysis of what it has accomplished and what it has failed to accomplish is far more useful than glib assertions that pass as rare insight into present and future events.

The British refusal to risk a fleet in the Skagerrak in April 1940, and the heavy losses they suffered in the sea north of Crete in the following year have proved beyond cavil that under current conditions no fleet unprotected by a substantial screen of fighters can operate for any length of time in coastal waters *near powerful enemy land-based air forces*. This does not mean, as frequently supposed, that a fleet cannot operate near a hostile coast. There are bound to be great expanses of "hostile coast," some very important, where the enemy does not have great concentrations of air power, and even where he does a surprise raid may still be possible. British naval operations along the North African coast, in the Strait of Otranto, and in the Gulf of Genoa have demonstrated these facts, as have also the many Japanese successes with landing operations in the Western Pacific and the Bay of Bengal. British naval-Commando forces have even raided, under the cover of night, bases like St. Nazaire in the very heart of German air power.

Nor is it caviling to point to some qualifications of the lessons of Norway and Crete. In the Norwegian campaign the crucial area, the Skagerrak, was swarming with submarines as well as bombers; it was not merely next door to German air bases but 500 miles from the nearest British naval base, a factor to be considered in getting damaged ships home. Even more important was the British shortage of warships. Had the Royal Navy been prepared to pay the cost, it could have stopped the invasion. The Germans could afford the sacrifice of one-fourth of their naval strength to win the victory, but the British could not sacrifice any comparable portion of their own fleet to prevent it. Germany's fleet, as one British naval officer put it, was a luxury, an "expendable commodity"; Britain's was a necessity. The British were already woefully short of the destroyers and cruisers which would have been the first victims of air assault. British naval strategy in her second war with Germany must always be appraised in the light of the fact that Great Britain had no such superabundance of warships as she had enjoyed in the latter stages of the first World War. And if she once lost command of the sea, no victories on land, nor even the strongest air force in the world, could save her from destruction.

In the battle for Crete, the British Navy anticipated the price it would have to pay, decided to pay it, and *succeeded in its share of the operation*. In a remarkable speech in the House of Commons after the event, Mr. Churchill outlined the Navy's share in the plan of strategy for the defense of Crete. "Our Army," he said, "was to destroy the air-borne attacks, while the Navy held off or destroyed the sea-borne attacks. But there was a time limit. The action of the Navy in maintaining the northern sea guard without adequate air defence was bound to be very costly. . . . We could only stand a certain proportion of naval losses before the northern sea guard of the Fleet would have to be withdrawn. If meanwhile the Army could succeed in biting off the head of the whole terrific apparatus of the air-borne invasion before the naval time limit, or loss limit, was reached, then the enemy would have to begin all over again, and, having regard to the scale of the operation, the enormous, unprecedented scale of the operation, and the losses he would have to incur, he might well have, for the time being at least, broken it off—at any rate, there would have been a long delay before he could have mounted it again. That was the basis on which the decision [to defend Crete] was taken."

The Navy did succeed—at the very serious cost, to be sure, of four cruisers and six destroyers sunk and several other warships damaged—in keeping any appreciable German forces from landing on Crete by sea, and in fact drowned thousands of troops that tried. That not only limited the volume of men which the Germans could pour in during any period of time but absolutely prevented them from bringing large tanks or heavy guns to the Island. Had the British land forces not been so ill-equipped themselves, with only six infantry tanks, scarcely any artillery, and no air support at all, that fact might have made all the difference. Had the British merely had the foresight to place obstacles across the airdromes which their planes had evacuated, they might have prevented the successful landing of the transport planes in which the major part of the invading troops were brought. At any rate, it was the Army's failure—by a very narrow margin—to "bite off the head" of the air-borne invasion that lost Crete.

The British had been similarly willing to pay the price in the evacuation of Dunkirk a year earlier, and succeeded there also. The price paid in destroyers and other small vessels—though not cruisers—was even greater than at Crete, considerably greater, a fact which those who attribute the success entirely to the "umbrella" of British fighter defense generally overlook. The role of British fighters was crucial, but so too was the intense anti-aircraft barrage of the British warships. And in the evacuation from Greece the British succeeded in removing under incessant German bomber attack, with practically no defending fighters of their own on the scene, 45,000 of the 60,000 troops they had originally sent to that country. There were tragedies of course, particularly at Nauplia where a fully loaded transport and the destroyers *Diamond* and *Wryneck* were sunk, with the loss of several thousand men. But war is synonymous with tragedy, and the cold statistics of accomplishment must be given their due.

Naturally, the fact that navies are far more restricted than formerly in coastal operations is of the greatest strategic consequence. Norway and Crete are sufficient evidence of that, and one must consider too the sum total of wastage from air attack of warships engaged in less spectacular operations, such as convoying British and American war materials to northern Russian ports—a route which runs down the entire length of the German-held Norwegian coast. But it is an error to assume that in the past the chief purpose of navies was to attack enemy coastlines and harbors and fortresses, or that inability to attack such objectives means that navies, to quote one writer, "have definitely lost their former *initiative* in the matter of offensive action." Such an argument bespeaks a total lack of understanding of what constitutes offensive or defensive action in naval strategy. It was in a defensive action at Crete that the Royal Navy was obliged to expose itself to air attack. If the Germans had attempted an invasion of England in 1940, the Royal Navy would similarly have interposed itself, and in doing so might have suffered catastrophic losses.

In one of the shrewdest of the many brilliant strategical analyses that Mr. Churchill has vouchsafed the House of Commons he said when summing up the lessons of Crete, "We rely [in England] upon a strong superiority in air power, and certainly upon a much greater air power, both actually and relatively, than was proved sufficient last autumn. This sustains not only the land defence but *liberates again the power of the Navy from the thraldom in which it was held round Crete*" (italics mine). In other words, growing British air power at home not only meant that the Royal Navy could intervene against German invasion attempts with less relative cost than at Crete, but also meant that once the R.A.F. became capable of taking over entirely the job of defense, it freed the Navy for other and offensive purposes, just as reconnaissance aircraft relieved the Navy of the necessity of maintaining cruiser and destroyer squadrons in exposed positions near enemy bases.

What, then, constitutes the naval offensive? The Japanese sea-borne invasion of the many United Nations possessions in the Western Pacific is the most spectacular kind of offensive possible to a navy, and this, it must be admitted, is precisely the kind that large air forces should be able to counter. But that is only another way of saying that in amphibious warfare the airplane has greatly favored the defensive, just as the machine gun favored the defensive in the land combats of the first World War. That by no means signifies that the offensive must also be air-borne. On the contrary, no aircraft coming from a distance can begin to compete in military performance of any kind with aircraft operating close to home, and if the experience at Crete means anything, the defenders with a very modest amount of equipment in anti-aircraft armament and fighters will be able to knock troop transports out of the air like kites. It means simply that a greater concentration of naval strength than formerly is necessary to accomplish sea-borne invasion, and also that that naval strength must be modified to give greater protection against the air menace.

It must be remembered that the Germans did not choose to make an air-borne invasion of Crete because that was the better way. On the contrary, the terrific pounding they took from the weakly-armed defenders evidently dissuaded them from at once repeating the feat elsewhere. The Germans used air-borne invasion because *that was the only way open to them*. British naval strength prohibited sea-borne invasion. And Crete was only sixty miles from German-occupied territory.

The reason that the United States put most of its money on a great navy rather than on a great air force prior to the Second World War was not so much that naval experts underestimated the airplane as that they pointed out to Congress that such a policy would be a commitment to the strategic defensive. Experience of the Second World War up to July 1942 did not invalidate that conclusion. In almost every case where aircraft achieved notable successes they operated either from carriers or over short distances. It must not be forgotten that the brilliant American success at Midway in June 1942 was a defensive achievement; it was Japan who had taken the initiative strategically. The very loose use of the words offensive and defensive is unfortunate, because the persons who use those terms most glibly never pause to distinguish between tactical and strategic concepts.

Where long maritime distances are involved, ships, including of course aircraft carriers, are the only means at present existing or likely to exist for a long time of carrying on large-scale attack or, what is more meaningful, the invasion and occupation of enemy territory. So long as the whole of a nation's navy can be concentrated far more completely at a distant point than the whole of a nation's air force, so long as radius of action is much greater for warships than for aircraft, and especially so long as armies need something like fifteen tons or more of equipment per man for offensives against well-armed defenders, we may confidently expect that invasions across oceans and even narrow seas will be predominantly sea-borne.

Moreover, as we have seen in the preceding chapters, sea-borne invasion is not the only kind of offensive possible to a fleet, and is usually not the most important. There is another kind which is all too seldom regarded as such—the most pervasive kind of naval offensive of all—blockade. And if the experience of almost three years of the Second World War is worth anything, it indicates that blockade is carried on chiefly by surface and submarine vessels.

From the moment she went to war in 1939, Great Britain established a blockade of Germany—a blockade which, seemingly of little consequence at first, was unquestionably destined to have as far-reaching effects on the struggle as had the blockade of 1914–1918. This blockade she instituted when she was enormously inferior to Germany in air power. However great the accomplishments of the Luftwaffe, it completely failed to open the sea lanes to German ports. The vessels which closed the shipping routes to Germany kept stations which for the most part were far beyond the reach of substantial German air strength. On the other hand, by the autumn of 1941 it was clear that the aerial component of the German effort to raise a counter-blockade against the British Isles had failed. Major De Seversky's assertion that "the blockade of an enemy nation has become a function of air power" and that warships are no longer useful for this purpose is simply an inversion of the truth.

Most of the debate on air power versus sea power has concentrated on the question of the continued usefulness of battleships. Persons who are quite ready to concede the value of the cruiser, destroyer, and submarine nevertheless insist that the battleship should be "consigned to museums of outlived weapons along with the bow and arrow and the blunderbuss." This is no new story. As already noted, in the mid-nineteenth century the shell-gun was generally supposed to have sounded the doom of the large warship, but the battleship of that day simply adopted iron armor and grew bigger than ever.

In the 1880's, the Whitehead torpedo had made such progress that at the launching of the *Trafalgar* in 1887 the First Lord of the Admiralty proclaimed this to be "probably the last battleship that would be built for the British Navy." But the naval architects met the new threat by a drastic scaling upward of tonnage to secure the increased defense factors needed, and the destroyer came into being as a protector. The torpedo has developed far beyond the expectations of its most enthusiastic supporters of the 'eighties, but until the development of the modern torpedo plane it had not displaced the gun as the main arbiter of naval battles, and it is by no means clear that it has done so yet in the great and decisive battles. Before the First World War, Admiral Sir Percy Scott proclaimed that the submarine had "driven the battleship from the sea." But surface warships adopted detecting devices and depth charges, and the submarine became the hunted rather than the hunter where combat with warships was concerned.

Of course, historical precedent is no certain guide to future development. But it ought to remind us that an instrument which has developed defenses to each new menace in the past may do so again in the case of the airplane. In fact, it has already done so in great part. The more modern battleships are more than adequately protected in their deck armor against vital damage by the heaviest of existing aerial bombs. And architectural defenses against torpedo attack can certainly be further improved. The *Prince of Wales* proved more vulnerable to torpedoes than she should have considering the date of her design—due no doubt to the treaty limit restrictions of 35,000 tons under which her plans were drawn up. But the broader-beamed *Bismarck* showed an astonishing resistance to torpedo attack. Present battleships are liable to destruction by submarines and aircraft not because it was impossible to make them relatively immune but because they had to be designed on a limited tonnage to fight enemy capital ships as well as to resist underwater blows.

There is a popular passion for the belief that Goliath must be vulnerable to David, and as a result the battleship has been indicted on the basis of a few selected incidents without regard to the message actually contained in available facts. By July 1942 it was abundantly clear that the battleship fared far better under air attack than any other warship type. Every belligerent navy, possibly excepting our own, had lost greater proportions of its cruisers, aircraft carriers, and destroyers to attack from the air than its battleships. Even Italy, who had suffered the Taranto disaster, apparently still had five of her original six battleships, although her formerly splendid cruiser force was half gone.[2] Britain had lost only two battleships to air attack, but the toll exacted by enemy airmen among her

[2] Far the greater part of Italian crusier losses, however, had been to British surface craft and submarines.

lighter classes had to be counted in scores. So far as was definitely known, Japan had not lost a single battleship, despite huge losses in other categories. In fact, among the many warships destroyed from the air in the fourteen months following December 1941, not a single battleship was to be counted. The one or two that the Japanese lost in the Solomons were victims primarily of our surface ships, and the British *Barham* fell to an Axis submarine.

Nor can this disparity in fatalities be laid to the inactivity of the capital ships. They were often at sea, and a large total number of aerial attempts against them had been made and reported. In many battles in which cruisers, destroyers, and aircraft carriers were struck down from the air, battleships were present, and we may be confident they were not ignored by the airmen. There were apparently as many Japanese battleships present in the Battle of the Midway Islands of June 1942 as carriers, yet none was sunk. Both sides had battleships in the events of June 13–15, 1942, in the Mediterranean when at least half a dozen cruisers and destroyers were sunk, yet none of the capital ships went down. The British had battleships in action in the defense of Crete when they lost so heavily in cruisers and destroyers. And this was the record of a class of ship of which most existing specimens were over twenty-five years old. To be sure, many battleships had sustained damages in air attack, damages varying from insignificant to serious, but since the battleship is the weapon of the once-and-for-all showdown rather than the constant patrol, the weapon whose contacts with the enemy have always been infrequent in war, the strategic significance of a few weeks or possibly even months of retirement for repairs can easily be exaggerated.

In the further changes in naval architecture that must indisputably result from the great and rapid development of the air arm to its present stature, the battleship is probably the type that needs to change least. Cruisers, which have customarily been protected only against the fire of their own kind, must either acquire adequate protection against 1,000-pound bombs or pass out of existence. American cruisers have already gone far toward acquiring such protection. Destroyers, which have relied upon their speed and maneuverability to protect them from larger warships, are not able to outrun aircraft, and they have proved insufficiently maneuverable wholly to escape bombing. Either they will become somewhat smaller, and therefore more maneuverable and more numerous, or they will become enough greater in size to carry the burden of deck armor or more anti-aircraft armament.

The fundamental irrelevance of the "airplane-can-sink-battleship" argument is that it assumes that the battleship is a particular genus of vessel of immutable qualities. The battleship is by definition merely the "predominant surface ship," a warship which can give and take harder blows than any other. It has changed from the 2,600-ton (burden) *Victory* which carried Nelson at Trafalgar to the 45,000-ton *Iowa* of today. If it is doomed because of vulnerability to air attack, then it is logical to assume that weaker warships and certainly the merchant ship are also doomed. A battleship may cost as much as three or four cruisers, but it will outlast that number under heavy air attack. The real question is: Will the predominant surface ship of the future be greater or smaller than it is today? And naval architects are practically unanimous in their belief that it will be greater.

The question of relative expense must be faced. Battleships already are very costly (about $85,000,000 each for the new *Iowa* class), and are promising to become even more so. But if one considers the huge number of long-ranged super-bombers and super-torpedo planes that would be required to take over all the functions of a modern battle fleet, assuming that planes of the required performance could be produced, one would be contemplating something that was also expensive.

The public eye is focused too much on the single plane which makes the torpedo hit. The idea that air power is a cheaper means of doing what the warship can do is a myth, and is readily seen to be such when one considers the cost of air forces large enough to accomplish really decisive results and the terrible losses which they sustain in carrying out their missions. If we had spent on capital ships during the last twenty years one-half the sum we are now spending yearly on aircraft, we would have such a fleet as would enable us to take calmly the loss of a few battleships. The same is true of the British. On the morning of Jutland they possessed altogether forty-two dreadnought capital ships, none over ten years old, besides many predreadnoughts. On the morning of September 3, 1939, after an era of "Faith, Hope, and Parity," they entered another war with fifteen capital ships, none less than fourteen years old. No wonder the loss two years later of the *Prince of Wales* and *Repulse* was such a disaster!

As a matter of fact, the costliness of battleships has been enormously exaggerated. In October 1942 we were spending *each day* on materials of war alone the price of three modern battleships. Admirals are cautious with their battleships not because of their monetary value, which is trifling compared with the issues at stake, but because each battleship represents to the navally dominant power an incalculable military asset which is practically irreplaceable during war. In the ten or fifteen years preceding 1941 this country could have built forty battleships of the *Washington* type with scarcely any perceptible strain on our national economy. And what a different position we would now be in had we done so! By agreeing with Japan not to build new capital ships we simply cancelled out of the equation of power the two factors in which we clearly outclassed her—wealth and industrial strength.

Naturally, the constitution of fleets will always be determined by the military utility of the individual units rather than by their cost. But cost is by no means unimportant, since a navy during peacetime will seek to acquire the maximum of fighting strength out of the funds allotted to it (during wartime all sorts of complicating factors arise, particularly in respect to the availability of materials). But on the basis both of military utility and economy, one may confidently look to a balance between surface and aerial weapons comparable to the existing but ever-changing balance between the different types of surface warships.

Air enthusiasts usually talk in terms of aircraft of the future being opposed to battleships which are antiquated even now. Major De Seversky, for example, describes planes carrying fifty torpedoes each—more than six times the load of the experimental B-19, the largest bomber existing in July 1942— making attacks on battleships which can be destroyed by five torpedoes each (the *Bismarck* absorbed about ten). He insists on the basis of simple arithmetic that twenty-five such super-planes "would be strong enough to sink some 250 battleships," and envisages an attack not only where none of his large and unhandy aircraft will be shot down and where none of his torpedoes will miss (the *Repulse* successfully dodged nineteen before the first one hit), but also where there will be a perfect distribution of torpedoes against targets. At Jutland the German destroyers carried enough torpedoes in their tubes to destroy the entire British line of twenty-eight battleships twice over, but not a single British battleship was put out of action and only one received a torpedo hit.[3]

---

[3] The *Marlborough*, which was struck in the encounter but which did not leave the battle line until 2:21 o'clock the following morning. Several recent newspaper and magazine articles have stated that the *Warspite* re-

It is, of course, to the fighter airplane that we must look for the chief defense of the capital ship against air attack. Such fighter planes must be in attendance with the fleet on carriers, for experience in the Mediterranean, round the British Isles, and off Malaya has proved that land-based fighter planes which are called in only when the enemy attacks usually arrive too late to be of value. And the fighter has too brief an endurance for continuous escort of warships from land bases, unless the warships are within easy proximity and the fighters are available in great numbers to provide relays. Even then this system is extremely wasteful, inasmuch as the enemy holds the choice of the time of attack. The carrier-based fighter is somewhat inferior in combat power to the best land-based fighters, but it would not be inferior to any land-based fighters designed for operating far out at sea. And the best carrier-based fighters will always be able to cope with the best land-based bombers.

That is not to say, however, as is too generally believed, that warships can go nowhere unless they have their defensive "umbrella" of fighter aircraft. There are bound to be great and important areas of the sea where the enemy cannot marshal substantial air power. It would be an intolerable restriction on the movements of warships to insist that unless they have fighter protection they keep out of any areas into which the enemy may be able to send even a few attack planes. War is made up of risks, and a wise strategy is hardly more than an intelligent choice of risks. In the Second World War the British have been totally unable to dispatch carriers with all their numerous patrolling squadrons; and although they paid for it in many instances with losses that could otherwise have been avoided, they did not for that reason abandon control of the sea.

---

ceived three torpedo hits at Jutland, but those statements have no foundation in fact. The *Warspite* was of course heavily hit by shell fire.

Just as in land warfare infantry must often attack without tank support, so in naval warfare no temporary or local inadequacies in air support must be permitted to hamper unduly the offensive action of the fleet. Anti-aircraft armament must be relied upon to a large extent whether fighter defense is available or not, and its effectiveness is much greater than the air enthusiasts usually admit. The obverse side of the argument that the *Prince of Wales* and the *Repulse* would have been saved by fighter planes is that they might also have been saved if they had carried a better and more numerous anti-aircraft armament—such as enabled one of our new battleships less than a year later to shoot down in one day thirty-two attacking Japanese planes, including the whole of one wave of twenty, without suffering any noteworthy damage (other than a wounded captain) from the one bomb hit.

Major De Seversky bases his contention that the airplane will drive out the warship on the quite reasonable thesis that the limited range and bomb load of present-day aircraft are no indication of what they will be in the future. With increased range, he says, land-based aircraft will be able to make their influence felt over the entire globe, marine and land alike, from any base. With increased bomb and torpedo loads, they will be able to overcome any kind of passive resistance adopted by the warship. More than that, once aircraft have the requisite range it would be a waste of time and effort to send them against enemy navies, since the enemy will be quickly overcome by direct assault on his home territory. The separate phases of this argument must be considered in turn.

Obviously aircraft can be given both greater range and heavier bomb load, but there is only one way to do that and that is by giving them greater size. And to make an airplane larger means robbing it of many of the advantages which are now peculiarly its own. The large aircraft is enormously expensive, yet it must retain much of the fragility inherent in any flying machine, and it is easier to hit with defense fire. Its "armor" is of thin gauge, intended only for the defense of the more important personnel and of vital parts of the power plant against machine-gun bullets, and is confined to a few portions within the fuselage and on the engines. The huge wings remain exposed. To the ordinary anti-aircraft gun such armor means almost nothing whatever; and it is obvious that the power even of air-borne armament, which already includes cannon of 37 mm. caliber, can more than keep pace with the development of air-borne armor.

It cannot be supposed that the history of armor in a craft where weight means so much can ever approximate the story of armor in warships. The first sea-going armored warships carried wrought-iron plating of 4½ inches thickness extending over all or most of the ship's length. Ship-borne armor has varied between 25 and 43 per cent of the weight of the vessel, whereas the modern fighter devotes only 5 per cent of its far lesser weight to protection, and the bomber carries an even smaller proportion.

One of the essential differences between the warship and the heavier-than-air flying machine, a basic difference which must over-ride all possibilities of development in either type, is that the former floats in its element merely by its displacement of water while the latter must consume energy in order to keep afloat in the air. The warship floats at practically the same trim whether stationary or travelling at top speed. It can carry heavier guns and heavier armor simply by increasing its dimensions and therefore displacing more water. And as it grows larger its propulsion efficiency increases, so that the ratio of power consumed to displacement actually diminishes for any given rate of speed. An airplane, on the other hand, not only derives its support in the air from its rapid forward motion, but consumes a good deal more power to achieve that motion than would be necessary if it were merely trying to cleave through the air without being upheld by it. The force of gravity is not defied by wings; it is exacting its toll at every moment of flight in pounds of gasoline. The heavier the plane, the more fuel consumed for support, and the ratio between the two for any given speed may be regarded as practically a constant.[4]

This distinction may seem too self-evident to merit discussion, but its consequences are all too often forgotten in popular speculation on the potentialities of aircraft. The modern battleship, constructed without too nice a regard for the possi-

[4] This factor has direct bearing on the now much debated question of whether aircraft can replace ships as the major means of transportation across the seas. Mr. Grover Loening, in an article pleading for the construction of great numbers of transport planes, envisages a type of craft, of 82 tons loaded weight, more efficient than any existing in 1942. According to his estimates, this plane could carry 40,000 pounds of cargo a distance of 4,000 miles, but in doing so would consume 40,000 pounds of high-octane gasoline, or one pound of fuel per pound of cargo. To make round trips possible, fuel would have to be brought to the terminus by some other means. And again according to his rather optimistic figures, it would require twenty-one such planes to carry in one year the cargo transported in the same period by one C-3 class freighter. The twenty-one planes would cost $10,000,000, as opposed to the $3,000,000 of the far more cheaply run surface ship. It has been argued that cost means nothing in wartime, but cost after all reflects largely construction effort in manhours of labor, which is certainly not unimportant in war.

It would of course be foolish to say that a change to aerial transportation is impossible in the future, but it is certainly impossible during wartime to build a sufficient fleet of transport planes to take over a major portion of our shipping burden, particularly in view of the great need for combat planes. The more we have the better, but that is not the question.

In so far as the argument for air transportation rests on the contention that the submarine menace cannot be overcome, it is defeatist, untrue, and irrelevant. Solution of the crucial transport problems of 1942-43 lies not in thousands of huge air transports available at best some five or six years hence, but in more effective suppression of the U-boat, which can be accomplished by rapid production of escort and patrol craft. Meanwhile, of course, aircraft will be increasingly used, as they have been used, to transfer key commodities and personnel where swift movement is essential or where no other means of transportation is available.

bility of saving a few tons of weight here or there, can easily travel 5,000 miles with a fuel load of oil amounting to 8 per cent or less of its loaded weight. The engines will account for an additional 8 per cent of total weight. It can have five-sixths of its top speed at two-fifths of its power, and if it wishes to conserve fuel in order to keep a certain station it can reduce speed as much as it likes. It will carry the same load of shells and have practically as great a combat efficiency at its maximum radius as it will close to home. The hundreds of one-ton shells and the thousands of lesser shells aboard a *North Carolina* can be hurled against an enemy at any point the ship can reach.

The airplane, on the other hand, is a masterpiece of parsimony in weight. Hardly a spare ounce is to be found over the whole structure of the craft. Its power plant particularly (amounting in some fighter types to about half the weight of the plane) is a modern miracle in pounds per horsepower. Its fuel is uncommonly expensive but efficient high-octane gasoline. And yet, under the existing state of knowledge in the art of aeronautics, a well-designed bomber will consume on a flight of 5,000 miles in still air at its most economical speed about 44 per cent of its loaded weight in fuel and oil.

However, one never flies in still air. Reserves of fuel must be allowed not only for adverse winds but also for errors in navigation, for the possibility of being forced to fly around storms, for maneuvering round the target, and for the likelihood that the bomber will have to forsake its most economical speed and fly at nearly its top speed when engaged with enemy fighters or proceeding through areas heavily defended by anti-aircraft guns.

The rough general rule gained from experience is that a bomber should carry at least 2½ times the fuel and oil necessary to carry it to its target in still air at its most economical speed. That means that our bomber loaded with 44 per cent of its weight in fuel should be able to travel to a point 2,000 miles away and return. But any military plane has a high "overhead" of weight, that is, it must carry not only its fuel and bomb load but also itself and its power plant, its crew and all their paraphernalia, its instruments, ammunition and armament. Few military planes can carry 44 per cent of their weight in fuel; and even in those heavy bombers that can, such a percentage would ordinarily absorb all the weight-carrying capacity of the plane and preclude any bomb load whatever.

The percentage of initial weight available for fuel, oil, and military load can be increased by allocating less weight to engines, but the sacrifice in power reduces the speed and ceiling of the plane and greatly increases the space needed for take-off. The rate of economical cruising speed (about 140 miles per hour in the ordinary large transport or bomber) can be reduced—to diminish the effects of air drag—by decreasing the wing-loading, but that also reduces top speed. It might be observed that the largest bomber in the world at this writing, the 82-ton (loaded) American Army B-19, can cruise over 7,000 miles with a bomb load of eight tons, but its top speed is less than 200 miles per hour.

The problem of finding airdromes for long-range bombing is not so easy to solve in many regions of the world. An airplane which can carry enough fuel for a 4,000-mile flight but which needs a 5,000-foot field for a take-off with that amount of fuel may have its extreme range reduced to 2,000 miles if only a 3,500-foot field is available. It must be remembered, too, that mud, snow, and enemy action often reduce the length of available runways. Even with present types of planes, paved runways 4,000 and even 5,000 feet long are considered desirable for long-range operations.

Obviously these figures will change as the art of aeronautical engineering progresses, particularly as higher octane fuels become available and as lighter and stronger materials are found for aircraft construction. But it is easy to exaggerate possibilities in this direction. The airplane is already a highly perfected mechanism. As Mr. Edward Warner, one of the most distinguished of American aeronautical engineers, observes: "Laymen rather generally seem to picture the designing of airplanes as a field in which revolutionary inventions come fairly tumbling on one another's heels. This is strikingly inaccurate. The general history of the last dozen years has been one of gradual refinement in detail." Most of the spectacular advances in the performance of aircraft in the last eight years have been due not to any substantial improvement in structural or aerodynamic design but to improvements in the power plant and to increases in the proportion of weight devoted to power. The Hawker Hurricane design was six years old when war started in 1939, but except for a more powerful engine and all-metal instead of fabric wings, the latest Hurricane is very little different from its prototype.

What is even more important, there is always a strong tendency in any military vehicle for improvements in efficiency to be absorbed in the pursuit of tactical advantage. That has been conspicuous in the case of warships. The battleship has gained remarkably little in range in the last fifty years despite ever-increasing tonnage and efficiency of engines, which have been absorbed in greater speed, armament, and armor. We see the same sort of thing happening in aircraft. In any given size or type of plane, longer range is gained only by devoting to fuel weight which might otherwise be put into additional power or armament. Additional power means additional speed, rate of climb, and height of ceiling, which seem at the present stage of development to be the factors which designers are most ardently seeking.

The dream of every advocate of long-range bombing is a long-range fighter for escort, but such fighters must always be at a disadvantage when meeting enemy fighters designed for operating close to home, for these can use the weight saved in fuel for additional armament and power.[5] The speed of both fighters and bombers tends constantly to increase, and those speeds are already at such levels that every additional gain is purchased at extremely high cost in power. The weight of armament carried by fighters is also bound to increase, which in turn will require strengthening of the already heavy structural features of the fighter type.

The limit of size in bombers will not be the maximum size possible for aircraft but the point in growth at which diminishing returns set in. And diminishing returns must be considered not only in terms of aerodynamic efficiency, but in military efficiency and economy as well. The huge dirigible of the first World War went beyond the point of diminishing military returns, and for the time being we have only the much smaller blimp; the submarine passed the point of diminishing military returns when it reached the size of the *Surcouf*, which subsequent submarines have not approached.

Certainly there are advantages in large size to compensate for the disadvantages. The large plane not only has greater range and weight-carrying capacity, but the weight ratio of crew to bomb load is smaller, and in large-scale raids the organizational problems and the congestion of traffic over the target area are reduced. The present trend is all towards larger bombers for night bombing of land targets, but for operations against warships at sea large size has been proved a definite disadvantage.

[5] Most military planes are equipped to carry jettisonable tanks, by which they can extend their range somewhat for special missions. It has been reported that the Japanese fighter planes in some of their longer range operations carried such tanks, which they dropped before going into action. The possibilities of extending range in this manner are limited by the weight-carrying capacity of the plane and the performance demanded upon take-off.

In modern bombing attacks, aircraft are loaded with enough fuel to get them to their objective and back with a reasonable reserve, and the remainder of the weight-carrying capacity is given over to bomb load, which thus varies inversely with the distance of the objective. But that is only one aspect of the inhibiting influence of distance on bombing capacity. Since one's aircraft are bound to be of varying types and sizes, the more distant the target the fewer are the aircraft that can be used. With greater distance there is also greater personnel fatigue, more likelihood of adverse weather, less likelihood that the cover of night will be available for the entire trip, and a greater frequency of engine overhaul between trips. All these factors have proved of the highest importance in bombing raids in Europe, and they add up to the fact that *regardless of the range designed into an airplane,* the longer the distance to the target, the fewer the trips that can be made and the smaller the bomb load. And only a large volume of sustained bombing can achieve decisive results.

In operations against targets at sea there are two additional drawbacks in long-range bombing. In the first place, navigation is far more difficult over sea than over land, since terrestrial markings are absent. A surface ship proceeding under an overcast can find its position fairly accurately because the ocean currents in which it floats are extremely slow moving and of well-known direction and velocity. A plane is suspended in swift-moving wind currents, the direction and velocity of which may be entirely unknown to the plane's navigator. Secondly, while a city can be bombed tomorrow or next week if the weather does not permit it today, there can be no such delay in attacking an enemy warship or fleet or convoy at sea. If a powerful German ship leaves her anchorage at Trondheim to waylay the Russian convoy, it will do no good to strike at her two days hence. Even if the weather permits flying, the presence of the German may not be known until she is seen on the horizon from the decks of the convoy itself. The fastest moving land-based torpedo planes will get to the spot in time to see a few survivors of the convoy struggling in the water.

Respecting super-bombs (Major De Seversky speaks of a fifty-ton bomb which could shake a battleship apart even if loaded only with bricks), it is clear that in sea fights it is not feasible to use even the largest of the bombs already developed. The most obvious reason for this is that the larger the bomb the fewer that can be carried and the less chance of making a hit on maneuvering targets. And anything not a direct hit or a hair-breadth miss is totally wasted in the sea. "Block-busters" merely make bigger splashes.

Obviously, none of this discussion is intended to cover the remote future. What war will be like fifty years hence may be left to the astrologers. If our present predictions are as wrong as were those of even the most farseeing men of fifty years ago, we are wasting our time in attempting to predict. For the present, two homely observations apply to the airplane-battleship controversy. The first was made by the British statesman Palmerston about a hundred years ago when he said, respecting a similar controversy of the time, "Until I see that other nations have ceased to build line-of-battle ships, they are not yet an antiquated prejudice."

The second was made by a British commission studying the problem before the outbreak of war in 1939, and can be paraphrased as follows: "If we build battleships which turn out to be useless, we have wasted money; but if we abandon battleships *before* they have been proved useless, we will have forfeited our national independence." In the war that followed, battleships turned out not to be useless. The overwhelmingly superior German air force failed to destroy the British battle fleet despite the fact that that fleet operated for the most part *within range* of the larger German bombers.

"Once a country has air power enough to guard a battle fleet in enemy waters, why not unloose that air power directly at the heart of the enemy instead of wasting it to shield a less effective force?" This observation by Major De Seversky overlooks the fact that the air force necessary to protect a fleet is a very different thing from the air force required to achieve decisive results against enemy territories. Nevertheless, it does posit a fundamental question which must be scrutinized. If nations can be pounded into submission from any distance by air forces alone, it naturally will make little difference how control of the seas is maintained.

When the Luftwaffe was hurled against the British Isles in the summer and autumn of 1940, the world was presented with a test case in which everything favored the attacker over the defender. The disparity in air strength between Great Britain and Germany in favor of the latter was greater than could reasonably have been anticipated in any conflict between great powers. The Germans had innumerable, excellent air bases at their disposal and these bases were as close to the target as could well be imagined. That meant that the terrific total of German air strength, light bombers and even pursuit-bombers as well as long-range ones, could be hurled into the attack with maximum bomb loads, and each plane could be used a maximum number of times. The initiative rested entirely with the Germans, and the British had to improvise their modes of defense as the battle progressed.

Yet the attack was a failure. It failed not only to put Britain out of the war but also to open the way for invasion, or even to halt the upward trend of her munitions and armament production. At first much time was lost by workers going to shelters prematurely, but later this was rectified. England went into the war expecting to sustain casualties amounting to 3,000 killed and 12,000 wounded in a single night, and to suffer such losses night after night; hospitals made arrangements merely as a first provision for a quarter of a million casualties. Instead, in all the raids ending with November 5, 1940, some 14,000 British civilians were killed and 20,000 wounded, and the ratio of casualties to bombs dropped steadily declined; 150,000 hospital beds stood open—and empty. And, as the Prime Minister announced in Commons, "None of the services upon which the life of our cities depend—water, fuel, electricity, gas, sewage—not one has broken down."

By November 1940 it was the recrudescence of submarine warfare—not the air raids—to which British ministers in Parliament referred as "touching the life of the state." And in the spring of 1941 Mr. Stephen King-Hall of the Ministry of Aircraft Production was able to write, "There is not the slightest doubt that up to the moment of writing the material damage done by the German submarine service to the war effort of Great Britain is greater than that which has been achieved by their air force."

The idea that the attack failed because of the tactical unsuitability of the German planes is lent plausibility by the performance over France two years later of our B-17F's ("flying fortress") and B-24's. It is equally plausible to say that in those American types bomber development had temporarily outrun fighter development. Other things being equal, a plane designed for shooting should be able to defeat a plane designed for bombing. The American planes were in fact compromise types, for their design sacrificed bomb load for speed, and in day operations more bomb load was sacrificed to gain high altitudes. In Europe they were not commonly sent outside fighter escort range in daylight, and in any case their immunity was not typical of contemporary bombing raids.

It has been stated that a raid is militarily profitable when the losses are less than 10 per cent of the attacking force, but that is a wholly arbitrary figure. Everything depends on how much damage is done as well as on the rate of replacement. The Japanese clearly lost a good deal more than 10 per cent of their attacking planes at Pearl Harbor, but that was a highly profitable attack. On the other hand, the British in their 1,000-plane raid over Bremen on the night of June 26, 1942, may or may not have done enough damage to compensate for the fifty-two heavy bombers lost.

It is easy enough to say that if the Germans had possessed *unlimited* air power, if they could have taken their colossal losses without flinching, they would have defeated Britain. That is clearly true. Any nation can be overwhelmed by an air attack of sufficient magnitude. But when will a nation possess unlimited power of any kind, and, if the number of aircraft and flying personnel be put somewhere below infinity, the question should be asked: "How much is enough?"

By the winter of 1942–43, after six years of the most intensive aircraft building effort on the part of Britain and with the help during the latter part of that period of the colossal production of the United States, British and American air forces based on England were able to carry out frequent devastating raids upon enemy-held territory—raids which undoubtedly were having great effect upon the fighting fronts —but apparently were still far short of being capable of forcing a decision by their own power alone. And it should be noted that the successes our air forces were achieving were due partly to the fact that land operations in Russia and North Africa were tying down a major portion of German fighter plane and anti-aircraft strength, as well as to the general attrition suffered by the Luftwaffe in over three years of war. Moreover, by March 1943 the reduction of German production due to R.A.F. raids was still in no sense comparable to the injury which Germany had heaped upon her enemies by the rapid advances of her armies in 1939–41.

The campaign in Europe is one where the adversaries are

practically contiguous. Some air enthusiasts would have us understand that one nation can defeat another by direct air attack alone from a position half-way round the globe. No doubt it is possible, but the effort involved as compared with that in Europe would have to be computed by the professional astronomer or mathematician.

The naval force necessary to acquire and exercise command of the sea is computed in terms of the forces of the enemy. The superiority required in battleships, cruisers, and aircraft carriers is certainly not large, and the number of escort vessels required depends on the magnitude of one's shipping. The army necessary to invade the territory of the enemy is not expressed in absolute figures but in terms of superiority to the enemy. Only when we talk of winning a decision by the air offensive alone must we talk in terms of absolute rather than relative figures, and the figure of strength required is extraordinarily high. And with allies fighting with their backs to the wall, the time required might easily be too long.

If one chooses to escape from the present to the future, one must remember that aerial defenses also have a future. The progress of the so-called "static defenses" during the last twenty years has been uninterrupted and has reached astonishing effectiveness. Anti-aircraft armament, which was a joke to airmen in the First World War, is no longer amusing. American anti-aircraft guns capable of firing over 45,000 feet high are already in quantity production. Blackouts, smoke screens, camouflage, and intensively organized A.R.P. services greatly reduce the damage inflicted in air raids. The proportion of casualties to weight of bombs dropped in London was one-thirteenth as great in the autumn of 1940 as during the First World War. As experience accumulates, these defenses become more adequate. One British observer stated that "it was radio-location, almost as much as the bravery of R.A.F. pilots, which won the Battle of Britain." He might have said as much also for the volunteer fire fighters of London and other cities.

Naturally the greatest defense against air power resides in one's own air power; in the fighter plane we have the means of robbing the air assault of its sting. So long as the great powers keep themselves well armed at least with fighter planes, as they may be expected to do, military decisions will not be won by air attack alone.

The British in the auspicious year of 1942 were looking upon their already superior and still mounting air power chiefly as a means of supplementing and making more effective the blockade established by their navy. This was apparent not only in the great effort expended on German-held ports and naval bases, but also on the bombing of stores of materials, particularly oil, which the blockade had made almost unobtainable. The bombing of factories producing war materials is exactly analogous to blockade in its restricting consequences on the enemy's war effort. German railroads, which were already overstrained by war needs and British denial of sea-borne transportation, were given their share of bombs to make confusion worse confounded. The integration of the Bomber Command's effort with that of the Ministry of Blockade was repeatedly described in the writings and public statements of officials in both organizations. But neither in their blockade alone, nor in their bombing alone, nor in the combination of both, did the British expect the final defeat of Germany. That could be achieved only by the defeat of German armies in the field, to which blockade and "strategic bombing" merely contributed, however powerfully.

To be sure, the gigantic air power being built up in 1942 among the United Nations, especially in the factories of America, was bound to be an instrument of stunning force. It was by no means impossible that when launched upon Germany from bases in nearby England, the additional devastation and grief it would inflict upon a population already engulfed in misery—suffering blockade and despairing of any final victory—might be enough to turn the scales between will to resist and capitulation. In such an event, it would be all too easy to regard as the decisive weight that which was laid on last.

The airplane is an instrument of almost miraculous accomplishments. A weapon which can lay large parts of Rostock, Essen, and Cologne in ruins while the German armies are everywhere on the offensive needs no apologists. But it needs to be placed in its proper place in the scheme of things, if for no other reason than to derive from it its maximum effectiveness. Since every weapon of war has peculiar limitations, different types will complement each other to the mutual advantage of all. Air forces at least comparable to those of the enemy are necessary for victory, certainly for economical victory. Great air superiority over the enemy is unquestionably of tremendous advantage, whether on land or sea, though it is not true, as the Russian, North African, and Chinese fronts have indisputably shown, that such victory is impossible without "complete mastery" of the air or that such mastery, where attained, is itself a guarantee of victory.

On the seas the airplane is of enormous utility. It may be true, as some believe, that fleets should be used chiefly to secure and supply advanced bases from which aircraft can strike at enemy shipping. But obviously in such a scheme ships of all classes, battleships included, are needed as well as planes. The value of the airplane in the anti-submarine hunt needs no emphasis, but since the airplane cannot carry sufficient depth charges and cannot use the detecting devices which warships carry, it is helpless against submarines which have succeeded in submerging before being bombed. Why not, then, combine aircraft with destroyers?

So the story might go on endlessly. By properly combining weapons we achieve maximum strength. Which weapon becomes the "dominant" one is of no consequence except to the operating personnel involved. The nation is interested only in victory, and victory at the least possible cost. But to insist that only the airplane can achieve victory, or that the airplane can do everything the warship can do and a good deal else besides, is simply to ignore Samuel Johnson's famous warning, "Beware of cant!"

CHAPTER IX

The Tactics of Fleet Actions

NAVAL strategy is reducible to a set of simple aims and of principles governing the pursuit of those aims, but naval tactics is an immeasurably more complex field. Combats at sea are marked by infinite variety, and the circumstances peculiar to each meeting between enemy forces must determine the tactics used. Moreover, while the science of naval strategy remains relatively unchanged over a long period of time and is only moderately altered by changes in weapons, tactics change almost from day to day and tend to become constantly more complicated. The full-time occupation, therefore, of all naval personnel, flyers naturally included, is to perfect the science of tactics and to develop individual adroitness at its pursuit.

It is thus obviously impossible in a book of this size to present anything like a comprehensive review of naval tactics. But there is one kind of action which is at once the rarest and the most important, the least understood and appreciated by laymen and the kind upon which naval chiefs have their gaze most intently fixed—the action between whole battle fleets. In the naval history of the last two centuries, there are relatively few instances of engagements between the main bodies of the belligerents and even fewer instances of such engagements reaching a decisive conclusion. Naval wars may take place in which no such action occurs at all. Yet, not only are decisive actions of this type conclusive of great issues, but willingness on the one side and unwillingness on the other to fight such a battle may be itself conclusive. The side which chooses not to fight forfeits to its opponent most of the fruits of victory. The only reason the Battle of Jutland was not followed by another and more conclusive fight was that the

Germans knew they could not best the British Fleet. As a result they conceded to the British command of the North Sea and of all the oceans to which it opened. But the British in order to achieve that result had to stand ready at all times to fight a fleet action.

It has been said by some naval men that the engagement of whole battle fleets is a thing of the past, that modern naval operations are concerned exclusively with task forces—that is, forces of various sizes gathered round one or more important warships and assigned a specific mission. Naturally, such operations are the kind which fill the news columns, since they are going on all the time. But there has been no change, technological or otherwise, over the last decade or the last century, which alters the two elemental principles that in concentration there is strength and that command of the sea is likely to be conclusive while hit-and-run raids are not. From the strategic point of view the airplane and the submarine are only additional instruments for disputing the enemy's command of the sea or of intensifying one's own command.

To say that vast distances, such as obtain in the Pacific, prevent command of the sea is to acknowledge distance as one's master, whereas superior strength can be made to conquer distance by the seizure of bases nearer the enemy. Of course, it is an old story in naval history that neither side may have quite the strength to do more than challenge or deny the enemy's efforts to establish command, and that the sea thereby remains permanently in dispute. But that reflects either weakness or an exceptional set of geographical circumstances.

The weakness of the "task force" theory lies simply in the fact that each task force can be beaten by a larger task force, and in penetrating enemy waters it is always beset by the anxiety that the enemy will interpose just such a superior force. The only conclusion to this endless chain of matching big by bigger is a showdown match of maximum strength, in which one side stands ready at all times to intervene in the active theater with a force larger than the largest available to the enemy. It can never be too much stressed that the chief reason the American Navy had to stand by virtually helpless while the Japanese seized position after position in the Western Pacific was that after December 7, 1941, the American Pacific Fleet was in no position to challenge the combined battle fleet of Japan, even if reinforcements had been rushed from the Atlantic. The small squadrons in the Far East were, as at Java, hopelessly ineffective.

The Japanese failure at the Midway Islands in June 1942 proves that no navy can afford to flout principles evolved from long experience. The Japanese force was a formidable one, to be sure, but it was nevertheless only a portion of their whole fleet. We struck at it with all the strength we had on the spot and which could be rushed to the spot, and that strength proved to be sufficient to administer a severe defeat to the Japanese. Had the enemy come in much greater strength, our own opposition could not have been greater than it was. Since the Japanese squadron included three or four battleships, they were already risking a force whose loss would have been a catastrophic blow to their naval position in the Pacific.

They would have been risking not more but less to have used their whole fleet. Their defenses against our aircraft would have been much greater. All the experience of war indicates that with greater force they would have suffered not more but less total damage, and they would have had a far better chance of attaining their objective. Part of our Fleet was at Pearl Harbor 1,140 miles away. Our capital ships were undoubtedly sent out the moment we learned of the threat against Midway, and since we knew they had only a few battleships present we could afford to let our fastest and most powerful battleships run ahead to counter or pursue them. But if they had come with their whole fleet, we should have been obliged to keep our own fleet together and it would have proceeded at the speed of the slowest member, which at such a distance would be under 20 knots. Thus, if the Japanese had come in full strength, they would have been better able to overcome our aircraft opposition and they would have had more time for their landing operation before the intervention of our battle fleet. They in fact retired, without attempting a landing, before our battle fleet reached the spot.

The side with the initiative will sometimes disperse its forces to persuade its opponent to an even greater dispersion, but it should be noticed that it is easier to dictate concentration upon the enemy than dispersion. If two widely separated Japanese forces were operating against us simultaneously, we might choose to ignore one temporarily or in part in order to overwhelm the other. But if the Japanese assaulted us in one concentrated force, no choice would be left to us. We should either have to combine our own forces or accept defeat. We should therefore consider with extreme care the new gospel that fleet actions are an obsolete form of war.

The constitution of battle fleets has always been determined by the prevalent tactical theories of the time. Until very recently the battleship was considered as indisputably the arbiter of great battles. Today its position is, to put it mildly, no longer unchallenged. The attack airplane is considered by many the dominant weapon in naval as well as in land warfare, though there is a marked conflict of opinion as to whether carrier-based or land-based aircraft will rule the seas. This writer's conviction, developed in previous chapters, is that aircraft are inherently of such limited range and seakeeping capacity that in the foreseeable future land-based aircraft cannot hope to control sea lanes outside of narrow zones along certain coasts. But this still leaves open the question of whether the decision in major battles at sea will be won primarily by guns or by carrier-borne aircraft. If it is the latter, the aircraft carrier becomes the dominant surface warship, and battleships will either disappear entirely or take on a role of mere escort to the carrier. In that case fleet tactics will become wholly different from what we have known in the past.

The advantages in favor of the carrier as the chief offensive instrument in a fleet are, first, the extraordinary range of its weapons, which far outreach any naval gun; and second, the fact that the aircraft which deliver the carrier's blow are an excellent means of launching torpedoes, which generally are more disabling, pound for pound, than shell or bombs.

Against these two advantages the carrier is beset with several vital handicaps. First among these is its vulnerability. Once carriers get within gun range of enemy battleships or heavy cruisers they are quickly destroyed, just as the *Glorious* was destroyed by the *Scharnhorst*. Outside of gun range they have proved a much easier prey to air attack than battleships or well armored cruisers.

There are many conditions of wind and weather under which the carrier cannot operate its aircraft, just as the *Ark Royal* could not launch her planes on the day after she had scored hits on the *Bismarck*. In some of the higher latitudes, the days of weather unfavorable to the operation of aircraft from carriers often amount to fully half the days of the year. It also appears, from experience in the battles of Cape Matapan and the Coral Sea, that carriers and their aircraft are not likely to be as effective as other warships in night actions.[1] Thus, the aircraft carrier might be the dominant ship in fair

[1] During the night following the destruction of the *Hood*, however, some torpedo bombers from the aircraft carrier *Victorious* found the *Bismarck* in the darkness by the aid of radio bearings flashed by the cruisers *Norfolk* and *Suffolk*, which were shadowing the German battleship. One hit was registered. This is one of the more spectacular examples of the effectiveness of ship-plane coordination.

weather and in daylight, with the battleship retaining its ascendancy at other times.

The carrier suffers also from the fragile nature of the aircraft which transmit its blows. Considering the fighter aircraft and anti-aircraft armament defenses available to a strong enemy, carriers might lose their attack aircraft before a decision was reached. It is altogether possible that a fairly large superiority in attack aircraft might be reduced to equality before the battle was well begun. During one phase of the Solomon Islands campaign, some of our scouts discovered a Japanese carrier hurriedly retreating from a scene of previous action without a single plane on her flight deck and with none of her planes in evidence in the air.

And since the carrier can defeat heavily armored warships almost exclusively by means of the torpedo, its future as the dominant ship of the battle fleet stands or falls with the future of that weapon. Modern battleships have been built on the presumption that while the torpedo put certain restraints on admirals in command of battleships and widened the range of fire, actions at sea would still be determined by the naval gun. But inasmuch as the airplane furnishes a new and better means of launching torpedo attack than the destroyer or cruiser, battleships will have to be redesigned accordingly.

Torpedo protection will certainly be improved, and the battleship of the future may be so constructed that torpedoes are less effective against it than shell.[2] If this should come to

---

[2] For example, Franklin G. Barnes, inventor of the anti-magnetic mine device which has now been generally adopted on merchant ships and warships, announced in the spring of 1942 that he had a device which would prevent any torpedo from reaching its target, and he declared further that he was working upon a system for reducing gun recoil to such an extent that an 8-inch gun could be substituted for one of half that caliber. If these two projects of this established inventor should prove successful, we would be embarked upon a new era in which the gun will enjoy unchallenged dominance.

pass, the possibility that the carrier will usurp the present position of the battleship will be at an end, for no carrier whose planes use bombs can begin to match the fire of the battleship in volume, accuracy, and penetrating power. Even without such a revolution in naval architecture, however, it must be remembered that the battleship has in its own carriers a protection against enemy carriers, just as it has in its cruisers and destroyers a defense against torpedo attack by enemy vessels of similar types. Its own secondary armament, torpedo protective layers, and its maneuverability are of course an additional protection.

The battles of the Coral Sea and of the Midway Islands in May and June 1942 have been hailed as prototypes of the battles of the future. In neither of those battles did the opposing warships come within range or even within sight of each other. The tactical activity in the vicinity of each of the opposing squadrons was exactly comparable to the attacks of land-based aircraft upon naval squadrons, and it followed the now familiar pattern of simultaneous bomb and torpedo assaults. A thousand journalists over the country leaped to the conclusion that never again would fleets close to gun range. The Coral Sea Battle, it was predicted, would hold the same position in history as the engagement between the *Monitor* and the *Merrimac*.

It might, incidentally, be pointed out that the historic battle in Hampton Roads in 1862 was almost universally misinterpreted at the time. Many people, including some naval experts, predicted that never again would a warship be built without armor. They predicted also that the gun would never be able to overcome ship-borne armor—that the only means of sinking enemy vessels in the future would be by ramming or torpedoes. Both forecasts proved wholly wrong. Today the most numerous combat ships in any navy—destroyers, and lesser combat craft—are virtually unarmored. And the battle between the *Monitor* and the *Merrimac* was not only the first but also the last naval battle in which guns failed so dismally against armor. During the same Civil War, better armorclads than the *Monitor* and *Merrimac* were penetrated by enemy shot.

That it is still possible for fleets to close each other, despite the use of aircraft carriers by one or both sides, has been proved during World War II not only in the sinking of the aircraft carrier *Glorious* by the battleship *Scharnhorst*, by the Battle of Cape Matapan, and by the *Bismarck* episode, but also by the Battle of the Coral Sea itself. On the evening of May 7, American flyers reported to their squadron that a big Japanese air and sea force was *only thirty miles away*, lurking in the dense rain squalls, fog, and clouds of the miserable weather that surrounded the area. Had the American squadron contained one fast battleship, it could have closed the enemy force and probably destroyed a good part of it before either side could organize an attack by torpedo planes. As it was, neither side cared to attempt an airplane attack in the gathering darkness, and action was postponed until the following morning when the two fleets had moved 190 miles apart.

That, however, is a deduction from what might have happened in the battle. But there are several things that did happen both in the Coral Sea and at Midway which throw a good deal of light on the battles of the future. In the first place, both sides lost heavily and rapidly in aircraft, and the Japanese at least were deprived of all their carrier strength very early in each of the engagements. Here we have the consequence of vulnerability in aircraft and in carriers. This indicates not that carriers and their aircraft will play an unimportant role in the great naval battles of the future, but that their influence will be felt chiefly in the opening stages of the engagement. They may do decisive damage before they are eliminated, but it is logical to assume they may be eliminated as a major force fairly early.

What kind of decisive damage may they do before they are knocked out? They will do a good deal more than merely neutralize each other's aircraft. The communique issued by our Navy after the battle at Midway indicated that three Japanese battleships had been damaged. The kind of damage was not described, but let us assume that some of it was torpedo damage. If so, the chances of closing the enemy on the part of the American forces rushing up from Pearl Harbor were enormously enhanced. Unfortunately, the American battleships failed to close because of the great distance they had to come and also because of the quick Japanese retirement after their initial heavy losses.

One important fact about both the Coral Sea and Midway, the significance of which was universally overlooked in the press, was that in each case the Japanese force was an invasion force. This meant not only that the Japanese naval forces were attended by a vulnerable convoy which embarrassed all their movements, but it meant also that as soon as the land and air forces which the naval squadron was escorting fell below the level necessary for a successful landing, there was nothing to do but retire. That factor would be completely absent in a fleet action fought to determine command of the sea.

Naval history records few instances of battle in which both sides were anxious to engage. The side which recognizes itself to be clearly inferior in strength and which sees little hope of overcoming its disadvantage by a favorable position will seek to avoid action. It is clear that if Scheer had been able to maintain aerial reconnaissance ahead of his fleet at Jutland, he would never have run into the jaws of the Grand Fleet, and there might have been no battle at all. Incidentally, the

Germans did have Zeppelin airships over the North Sea that day; they were supposed to be working with the High Seas Fleet, but none of them saw any warships, either British or German, though they were in the vicinity of the action. One saw some firing during the night and thought it was directed at her, though no vessel in either fleet was aware of her presence. This experience, confirmed also by several events in World War II, seems to indicate that shore-based aircraft cannot be depended upon to cooperate with fleets well out at sea if visibility is not good. That is especially true if radio silence has to be observed. Aircraft based on carriers will at least know where their own fleet is and have only to find that of the enemy.

However, granting that in battles of the future aircraft will discover the enemy's presence before the fleets are in gun range, such a discovery will not take place simultaneously for both fleets. If the superior side first receives the intelligence, the fleets will begin to close. Under those circumstances the airplane tends to favor engagements rather than the contrary. Aircraft may also succeed in driving off the enemy's aircraft, so that the latter may remain in ignorance of approaching contact. The many battles of the Second World War have proved that while airplanes have reduced they have by no means eliminated the chances of surprise at sea.

It is to be expected, however, that the stalked fleet will finally be made aware of its danger before contact. One of the differences between aerial and surface reconnaissance is that the sky is too big to be shut off to prying enemy eyes even by superior forces, whereas strong cruiser forces can not only reconnoiter themselves but can also prevent enemy cruisers from approaching their own battle fleet. What happens, then, when each fleet is aware of the other's presence but still out of gun range?

Obviously, the first blows on each side will be struck by aircraft, some of which will attempt to torpedo enemy battleships. Let us suppose that both sides make torpedo hits on major ships of the opposing side. The chances are that such hits will at least cut down the speed of struck vessels even if they do not disable them. At this point each commander is placed in a very different position from his opponent. The one commanding the superior fleet may feel that one or two battleships dropping out of his line still leaves him with sufficient superiority to best the enemy. If his damaged ships fall behind, they are relatively out of danger, save from planes. The fleeing admiral, on the other hand, is not only less able to spare the same number of ships as his opponent, but he knows that to leave a ship behind is to sacrifice it. Considerations of prestige and of morale within the fleet as well as of material loss will be opposed to such a sacrifice without battle. Thus, unless the superiority of the pursuer is overwhelming, a few torpedo hits on important ships of the retreating fleet may force its admiral to commit himself to an action he would otherwise decline.

It is therefore obvious that the airplane can be responsible in some instances for producing decisive actions, just as in other cases it may prevent such actions. The American Navy has been so confident that the speed of fleets will be determined by the speed of torpedoed vessels that it has built battleships somewhat slower than those of rival navies, feeling that this initial inferiority in speed will be of minor importance in determining whether action can be joined or in determining range. This might prove to be an unhappy miscalculation, but the lessons of Cape Matapan, of the *Bismarck*, the *Prince of Wales*, and the *Repulse* seem to indicate that the decision to sacrifice speed for armor and gun power was shrewd.

The Battle of Cape Matapan of March 28-29, 1941, gives

an interesting hint of what might happen in a great fleet action under modern conditions. Three battleships were involved on each side, and the British were aided by carrier-based aircraft. The more advanced portion of the Italian force consisted of the new battleship, *Vittorio Veneto*, eight cruisers, and nine destroyers. Two *Conte di Cavour* class battleships, three cruisers, and four destroyers were later sighted eighty miles west of the advanced group, furnishing a support upon which the fast advanced force could fall back.

Contact was first established between the British and Italian cruiser forces. Having been led toward the *Vittorio Veneto* by the retreating Italians, the British cruisers then began to retreat toward their own battleships, leading the Italian battleship after them. When the *Vittorio Veneto* was within thirty miles of the British battleships, she was attacked by a formation of torpedo planes from the aircraft carrier *Formidable*. Apparently undamaged, she wheeled at once in retreat, her cruisers and destroyers turning with her. The speedier Italian ships soon outdistanced the British battleships, but shortly afterwards the British torpedo planes began to make hits. Four in all were claimed on the *Vittorio Veneto*, and her speed was drastically reduced. At least one Italian cruiser, the *Pola*, was also damaged. Unfortunately for the British, night fell before contact was established, and the Italian battleship got away entirely. But the *Pola* and several of her cruiser and destroyer consorts were caught by the British in the darkness, lighted up by the searchlights of a British destroyer, and blasted by the guns of the battleships. The British remained in the area until the following morning to pick up survivors, but withdrew when German dive-bombers attacked. The British fleet returned to its base without damage or casualties.

The Italian battleship escaped because of her initial speed, which gave her a considerable lead over the pursuing British before she was torpedoed, and because of the narrowness of the sea, which permitted her to gain her base. Some reports had the ship sunk, but the British never officially claimed it. Had the action occurred on a broader sea, the Italian ship would probably have felt the guns of the British battleships on the following morning. That is exactly what occurred two months later in the destruction of the *Bismarck*.

Thus, from all these battles the pattern of modern engagements emerges: initial contact made by cruisers or, more likely, by reconnaissance aircraft; torpedo planes used to destroy the floating bases of enemy aircraft and to clip the speed of the retreating enemy main body; and battleships brought in for the kill.

The air-minded will of course point to the *Prince of Wales* and *Repulse* and ask, "Why use battleships at all?" To answer that one can point to the Midway Islands, where Japanese battleships got away, and to a dozen similar instances. Apparently aircraft, even large numbers of land-based aircraft, are usually not enough. Besides, the *Prince of Wales* and *Repulse* had no fighter plane protection whatever.

Summing up all the experience of the Second World War up to July 1942, it is clear that in order to get the most in all-weather fighting value out of a given amount of resources, one must balance battleships with carriers. Just what balance to strike is not yet clear, though there will unquestionably be a greater proportion of carriers in the battle fleet of the future than at present. On the other hand, it still seems logical to interpret the tactics of fleet actions on the assumption that the battleship remains the final arbiter of major fleet actions, with the various torpedo craft including airplanes playing highly important though nevertheless subsidiary parts.

A fleet is uniquely adapted to realization of the fundamental principle in strategy that strength lies in concentration. It is more readily coordinated and directed by a single man than is an army in the field, and superiority in total strength can therefore more easily be made to register on the enemy. A fleet on the offensive is permitted a more complete concentration than is possible to an attacking army. The latter must disperse a great deal of strength, perhaps a major portion, in defending long fronts and lines of communications outside the immediate area of the offensive. The fleet has its obligation to provide escorts to convoys, but these do not usually require important ships of the larger categories, and there are no such things on the sea as positions which need to be defended. All the vital positions which must be secured to a navy are on land and are protected by land forces. A navy might therefore be regarded as inherently an offensive force.

In an action the units of a fleet are not only mutually supporting, each adding to the fire of its neighbors and sharing the burden of providing a target, but are also contributing to the group effort at the same moment of time. No important vessels present are held in reserve or prevented from taking part by the narrow confines of the field. It is the first preoccupation of the admiral to prevent such a thing from occurring. He wants all his battleships speaking against the enemy in the same instant. In land warfare, on the other hand, there is an old axiom that he who throws in his reserves last will win the battle. The general is also determined to let none of his force go unused and therefore wasted—the true meaning of the principle of "economy of force" [3]—but he has no thought of having all his force engaged at the same time.

[3] This principle has been erroneously interpreted by some writers as referring to the attainment of one's objective with the least possible force. It is possible that one's superiority at any one point may be so excessive as to indicate a waste of strength that is much needed elsewhere, but in such a case it is better to speak of faulty disposition of force than of violation of a principle which has so specific a meaning in military literature as "economy of force."

There is another important difference between land and naval combat. In land warfare, though there is great advantage in having the strategic initiative, the defensive has had from the time of the invention of the breech-loading rifle to the present a considerable *tactical* advantage. The strategic initiative permits one to concentrate forces at positions of one's own choice and thus to gain local superiority, but wherever opposed forces are approximately equal, the side which attempts to advance will usually be hurled back with disproportionately large losses. In sea battles, on the other hand, advantages of position have almost nothing to do with being on the defensive or the offensive. The tactical defensive is symbolized by flight, the offensive by pursuit. It is true that a pursuing fleet is usually less able to use smoke screens and has in the past been somewhat more endangered by torpedoes and mines than a fleeing one. But in these days when torpedo attacks during fleet actions are as likely to be delivered by aircraft as by destroyers, the advantage of the escaping fleet even in the case of torpedoes is diminished. At the Battle of Cape Matapan the fleeing Italians suffered more from torpedoes than the pursuing British.

The absence of any special advantage to the defensive in fleet actions means that a superiority in guns and armor is more telling than it otherwise would be. And in fact a margin of superiority in numbers confers a disproportionate superiority in actual combat power. Let us consider a case where one fleet has a two-to-one superiority in numbers over its opponent. Each of the warships of the inferior side will either divide its fire between two adversaries (which complicates the problem of fire control), or, as is more likely, will concentrate on one enemy ship at a time. In the first instance each ship in the superior fleet is receiving only half the fire (and less than half the effect) it is giving, and in the second instance half the ships in the superior fleet will be undergoing

229

no fire at all. In either case, each vessel on the inferior side is receiving the fire of two ships and is likely to go down or be put out of action before it can silence either one of its opponents. The inferior side thus begins to lose its ships faster, and the disparity in strength between the opponents widens at a steadily accelerating rate, like compound interest.

It can be mathematically demonstrated that when luck and intelligence are eliminated, the ratio of power between opposed fleets of identical units is arrived at by squaring the strength of each side, which would make a superiority of two to one in numbers equal to four to one in combat power. Of course, such a formula cannot be too tightly applied to actual fleet actions, where luck and intelligence are always important and where opposed units are rarely exactly comparable. And the more nearly equal the opposing sides, the more luck cancels out the marginal differences.

It seems also that probabilities for victory vary not only with the ratio in numbers but also with the actual numbers involved. Where the forces engaged are very small, the element of chance plays a disproportionate role. For example, in the engagement between the *Bismarck* on the one side and the *Hood* and *Prince of Wales* on the other, the *Hood* was quickly blown up by a lucky hit. To be sure, the ratio of force in that case was not really two to one, since each of the British ships, and particularly the *Hood*, was weaker than its opponent. On the other hand, when the *Bismarck* was later engaged by the *Rodney* and *King George V*, the fire of the German ship was relatively ineffectual and the British vessels destroyed her without much damage to themselves, due chiefly to a lucky hit early in the action on the German's fire-control system. In a larger engagement the truly lucky hits on each side would tend to cancel each other out.

At the other extreme, where very large forces are involved,

the problem of coordination of effort looms so large that the admiral enjoying superiority may not be able to bring all his power to bear upon his adversary, particularly if he approaches the battle with an unfavorable deployment. And large forces are spread over so much space that conditions of visibility may prevent the advantageous use of superior strength. At Jutland, Admiral Scheer apparently was prepared to stand and fight if only he could catch the huge, unwieldy British Fleet at a disadvantage in position. And his opponent was determined not to fight a night action because it would minimize the advantage of his superiority.

Despite these various qualifications, however, two things are clear. First, the value of concentration is such that the total strength of a fleet amounts to much more than the mere addition of its parts. Second, a decided superiority in firepower, other things being equal, is a pretty certain guarantee of victory in a naval battle.

In fact, if one excludes the factor of surprise air attack, most modern combats tend to indicate that a superior fleet will not only win the action but will win it without itself suffering damage at all comparable to that inflicted on the enemy. This is of course particularly likely to be true where superiority includes superior range in guns and a superior speed enabling one to dictate the range. The Battle of Coronel on November 1, 1914, where Admiral Von Spee destroyed Cradock's inferior squadron, had that result, as did the Battle of the Falkland Islands on December 8, 1914, where Von Spee's squadron was in turn destroyed by a superior fleet under Sturdee. The Battle of Jutland, where the British lost more warships than the inferior Germans, is on the whole a confirmation rather than a contradiction of this conclusion, since all the important British losses occurred before the two main fleets were engaged. The Germans had for a time the much sought after advantage of meeting portions of the British forces with their whole High Seas Fleet. In the two brief periods when the opposing battle fleets were engaged, the Germans took a great deal more punishment than they gave.

True, in the initial battle-cruiser action between Beatty's six battle cruisers and Hipper's five,[4] the British lost two of their big ships and the Germans none, but in that instance the numerical strength was misleading. The British battle cruisers were much more thinly armored than the German; their gunnery was poorer, and Hipper was a better tactician than Beatty. That should remind us that while we ordinarily compare the firepower of two fleets on the assumption of "other things being equal," those "other things" generally are not equal.

There have, of course, been some remarkable upsets in modern naval battles. At the Battle of Montevideo in December 1939, the German pocket battleship *Admiral Graf Spee* should by all calculations have blasted Harwood's little squadron of cruisers completely out of the water, but instead the German was defeated. The reason is to be found in the brilliant tactics of the British squadron and in the relatively light protection of the German ship for a vessel of its firepower. But perhaps the most amazing performance occurred in the Mediterranean in March 1942, when Rear-Admiral Vian with a handful of cruisers and destroyers actually stood off for two hours, by a marvelous combination of aggressive tactics and skillful use of smoke cover, an immensely superior Italian force which included a battleship. The British warships and the convoy they were protecting escaped with little damage and put at least one torpedo into the battleship. These examples do not include whole fleet actions, but they prove, never-

[4] The *Queen Mary* was actually sunk after Evan-Thomas had brought his four powerful battleships into the action in support of Beatty. But as soon as these ships got well within range, Hipper sought to break off the action.

theless, what never should have been doubted—that naval battles like other battles are essentially contests of men, and not merely of armor and broadsides. It might be observed, too, that in the Second World War the British with their smaller and much more heavily burdened fleet have come a long way from the cautious tactics of Jellicoe in World War I. Without a great reserve of strength upon which to fall back, they have nevertheless used their available force with an aggressiveness worthy of their finest traditions.

The tactical theories prevailing at any one time will determine not only the constitution of fleets but also the design of the individual warship. During the nineteenth century there was considerable confusion as to whether ships should fight in line ahead or line abreast, but prevailing opinion finally returned to the old eighteenth century practice of major ships fighting in line ahead—that is, one following behind the other—or in several minor variations of line ahead which need not be here discussed. Ships proceeding in line ahead will obviously seek to have their enemy on either beam, since fire ahead or astern will be obstructed by their neighbors. The modern battleship is therefore without exception designed to be able to use all its primary guns on either beam.

The four French battleships of the *Richelieu* and *Dunkerque* classes carry all their primary armament in the forward part of the ship and can therefore concentrate all their heavy fire ahead as well as on either beam. This disposal would be of advantage in a pursuit, but in many actions it might be a serious disadvantage. The two British *Nelson's* also carry all their heavy armament forward, but since the third of the three turrets is lower than the second, these ships do not even have as compensation for absence of fire astern the ability to concentrate all their fire ahead, except possibly at extreme ranges. The British ships were built in that fashion in order to save weight and thereby bring the ships under

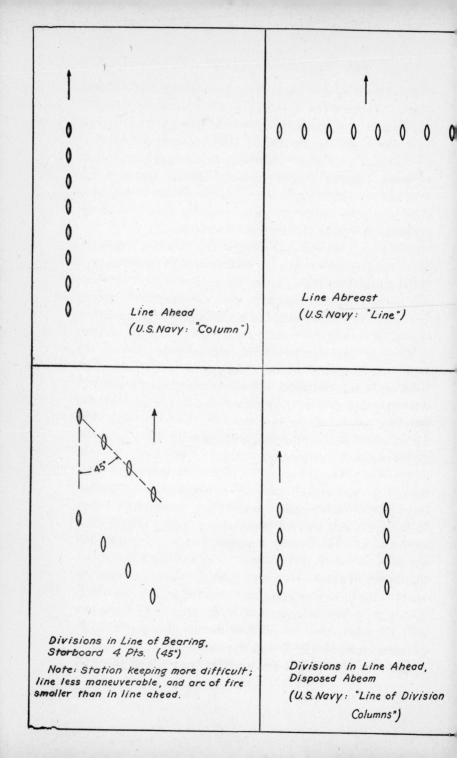

Line Ahead
(U.S. Navy: "Column")

Line Abreast
(U.S. Navy: "Line")

45°

Divisions in Line of Bearing,
Starboard 4 Pts. (45°)

Note: Station keeping more difficult;
line less maneuverable, and arc of fire
smaller than in line ahead.

Divisions in Line Ahead,
Disposed Abeam

(U.S. Navy: "Line of Division

Columns")

treaty limits. By grouping the guns together the armored citadel could be made shorter. Why the French chose a similar design is not known. All other battleships are designed with at least part of their heavy armament aft, and in most types the guns are equally divided between the fore and aft positions. But however disposed on the ship, the main guns are so arranged that an extraordinarily large arc on either beam (120° in the older battleships and more in the newer ones) can be commanded by the ship's entire main battery. The second turret of the British *Nelson's* can fire through 330° of arc, which means that despite its position in the forward part of the ship it can fire within 15° of direct astern on either side. The line-ahead position in battle, called "column" in the U. S. Navy, thus gives the fullest opportunities for the exploitation of the battle line's great firepower.

When two opposing fleets are drawn out in more or less parallel lines, neither having the advantage in position, the victory will go to the side with the superior firepower-armor combination. Firepower of course includes skill in gunnery, and the armor factor must be considered as covering the whole design of the ship. But the likelihood is that one side or the other will have, either from tactical skill or mere chance or a combination of both, certain advantages of position relative to light and weather—advantages which may augment superiority or compensate for inferiority. One fleet may be firing into a blinding sun near the horizon and the other away from it. On the other hand, one may be silhouetted against a lightened sky at dawn or dusk while the other is shrouded in darkness. Advantages of light played a very considerable part in the battles of Coronel and of Jutland. However, the modern practice of spotting artillery fire with aircraft has done much to diminish possibilities of substantial advantage from this quarter.

The direction and velocity of the wind may favor one side

or the other in the use of smoke screens. Firing against a strong wind is usually a disadvantage, particularly for one's secondary armament and lighter vessels, which have to contend with spray in aiming and firing. A condition of mist and bad visibility may be highly localized, and it is possible that one fleet will be shielded in it while the other is completely in the clear, which might mean a substantial advantage for the former if it were firing by indirect control. Such localized conditions were prominent at Jutland. Also, the *Scharnhorst* and *Gneisenau* undoubtedly owe their escape from destruction during their dash up the English Channel in part to the fact that they entered an area of mist just before the first of the 600 British planes attacked. And we have already seen how in one phase of the Battle of the Coral Sea the Japanese squadron was hidden in a local squall condition, which accounted for its not being seen until it was within thirty miles of the American squadron.

However, the tactical jockeying for position that marks the large fleet action is usually concerned not so much with light and weather as with the bearing of the opposing forces toward each other. Where small task forces with perhaps one or two heavy ships on each side are involved, the problems are very simple. Such an action is like a pistol duel between two men. But where large forces are engaged the problems are wholly different, which is the chief reason it is dangerous to draw too many conclusions from small-scale actions. Most of the maneuvers of fleet actions are determined by the importance of mustering one's whole fire against the enemy and preferably of preventing him at the same time from using his whole firepower.

The dream of every commander in battle, or. land and sea alike, is to be able to throw all or almost all of his entire force on a portion of the enemy's, overwhelming that portion and then proceeding to the next. It was because of his adeptness at such tactics that Napoleon was able to boast that he always had superior numbers at the critical point, even though his whole army was often smaller than his opponent's. The breakthrough or the envelopment in the tactics of land warfare has usually been motivated by the desire to roll up the enemy's line by an attack from the flank, that is, to destroy him by striking successively at portions which are not favorably disposed to support each other.

In naval battles there was for a long time none of this nice discrimination in tactics. A few of the great admirals of antiquity, like Phormio, had devised systems of attacking isolated portions of the enemy fleet, but their ideas were forgotten, and down to the eighteenth century most naval battles were little more than melees. Toward the latter part of that century, however, the English under Rodney adopted the practice of using an advantage of the wind not merely to attack but to concentrate their entire force on a part of the enemy's line. Many battles, such as St. Vincent and Trafalgar, were won by British fleets inferior to their opponents in numbers—at St. Vincent the British were fifteen to twenty-four —but by throwing their whole weight usually on the rear of the enemy line they forced the van to countermarch and sometimes to beat upwind to come to the aid of the engaged portion. By the time the disengaged portion arrived, its own destruction was in order.

Those were the days, however, when ships fought yardarm to yardarm. In modern times, with battles beginning and sometimes ending at long ranges, no fleet can throw itself on a portion of the enemy fleet in the direct physical sense known to the days before the long-range gun. But it is still possible to maneuver one's line so that a similar advantage may be gained.

If an admiral can contrive to get his line athwart the path of the enemy fleet in such wise that he forms the head of a

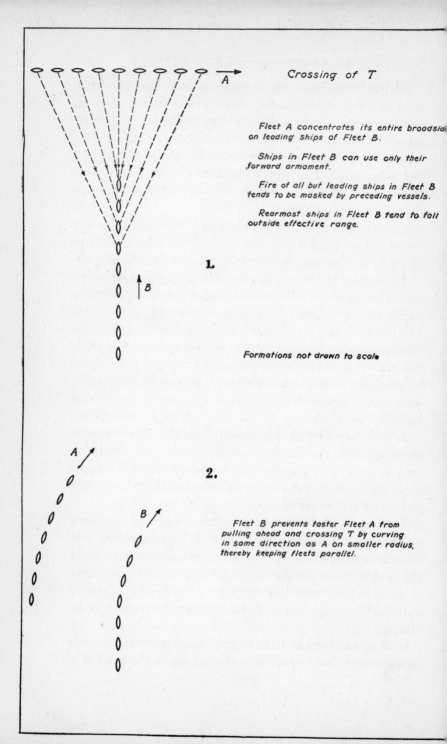

Crossing of T

Fleet A concentrates its entire broadsid
on leading ships of Fleet B.

Ships in Fleet B can use only their
forward armament.

Fire of all but leading ships in Fleet B
tends to be masked by preceding vessels.

Rearmost ships in Fleet B tend to fall
outside effective range.

1.

Formations not drawn to scale

2.

Fleet B prevents faster Fleet A from
pulling ahead and crossing T by curving
in same direction as A on smaller radius,
thereby keeping fleets parallel.

T relative to the latter, his advantage is enormous. His whole mass of fire is available and can be concentrated at the head of the enemy's line, its most important part. The fire of many ships on a few is bound to result in quick disaster to the few. In the line forming the stem of the T, on the other hand, the guns on the after parts of the ships will usually be unable to bear, the other guns will in many cases be obstructed by friendly ships, and if the line is long some of the vessels in the rear will be out of effective range altogether. Misses on one ship may hit the one next in line. The line in the stem of the T, in other words, is effectively enfiladed.

At Jutland, Admiral Jellicoe twice had Scheer in exactly this unfavorable position, and each time Scheer had no alternative but to reverse his line by a "turn together" of individual ships and to extricate himself as rapidly as possible. The second time he was in such imminent danger of annihilation that he sent his battle cruisers and lighter ships forward in a reckless charge to cover his retreat, thereby showing his willingness to sacrifice these valuable ships in order to save his battle line.

It is sometimes said that superior speed can be utilized to move ahead of the enemy's line and by turning athwart his path to cross the T. But the fleet menaced with such a movement can easily parry it by turning his head with the enemy so that his line is curved parallel to the latter's. The two fleets would thus tend to move in concentric circles with the slower on the inside. On the other hand, such a situation might be unacceptable to the slower fleet. It might thereby be sacrificing an advantage of light and weather or it might be anxious to break off the action. At the Battle of Tsushima in 1905 Admiral Togo not only had an advantage of speed over his Russian opponent of about 12 knots to 9, but he was additionally aided by Admiral Rojhestvensky's determination to proceed northward to Vladivostok and by his concern with covering a convoy. Since Togo already was favored by a superiority in fire power, the ensuing maneuvers could have only one issue. With the exception of a single cruiser which escaped, the Russian fleet of thirty-two vessels was annihilated.

In modern battles, however, the disparity in speed between opposing lines is hardly likely to be so great as it was at Tsushima, and the ranges at which fire opens are certain to be greater. Thus, the crossing of the T is not likely to result from maneuvers during battle except toward its close, when the issue has probably already been decided. However, the head of one line may be severely injured by concerted torpedo attack, which would tend to slow the whole line. Or the other side may have a division of exceptionally fast battleships, like our *North Carolina's* or the British *King George V's*, which might be sent ahead separately to effect such a movement. A line need not inevitably remain one unbroken whole if its separate parts can still be coordinated to the same end. Nelson's most brilliant tactical maneuver occurred when he hauled his battleship, the *Captain*, out of the line commanded by Admiral Jervis at St. Vincent and prevented the divided Spanish fleet from reforming. When Scheer was pursuing Beatty and Evan-Thomas in the first phase of the Battle of Jutland, he properly permitted the fast squadron that led his line to haul far ahead of the others.

But Scheer was pursuing a relatively small force, and he always had the option of slowing the leading division to close the line as soon as the enemy appeared in greater force. It must be admitted that dispersing the line in order to effect an envelopment of the enemy is a highly dangerous move, unless one enjoys an overwhelming superiority. In that case, breaking the line into separate portions which operate against the enemy from different sides may have many advantages even if the T is not crossed. One's whole strength is more effective, since a long line facing a short one tends to have its ends out of effective range; the enemy must maneuver relative to two lines rather than only one, which adds to his difficulties; he finds it more difficult to divide his fire; and it is likely that one portion of the superior fleet will get between him and his bases, making his escape impossible. But a division moving ahead to envelop the enemy's line or to strike at his disengaged side is apt to be out of range for an appreciable time when it might be supporting the rest of the fleet. It may also in the swift changes of battle find itself isolated and endangered.

In modern actions almost everything will depend on how the two fleets come into battle. A long line of battleships is not easily manipulated. If they happen at the outset to be disposed in the wrong direction or the wrong position relative to the enemy, it is exceedingly difficult to rectify that situation before irreparable injury is done. Consider the commander who finds himself in the stem of a T. He might do as Scheer did and reverse his ships to take them out of battle, but in the turning movement the vessels nearest the enemy may take a terrific pounding. And he may not wish to break off action. If he swings the head of his line gently in the direction followed by the enemy with the remainder of the line following in an easy curve, the change of direction will be much too slow. By the time the line is parallel to that of the enemy, the leading portion will have been destroyed. On the other hand, if he has the leading ship turn abruptly in the new direction with the remaining ships turning in succession on the same hub, the process of changing the direction of the line is faster but until it is completed the enemy has the advantage of concentrating all his fire on the few ships which are making and have made the turn. Moreover, the enemy will have got the exact range of the knuckle of the turn, and will pound each vessel mercilessly as it comes up unavoidably into that position.

In the close-order drill of infantry there is a maneuver

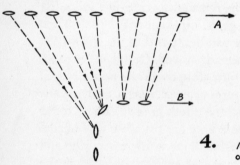

3. Fleet B tries to remedy
unfavorable position by curvi
in direction parallel to A.
Maneuver too slow.

4. Fleet A concentrates fire on
leading ships in Fleet B, especially
on ship in Knuckle of turn.

where a line of troops abreast swings around to form another line at right angles to the first, each soldier proceeding obliquely to his new position. But if the line is not to be badly broken and confused in the process, each soldier must adjust his speed to that of his neighbors and each will move at a somewhat different pace. The man at the fulcrum of the turn is almost stationary while the man at the other end moves

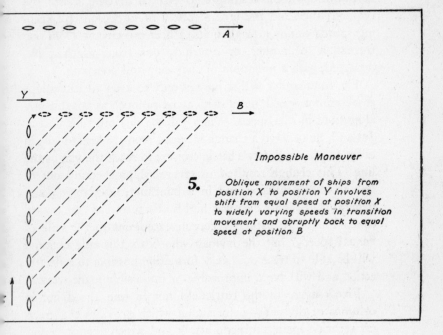

Impossible Maneuver

5. Oblique movement of ships from position X to position Y involves shift from equal speed at position X to widely varying speeds in transition movement and abruptly back to equal speed at position B

very rapidly. When the turn is completed, the whole line is ready at once to move off in any direction at a common speed.

Such a maneuver is completely impossible to a line of battleships. It would be difficult enough with a line of motor cars, and the speed of 35,000-ton vessels is not adjusted with foot pedals. Once contact is established with the enemy, a battle line proceeds by what are called equal speed maneuvers, all the battleships proceeding at a common speed. The formation and direction of the fleet may be altered, but this is done only by prescribing the degrees or points of turn (32 points in a circle), the direction of turn, and the units by which the turn is executed. The turn may be by individual ships, by subdivisions, by divisions, by squadrons, or by the whole line in succession. If the turn is ordered by divisions (usually three or four ships), the leading ship in each division makes the required turn and the others follow in succession. By keeping speeds common to all units, a fleet can change from one formation to another, or return to one from which it has departed, with a minimum of confusion and bunching.

The commander will strive not only to keep all battleships at a common speed, but also to avoid as much as possible any alterations in that speed. When Jellicoe deployed his fleet at Jutland, he ordered a change in speed from 18 knots to 14 in order to permit Beatty's battle cruisers to reach the van of the line. This change resulted in several ships sheering out of line to avoid collision and in a bunching, overlapping and general confusion which was highly dangerous at that critical time. There are naturally certain exceptions to the rule of "equal speed," but the layman who bears this rule in mind will be able to trace out every formation possible to a fleet in action and will avoid improbable or impossible maneuvers.

Fleets move to the battlefield not in line ahead but in columns of divisions—a formation which provides the greatest security against torpedo attack and which permits a line to be quickly formed. If the direction in which the enemy lies is known, the column can be wheeled to face the enemy (an unequal-speed maneuver but carried through before contact) and by a simple turn of divisions to port or starboard the line is formed. Most of fleet drill during peacetime consists primarily of swift and well-executed changes from one formation to the other so that in the day of crisis

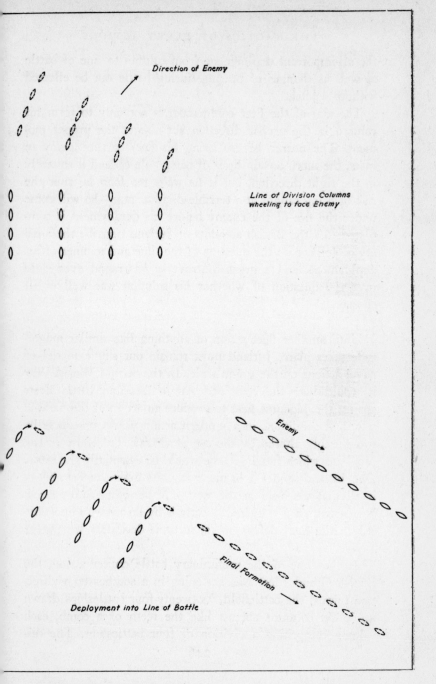

Direction of Enemy

Line of Division Columns
wheeling to face Enemy

Enemy

Final Formation

Deployment into Line of Battle

the all-important deployment from column to line of battle as well as changes of bearing during battle can be effected without a hitch.

The aim of the fleet commander is not only to form his column in the proper direction but also at the proper moment. The nearer he can bring his fleet to the enemy in mass, the more certain he is of being able to lead it squarely in the right direction, but if he waits too long he runs the risk of being caught at a terrible disadvantage—he will come under the fire of the enemy before his deployment is completed. All the British accounts of Jutland describe the anxiety of Jellicoe on the question of the time and manner of his deployment, and a great controversy has raged ever since over the question of whether his solution was well or ill chosen.

Until another fleet action of anything like similar magnitude takes place, Jutland must remain our single model of naval actions on the grand scale. In the Second World War it would take the combined Anglo-American battle fleets against the Japanese fleet to produce an action of comparable size, and conditions in a modern action would of course be considerably altered by the use of aircraft, but many of the problems which faced Jellicoe would be essentially the same. The Jutland model is in many respects unsatisfactory, but it is all that we have in the way of experience. And since a fleet action on a comparable scale is by no means impossible before the final defeat of Japan, it is decidedly worthy of study.

At the time of the preliminary battle cruiser action, the British Grand Fleet was hastening in a southeasterly direction toward the battlefield, its twenty-four battleships drawn up in six columns abreast like the teeth of a comb, each column comprising a division of four battleships. The dis-

JUTLAND
The Meeting 5:30 P.M.

British Grand Fleet
in Cruising Formation
(Jellicoe)

Note: Formations are not
drawn to scale

4th.
Light Cruiser
Squadron

3rd Battle Cruiser Squadron
(Hood)

3rd Light Cruiser
Squadron

1st Light Cruiser
Squadron

57° N.

6° E

Battle Cruisers
(Beatty)

2nd Scouting
Group

Battle Cruisers
(Hipper)

5th. Battle Squadron

German High Seas Fleet
(Scheer)

tance from one flanking column to the other was no less than five miles. To the south four more battleships of the *Queen Elizabeth* type were already engaged with the leading divisions of the German High Seas Fleet and were retreating toward the Grand Fleet, preceded by Beatty's four remaining battle cruisers. Ahead of Jellicoe and on his left were three more battle cruisers under Hood, who was seeking to engage the German battle cruisers on the opposite side from Beatty. Jellicoe thus had twenty-eight battleships and seven out of an original nine battle cruisers to dispose of, besides a large number of cruisers and destroyers. But his major problem was the deployment of the twenty-four battleships under his immediate command.

If he could be sure that his mass were headed in the exact direction of the enemy, he could postpone his deployment until almost the moment of contact, the armored cruisers immediately ahead of him guarding against surprise, and then turn the leading ships of each column to the right or left, the other ships in each column following in succession. In four minutes the fleet would have been drawn up in line of battle firing at its fullest strength. But Jellicoe was in fact by no means certain of the exact position of the German fleet. All kinds of conflicting reports began to come from the units already in contact with the enemy.

It must always be remembered that the cruisers which are in sight of the enemy are also in heavy action, zigzagging and turning suddenly to avoid gunfire or torpedo. They are bound to be out of their navigational reckoning. Their reports have to be written, ciphered, dispatched, received, and decoded before they reach the commander-in-chief. All that takes time and during that time the situation is rapidly changing. Today we have aircraft, but reconnaissance planes may also be engaged by the enemy; they, too, may be out of reckoning; their reports may also be conflicting. The layman usually conceives of reconnaissance aircraft operating under clear sky and brilliant visibility—conditions which in fact may often not occur. The situation may be ideal for aerial observation, in which case one or both commanders may have full and accurate information of the enemy's position long before contact is made, but conditions may also be such that visibility is in fact better from the decks or towers of cruisers.

Jellicoe, uncertain of the enemy's position but feeling it somewhere ahead and on his right, decided to deploy by sending the column on his left flank (the side farthest from the enemy) on ahead and having the other columns turn toward it and follow in succession ("deployment on the wing"). By this means the line formed at the end of four minutes had a bend in it. It took about twenty minutes before the line was straight and in satisfactory position for action. Jellicoe's choice of the flank farthest from the enemy has been condemned as creating too distant a range, and as causing the bulk of the fleet to be moving away from the enemy during the deployment; but the range was decided by the visibility anyway, and Jellicoe wanted to get to eastward of the German Fleet.

Action did in fact begin under circumstances the most favorable possible to the British. They were about to cross the enemy's T; they were moving into a position between the German Fleet and its bases, and they had the advantage of light. Had Jellicoe deployed on the right flank, all these advantages would have been lost. When Scheer saw the predicament he was in, his first thought was to turn away. Later he returned to fight, only to find his position worse than ever, with the Grand Fleet directly athwart his path and visible in the darkening mist only by its gun flashes while his own fleet was sharply silhouetted against the western sky. From then on his chief preoccupation was

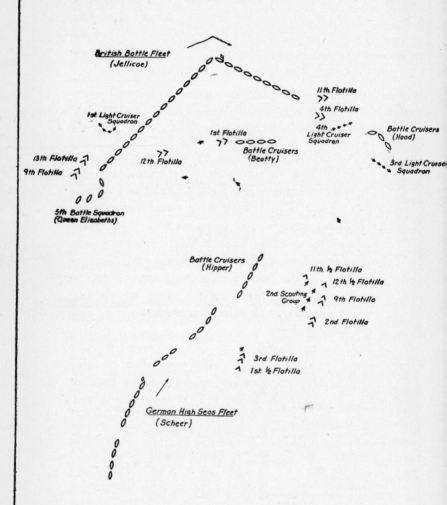

JUTLAND
The Deployment 6:19 P.M.

British Bottle Fleet
(Jellicoe)

1st Light Cruiser
Squadron

11th. Flotilla

4th. Flotilla

4th.
Light Cruiser
Squadron

Battle Cruisers
(Hood)

3rd. Light Cruiser
Squadron

1st Flotilla

Battle Cruisers
(Beatty)

13th. Flotilla

9th. Flotilla

12th. Flotilla

5th. Battle Squadron
(Queen Elizabeths)

Battle Cruisers
(Hipper)

11th. ½ Flotilla

12th. ½ Flotilla

2nd. Scouting
Group

9th Flotilla

2nd. Flotilla

3rd. Flotilla

1st. ½ Flotilla

German High Seas Fleet
(Scheer)

2nd. Squadron, 4th Scouting Group, 5th & 7th Flotillas
following some distance astern.

to leave the vicinity of the Grand Fleet as fast as he possibly could. That he was able to do so was due first of all to the fast gathering night, but it was due also to two other factors which are worth studying, since they are bound to influence in varying degrees naval actions in the future.

The first was the poor visibility obtaining on the battlefield. It is one thing to study a battle from charts prepared years after the event and showing almost the precise location of every important unit at various stages of the engagement and quite another to be an admiral on the bridge of the flagship peering into haze and mist and inevitable smoke, hearing the guns of the enemy but not knowing their precise location, and finally getting a glimpse, almost immediately obscured, of only the leading division of the enemy battle fleet. Jellicoe did not know that Scheer had actually turned away immediately upon sighting him. He might simply have been deploying his line for battle behind a smoke screen produced by his lighter forces, which, incidentally, could be expected also to be preparing a torpedo attack.

The next great battle fleet action may not occur in the almost perpetual haze of the North Sea, where the six to eight miles of visibility on the day of Jutland could not be considered unusually bad, but there are other regions of the world where poor visibility is the rule rather than the exception—the higher latitudes of the North Pacific, for example. And even if the weather be clear, there will be a great deal of smoke in the area of battle. The guns will be producing it, the funnels of the swiftly moving ships will be belching forth great quantities, and the lighter ships of one side or the other or perhaps both will be deliberately laying down smoke screens around their heavy vessels. With modern systems of indirect fire through spotting by cruisers or aircraft, it is not necessary for the battleship to see its target, and the heavy ships may therefore seek to envelop themselves in smoke for their protection. Under good weather conditions, aircraft will make concealment more difficult, but aircraft, too, are blinded by smoke.

The second factor which permitted Scheer to escape, and which is bound to influence future engagements even more than it did at Jutland, was the threat of torpedo attack by which he was able to keep Jellicoe from closing him. Only one British battleship, the *Marlborough*, was actually struck by a torpedo, and she was able to keep in the line until well after midnight, long past the last exchange of fire by battleships, but there is no question that if Jellicoe had not taken avoiding action a good many more British battleships would have been struck. The endless dispute which has gone on over this aspect of the battle is concerned with the question of whether Jellicoe took the proper kind of avoiding action.

At the time of Jutland the only craft other than submarines from which torpedo attack was to be feared were cruisers and destroyers. The British sighted numerous submarines which in fact were not there, but there was no question about the presence of a large number of enemy destroyers and cruisers. The British commander had reason to believe that there might be as many as 260 torpedoes in the tubes of the German lighter craft ready to be discharged in waves at any favorable opportunity.

When battleships are in line, the space between ships is about 400 to 500 yards and the length of each ship is some 250 yards. That means that any torpedo discharged in the general direction of the enemy battle line from a distance within its maximum range will have about two chances out of five of making a hit. Some torpedoes run erratic courses, but so long as they run at proper depth they would have to be extremely erratic to miss a battle line.

The battleship which is 250 yards long is only about 35

yards wide. It therefore enormously reduces its target area to turn its axis parallel to the course of the oncoming torpedoes. This it may do by turning away from or toward the origin of attack. The one time during the Battle of Jutland in which the British Fleet as a whole took avoiding action against a German torpedo attack, that is, at the second brief contact with the German Fleet, Jellicoe turned his vessels four points (45°) away from the enemy. For this he has been severely condemned, since it took him out of sight and range of the German Fleet, and he never regained full contact. It should be noted, however, that Jellicoe's purpose was to widen the range from the German destroyers and to place his ships in favorable position for *individual* avoiding action. The actual dodging of the missiles is not the responsibility of the commander-in-chief.

It should be observed too that Jellicoe turned his ships away by subdivisions, that is, by groups of two, one following behind the other. Such a maneuver reduces the target area offered by ships to torpedoes even more than a turn by individual ships. If the division consists of three ships instead of four, it is feasible to make the turn by whole divisions, depending on the range at which the torpedoes are fired.

Aside from the question of closing with or retreating from the enemy, the turn away and the turn toward each has its advantages and disadvantages. In turning away the vulnerable stern of the ship, with its screws and rudder, is exposed to the torpedo. On the other hand, the rate of approach of the torpedo is much diminished. The ship will have more time to dodge individual tracks. The speed of the ship in turning away is subtracted from the speed of the torpedo to give the velocity of approach; in turning toward it is added, so that the difference may be as great as 65 knots compared with 15 knots. If the torpedo has been fired at long range, the ship turning away may actually outrun it.

The choice of turn away or turn toward is also influenced by the bearing of the approaching torpedoes. They may be ahead of or astern of direct abeam position. A rule laid down by some tacticians is that if the attack comes from a direction between right ahead and 45 degrees before the beam it is better to turn toward, and that if it comes from a direction abaft this bearing it is better to turn away. The reason for the turn toward in the first instance is easily seen. A turn away would involve more than a 90° turn and would thus take longer and be more upsetting to one's tactical plan.

The choice is determined above all by strategic necessity. The distinction between tactics and strategy is in a sense arbitrary anyway. A battle is a crisis situation within a strategic plan, and it should be carried out in a manner to further rather than to compromise one's ultimate strategic purpose. The admiral who is bidding for command of the sea on a small margin of superiority must avoid losing ships to torpedoes at almost all costs. It is one thing to expose one's vessels to gunfire in order to hurl one's own shells on the enemy, but quite another to expose ships to a kind of attack which leaves no chance of inflicting any commensurate damage on the enemy. However, a fleet engaged with a much smaller fleet which has caused an anxiety disproportionate to its size might well afford to sacrifice a few ships to torpedoes in order to close and annihilate the enemy.

Admiral Sir Reginald Bacon has pointed out that at Jutland the British commander chose to turn away in the knowledge that only an hour of daylight remained and that there was little hope of a decision being reached before night anyway, that Jellicoe's thoughts were for bringing an intact fleet into action on the morrow. There was really more than an hour and a half of daylight left, and the fact that Jellicoe was carrying out a maneuver he had planned many months earlier vitiates this argument as an apology, but the weight of the observation must be acknowledged. If the turn away from torpedo attack were the only instance of Jellicoe's undue caution, his apologists would have an easy time.

In the action of the future there will be torpedo attacks from aircraft as well as from destroyers, and these will be in several ways more dangerous. Aircraft will probably be able to drop their torpedoes much closer to their targets, which will make avoidance more difficult. The torpedoes will form a criss-cross pattern instead of coming from one direction, which will make dodging more complicated and may throw a line into complete disarray. Ships placed close together make erratic avoiding movements only at considerable danger of collision, whereas lengthening the line by greater spacing weakens the fleet through dispersal.

On the other hand, torpedo attack even by aircraft is not likely to be so continuous that a disarrangement of the line cannot be remedied. The anti-aircraft power of the modern capital ship has risen so phenomenally since December 1941 that under present conditions it would require a very large force of torpedo planes attacking simultaneously to give any chance of success against a battle fleet, and such attacks could scarcely be mounted more than two or three times during a battle. Besides, the newest battleships, such as our *Iowa's*, have an underwater protection that makes it possible that they would hold station during a crucial stage in battle rather than turn to avoid launched torpedoes.

During the gunnery duel of the great ships the cruisers and destroyers will take up positions where they can instantly intervene between the opposing battle lines for purposes of scouting, launching torpedo attacks, fighting enemy torpedo craft, and laying smoke screens. The aircraft carriers will strive to remain on the disengaged side of the battle fleet, well out of range of the enemy's guns. By the time battle is fully joined, many of their torpedo planes will have been eliminated, but they are still of the greatest usefulness in providing planes which spot fire for the battleships, report the maneuvers of the enemy, and which attack enemy reconnaissance or torpedo planes. The destroyers and surviving torpedo planes will save their torpedoes for crisis situations in the battle, when they will be most effective, or for finishing off ships disabled by gunfire.

And thus in the thunder of great artillery and the swift rush of submerged missiles, the battle will move to its decisive conclusion.

CHAPTER X

The Men Behind the Guns

"THE moral is to the material as three is to one." If Napoleon's dictum sounds like an exaggeration, it is because in most modern battles the moral has been somewhat more evenly matched than the material. Instances are not lacking, however, where weak ships and strong men have triumphed over strong ships and weak men. Lord Cochrane taking with a little brig and without benefit of surprise a Spanish frigate of six times the manpower and at least ten times the gunpower; Nelson at Trafalgar defeating the better and more numerous ships of the irresolute Villeneuve; Togo crushing in two brilliant campaigns a Russian Navy which in aggregate strength was almost twice as powerful as his own; and, in our own time, Vian repulsing an immeasurably superior Italian squadron near Malta—these are examples which could be many times multiplied. "How many things apparently impossible have nevertheless been performed by resolute men!"

In the early months of the Second World War it became fashionable to speak of the conflict as being "a war not of men, but of machines." There never has been such a war in the past, and there never will be such. There are few other predictions about future wars which one can make with as much assurance. To be sure, the tools of war become ever more complex and more deadly, but the net result of those changes on the personnel factor is to place ever greater demands on the spirit and intelligence of the men who plan and wage battles.

We Americans in particular, who take such pride in our technological skill and in the tremendous productive capacity of our industrial plant, must beware of relying too much on the material alone. We are of such vast strength and of such happy geographical position that many more errors are permitted to us than to other nations—Britain could never have survived a Pearl Harbor—but there is a limit to war's tolerance even for our mistakes. It is not enough simply to build more and greater ships, or more and better airplanes than our enemies. We should remember also the words of du Picq: "The man is the first weapon of battle; let us then study the soldier in battle, for it is he who brings reality to it."

"An army," it is said, "is as brave as its privates and as good as its generals." But in a navy the admirals determine the bravery as well as the merit of the whole force. The admiral of a fleet or the captain of a ship shares the hazard of battle equally with the lowest ranks. He directs from the line of fire itself, not behind it, and if physical courage is needed for victory, as it is inevitably, he above all men must have it. The ships and crew members will go where he directs them—discipline and training will guarantee that— but his is the choice of the hazard that all will incur.

As a matter of fact, a brave admiral rarely lacks for brave personnel. The connection between a fleet and its leader is so immediate and intimate that the spirit of the commander tends to be suffused throughout all the personnel of the force. If the admiral is aggressive and resolute, the ships under him will reflect the tone of his command. This is even more true of a single ship when engaged in an isolated action. The crew of a resolute captain will fight as though inspired. A remarkable instance of this has been handed down in the court-martial proceedings against the captain of the *Serapis*, a fine British frigate with a picked crew which surrendered to the old converted East-Indiaman, *Bonhomme Richard*. The latter ship was commanded by John Paul Jones and manned by a polyglot crew of French, Americans,

Portuguese, and Malays. In his defense, Captain Pearson made this statement:

"Although more than half the crew were French—at any rate not Americans—long before the close of the action it became apparent that the American ship was dominated by a commanding will of a most unalterable resolution, and there could be no doubt that the intention of her commander was, if he could not conquer, to sink alongside. And this desperate resolve was fully shared and fiercely seconded by every one of his ship's company. And if the Honourable Court may be pleased to enter an expression of opinion, I will venture to say that if French seamen can ever be induced by their own officers to fight in their own ships as Captain Jones induced them to fight in his American one, the future burdens of His Majesty's Navy will be heavier than they have heretofore been."

By way of contrast one may remember the Italian Admiral Persano at Lissa, who left his flagship for an inconspicuous monitor just before the battle in order to be "better able to survey the battle line." The original flagship, sunk in the action, must have fought somewhat better for his absence, but the fleet generally showed the same sorry want of enterprise as its commander and was severely handled by the spirited Teghettoff, whose forces were decidedly inferior in material strength.

The commander of a fleet molds the fighting spirit of his men not only through example but also through a shrewd understanding of the psychology of morale. He seeks to give his men confidence in their strength and in their ability to win. The history of naval war is appallingly consistent in demonstrating the deterioration that overcomes inactive fleets—fleets which are held in port because the enemy is too obviously stronger. This inactivity and its cause are impressed on the minds of the seamen, with the result that on such occasions as they are actually brought to action by the opponent they are half-beaten before the battle begins. The admiral, therefore, whose material inferiority to the enemy enjoins him from rash ventures must always temper his caution with the knowledge of what inactivity means to the personnel.

The same kind of insight is necessary in action. During the desperate charge of the German battle cruisers against the British battle line at Jutland, Commander von Hase, chief gunnery officer of the *Derfflinger*, shrewdly continued to fire his remaining guns even though the target was totally obscured to him. "Without much hope of hurting the enemy, I ordered the two forward turrets to fire salvo after salvo. I could feel that our fire soothed the nerves of the ship's company. If we had ceased fire at this time, the whole ship's company would have been overwhelmed by despair . . . But so long as we were still firing, things could not be so bad."

The failure of spirit that comes from inability to hit back at the enemy perhaps explains why aerial bombardment against lighter warships, such as cruisers, is sometimes considerably more disruptive to morale than gunnery attack— a fact to which numerous survivors of bombed ships have testified. The warship which is the target for heavy bombs is not hitting back in kind. Its main guns are silent. A portion of its crew are firing a few small-caliber guns, which seem mostly to be uselessly filling the sky with puffs, but the men who would be feverishly active if the big guns were being fired stand by idle wondering if the next bomb will hit. Gunnery attack may in fact be more effective, but in the heat of a truly give and take action there is no time for worrying about danger.

The survivors of the *Bismarck* have told an amazing story of extreme oscillation in morale among the crew during her single brief cruise in the North Atlantic. Instilled at the beginning with a conviction that their ship was unsinkable and unbeatable, these men left their base in a spirit of supreme confidence. The action that terminated in driving off the *Prince of Wales* and sinking the *Hood* sent that confidence soaring to its ecstatic culmination. But after the first attack by British aircraft in which one relatively unimportant torpedo hit was registered, Admiral Luetjens, who seems to have shown manic-depressive tendencies, called the crew together and made a speech in which he implored them to meet death in a fashion becoming to good Nazis. This had a catastrophic effect on the morale of the ship's company, mostly very young men. It was the first they had heard of the necessity of dying. The rumors that swept the ship of violent disagreements between the admiral and Captain Lindemann did not improve their dispirited condition. Under the punishment administered by the *Rodney* and *King George V*, not a particularly greater force than they had bested only a few days earlier, the ship's company completely lost their heads. The gun crew of one turret fled their guns, and in another turret officers are said actually to have fired on the men to keep them at their posts. The result was an abysmally poor showing by the mighty *Bismarck* in her second and final action.

The quality most frequently lauded among our military personnel is physical courage, and it is well that it should be so because willingness to incur death is hardly a normal attribute of any human being. For some curious reason nature seems interested in our survival, and therefore endows us with certain emotional reactions to danger over which our intellects have only limited control. Men entering into battle must therefore be prepared by all sorts of psychological devices to act in a manner which from any sober point of view must be regarded as unnatural. Yet physical courage is a much commoner phenomenon among fighting men than one might be led to suppose. The accounts of most modern naval battles are almost redundant in their tales of heroism. No British or American naval action of either world war has failed to add to the catalog of epics. A fleet or ship which enters upon an action with good fighting morale may confidently be expected to give a good account of itself, however outnumbered.

There are, however, other and less common qualities which are also necessary, especially in the commander. Physical courage is not always attended by resolution, and professional proficiency naturally varies greatly with the native intelligence of the individual. It is the possession of high resolution plus a mental equipment capable of quick and correct decisions that distinguishes the great military leader from the mediocre.

There have been numerous historical examples of admirals who, while not lacking in the bodily courage which enables men to expose their own persons to hazard, were nevertheless incapable of taking risks with the forces under their command—risks which are usually unavoidable in the pursuit of decisive ends—or of persevering to the end in a chosen course. Admiral Villeneuve, whom Nelson defeated at Trafalgar, was no coward, but he certainly lacked confidence in himself and in his fleet. Admiral Cervera, whose force the Americans destroyed at Santiago, was a beaten man before he ever left Spain. And Admiral Witgeft, to whom command of the Russian Port Arthur squadron reverted after the death of the capable Makaroff, confessed himself to his captains as "no leader of a fleet." Makaroff, who had perished when his flagship struck a mine, was lamented by men who considered the loss of the battleship itself as small in comparison.

Witgeft commanded a squadron which was little inferior to the Japanese force which blockaded it. Yet, except for two efforts to escape to Vladivostok, he did nothing with this force, and it was finally destroyed ignominiously while at anchor in Port Arthur by Japanese howitzers ashore. Had he gone out to do battle with Togo he might have been defeated, but he would probably have so crippled the Japanese Fleet that it would have been unable to meet the second fleet which Rojhestvensky was then bringing from the Baltic. The Port Arthur squadron proved valueless in the campaign, and the irresolution of its commander caused not only the useless sacrifice of his own force but also of Rojhestvensky's fleet, the annihilation of which ended the war. It was the spectacle of Witgeft's incompetence which caused General Kuropatkin to exclaim that "the strength of a nation does not lie in armor, guns, and torpedoes, but in the souls of the men behind these things."

Leaders of great forces, and frequently their subordinate officers as well, have often shown a tendency to worry at the dangers facing their own fleet and to exclude from their minds those facing the enemy. It is only natural that this should be so, since one's own force is immediately at hand and its vulnerable points all too vividly apparent, while the enemy's fleet is distant and invisible. A commander feels his responsibility keenly, and usually has no time or inclination to attempt to imagine the worries facing his opponent. This magnification of dangers is the most frequent cause of irresolution in commanders.

Napoleon recognized the universality of this feeling among leaders, and in one of his many maxims on the subject urges that the general caught by surprise in a bad position should not immediately attempt a retirement but should adopt a menacing attitude toward the enemy in order to disconcert him and make him wonder whether he was right in assuming he had an advantage. Grant tells in his memoirs of his experience at the beginning of the Civil War when as a colonel he was put in charge of a regiment and sent on a detached mission against a Confederate regiment. On his way he kept worrying about what his opponent would do to him if they met suddenly, and he was losing his resolve step by step. All at once he realized that his adversary had exactly the same concerns and perhaps in greater degree, and from that moment on throughout the war he never ceased to remind himself of that fact.

Some commanders, however, have fought whole wars through without grasping the fact that the enemy's worries were at least comparable to their own, and in such cases the strategy of the war has usually not been brilliant. Frau von Pohl, widow of Scheer's predecessor as commander-in-chief of the German High Seas Fleet, remarked upon reading Jellicoe's *The Grand Fleet*, "How strange is the parallel between Germany and Britain, that in both navies the Admirals were in a stew as to the failings of their respective fleets!" Each side was obsessed by the fear of what the enemy fleet might do to it, the Germans, to be sure, with much more justification than the British. The dominant thought of each fleet commander while at sea was not to beat the enemy but to keep from being beaten.

Captain Grenfell has called attention to Admiral Togo's instruction to the Japanese Fleet in the interval between the capture of Port Arthur and the arrival of the Russian Baltic Fleet in the Far East: "Those who have little experience of actual fighting are apt to feel that the enemy is strong and we are weak; this because, while we cannot see the ravages wrought in the enemy's vessels, the damage in our own is always before our eyes. . . . When we think that the chances of victory are seven for the enemy and three for ourselves, the true chances are even." This remarkable statement, as Grenfell points out, was given to the officers not of a fleet trying to recover its nerve after a defeat, but one which had established its ascendancy from the war's beginning and had just seen the enemy fleet elect to be destroyed in port rather than come out and fight.

It will be noted that in order to overcome a specific kind of fear in his men, Togo was appealing to intelligence rather than to emotional symbols. Of particular significance was his observation that experience in fighting reduces the tendency to magnify perils. This is one of the important advantages of activity to a fleet. Experience in battle gives one a familiarity with danger, which does not breed contempt but which enables the seaman to assess hazards at their true value. Togo here demonstrated that he possessed what Napoleon regarded as the first qualification of a commander-in-chief—the possession of "a cool head, so that things may appear to him in their true proportions and as they really are," a disinclination to be unduly affected by good or bad news. Togo had suffered his share of setbacks, having lost one-third of his battleship force to mines on a single day.

Napoleon was a firm believer in boldness. He despised councils of war as usually resulting "in the adoption of the most pusillanimous or the most prudent measures, which in war are almost uniformly the worst that can be adopted." True wisdom, he believed, consisted for the commander in "energetic determination." He insisted that men who from their physical or moral constitution decked everything in the colors of pessimistic imagination were not fitted by nature for the command of armies and the direction of the great operations of war, regardless of whatever knowledge, talents, or courage they might have.

On the other hand, a too doctrinaire attitude about the merits of boldness may be exceedingly dangerous. An admiral must consider not only the tactical hazards of a contemplated course of action, but also the strategic consequences to be expected from both success and failure. A tactical hazard that would not loom unduly large if only the probabilities of success in an action were considered might be prohibitive if one were dealing with a force upon which the destiny of a nation depended. In other words, one could certainly take much greater risks with a task force than with a battle fleet. In this connection it is instructive to look at what has been perhaps the chief subject of controversy among naval officers and naval historians in the period between the two world wars—Jellicoe's caution at Jutland.

Jellicoe's apologists have stoutly maintained that his caution was well warranted by the strategic as well as the tactical circumstances under which the battle occurred. They hold that the Grand Fleet already enjoyed command of all the seas essential to Britain, and that there was no use risking that command and therefore the whole outcome of the war for the sake of sinking some German warships. An opposing opinion insists that in needlessly letting slip an opportunity to annihilate the German battle fleet, Jellicoe denied his country a victory which would have been of tremendous moral value at home and abroad, which would have made easier the handling of the U-boat menace, and which might have opened the Baltic to invasion. A crushing British victory, this school maintains, would probably have substantially shortened the war.

Choice between these arguments is not easy. To be sure, Jellicoe had a marked superiority over his opponent, and the British had a far greater reserve in dreadnought and predreadnought battleships at home than did the Germans. That should settle the issue, and yet it is logical that the fleet already enjoying the strategic advantages of command is risking more in a fleet action and has less to gain from victory than its enemy. Naturally it must fight if challenged, but there is no need for it to seek out the enemy at any hazard. In all fairness to Jellicoe it should be recognized that he desired a fleet action and that his initiative brought about the meeting at Jutland. But he wanted action only on his own terms and refused to take what he considered undue risks in order to bring the contact to a conclusive issue. He refused to advance upon torpedoes and refused to fight a night action.

Yet a crushing victory does have great psychological and therefore substantial strategic value. Jervis recognized that at St. Vincent when he looked out at a Spanish fleet almost twice his own in size and declared, "England has need of a victory." Victory is a potent tonic to the personnel of the fleet and the people at home, and it is comparably damaging to the spirit of the enemy. Allied and neutral nations are never blind to its implications, and their consequent actions are rarely unfavorable to the victor. Annihilation of an enemy's fleet releases vessels for service elsewhere, where they may be much needed, and makes possible passage into formerly prohibited seas.

It is interesting to observe the special dilemma which faced the American Navy in the summer of 1942. After the restoration of the Pacific Fleet to a fighting condition, which probably included the transfer of some American battleships from the Atlantic to the Pacific, that fine force was approximately equal, perhaps somewhat superior, to the Japanese Fleet. The mid-Pacific was in dispute, commanded by neither side. Except for the submarines of either side, which could not be expected to produce conclusive results, Japan held practically undisputed passage to the territories which she had conquered and occupied and the United States had easy access to her own bases and a relative freedom of movement to the outpost of Australia.

The passage of time was bound to mean a far greater accretion of strength to the American side than to the Japanese. A large number of mighty battleships and aircraft carriers were being speeded to completion in the United States. Events in Europe promised to release eventually large numbers of British warships as well. By waiting perhaps a year the United States Fleet could hope to have not merely superiority to the Japanese but overwhelming superiority. "The true speed of war," as Mahan so well expressed it, "is not headlong precipitancy, but the unremitting energy which wastes no time."

Under such conditions a policy of immediately seeking out the Japanese Fleet to engage in battle would seem to be hardly justified. Naturally, if the Japanese, fearing the threat of the future, came on their own initiative into American waters to challenge the American Fleet within range of American land-based air power, that would be another story. When the Japanese attempted to take the Midway Islands in June 1942, American naval forces properly showed themselves nothing loath to engage. On the other hand, a policy of watching and waiting was not only unpromising for the morale of our fleet but especially disheartening to our desperately pressed Chinese allies.

The policy of our fleet in that summer apparently combined aggressive minor operations with an essentially defensive strategy. The aggressive operations entailed the use of speedy task forces in raids upon the enemy. These brought to the fleet all the psychological values of activity and an offensive attitude, and harried and perplexed the enemy. At the same time any one such force, if it were somehow ambushed and destroyed, did not represent a vital part of American naval strength. If the raids of isolated task forces proved excessively costly, or if losses threatened to compromise our expectations for ultimate superiority, they could always be halted and a more passive defense substituted until we acquired the strength for an all-out offensive.

There has been too much loose talk about repudiating all

ideas of the defensive and about the gods favoring the bold. It is true that the gods favor the bold, usually, but they are notoriously harsh with the reckless. Those who are fond of quoting Nelson's assertion in his Trafalgar memorandum that "something must be left to chance, nothing is sure, in a sea action above all others," are inclined to overlook the significance of the word "something." It is true, as Lord Howe so neatly put it, that "some occasions in our profession will justify, if not require, more hazard to be ventured than can be systematically defended," but again we find a meaningful qualification in his first two words. A fleet which can confidently look forward to rapidly growing strength relative to the enemy is in a special position. It is certainly not impelled to risky moves.

Napoleon can be, and has been, quoted *ad infinitum* on the merits of boldness; but Napoleon, after all, finally lost his crown, and France lost a good deal more than an emperor. And in those days defeat did not have anything like the consequences it has today. Boldness is a great virtue in a fighter, and wars are won by hitting hard, fast, and often; but when an asset of the value of a battle fleet is at stake, an admiral must scrutinize risks well before he accepts them.

The admiral must have the ability to see things whole, to appraise the present in terms of the future, and to see the problems of both the present and the future in all their numerous ramifications. To understand strategy is easy, to determine upon a strategic policy is not. To determine upon a wise policy and stick to it through innumerable distractions and conflicting political demands requires something approaching genius.

The man who takes a fleet into action may be a different person from the one who plans grand strategy, but the demands upon him are equally heavy. He must comprehend intimately the framework of strategic policy within which he fights his battle, for it is within his power either to further or desperately to imperil that policy. The immediate responsibility is totally his. His proficiency as a tactician must be of the highest order, and such proficiency is gained only by constant study and contemplation of the problems of his profession. "To act correctly without reasoning," Napoleon said, "is not due to some familiar spirit which suddenly dictates to me what I have to do in a case unexpected by others, it is reflection, meditation." The admiral must have, in other words, a prepared mind, prepared through rumination over previously conceived problems.

The great speed at which modern fighting craft move in combat and the long ranges at which actions take place have placed on the fleet commander new demands for rapid thinking. When Nelson's *Victory* closed with the enemy at Trafalgar, Nelson himself had become little more than a spectator of the battle. His general orders for the engagement had been given some days earlier, and his functions as an admiral had practically ceased with his famous "England expects" signal, which preceded the first exchange of fire by almost half an hour. Today, on the other hand, the admiral keeps his grip on the action during every moment of battle, and in the swift rush of great ships and aircraft the situation is changing materially from moment to moment. The fleet commander's decision must be not only well chosen but also well-timed, and the time permitted him for major decisions is much less than is usually accorded the general of an army.

To be sure, admirals are ordinary mortals who will naturally make mistakes in action. The catalog of errors of the two fleet commanders at Jutland is a considerable one. Quite apart from his deliberate and much controverted turn away from torpedo attack, Jellicoe made several errors any one of which might be charged with having cost him the opportunity of a crushing victory. The most serious of Scheer's errors, that of turning eastward again toward the center of the Grand Fleet after his first successful disengagement, brought his fleet within a hair's breadth of annihilation. But Scheer redeemed his mistake by his coolness under terrific strain and hazard—a coolness which made him pause five minutes between his preparatory command for a turn away together and his signal to execute it, in order that every ship should be sure to get the order before the turn was begun. Cool-headedness and quick decision, more than cleverness, must be the attributes of the admiral in action.

A great deal has been made of the value of traditions in a service. It is true that the many splendid epics ingrained in the very souls of the men who take Britain's ships to sea are a real advantage to the Royal Navy. These men are accustomed to the ideas of winning and of fighting to the end, come what may. The same is true of the American Navy, which has on a less extensive scale the same inspiring history of valor and resolution in action. Yet many young navies have done splendidly without any traditions whatever. Our own navy did far from badly in its fledgling days, with a Paul Jones at the very outset, and shortly afterward leaders like Hull, Decatur, and Macdonough. The Japanese Fleet of 1904–1905 was practically a newcomer to the family of navies, but its accomplishments can be described only as brilliant. The German Imperial High Seas Fleet was an upstart in 1914, yet no serious historian has denied that its fighting inferiority to the British Grand Fleet lay in weight of metal alone. The fact is that the traditions of great spirits like Nelson or John Paul Jones are never the exclusive property of a single navy. The professional lore of naval men is highly internationalized. Precepts and even heroic legends are shared generously with rival navies. The monumental interpretation of the British Navy's aggressive spirit in the days of sail was written by the American naval officer Mahan, and his teachings were instilled into the personnel of all modern navies, German and Japanese as well as British and American.

The too frequent vaunting of traditions can easily become a substitute for thinking, and the constant emphasis among American naval writers upon certain of our supposed traditions sometimes looks like just such a substitute. The American Navy, we are told over and again, has "the tradition of the offensive." But so too does the navy of our chief naval enemy, Japan. And nothing could be more foolhardy than to choose one's path during a crisis on the basis of tradition. Cogitation, which is bound to take full account of the merits of aggressiveness, should be the foundation of policy, not sentiment.

Traditions, when used as a guide to policy, are like the frequently encountered superstitions which ascribe to the entire personnel of an enemy navy certain innate qualities likely to determine fighting performance. One American admiral, justly respected throughout the Navy and the nation, publicly declared *four weeks after Pearl Harbor* that the Japanese were not given to independent thinking either in tactics or strategy, that they were essentially and incurably imitators.[1] Japanese performance under the novel conditions of the Russo-Japanese War should have blasted that crude but much cherished notion long ago. Of course the Japanese Navy like any other navy learns from its rivals; if it did not we would have a much lesser problem. But to assume that Japanese officers are less able than others to improve upon what they have adopted is a particularly dangerous kind of fallacy. It may be useful for the ordinary seaman to

[1] During the Russo-Japanese War of 1904–1905, the Russian people were told that the Japanese feared horses worse than tigers, and that a few regiments of Cossacks in the Far East would defeat them.

feel that he is a match for three of his enemies, but admirals ought to have a more realistic perception of situations.

Anthropologists, whose life business it is to study racial differences, have long scoffed at the popular illusion that some races are inherently more courageous or competent than others. And if this be true among races, how much more true is it among nationalities, which cannot be identified by racial distinctions? The most varied peoples have at different times shown a high aptitude for war both on land and sea. And the Second World War has presented the spectacle of consummate bravery and skill in fighting among such diverse stocks as the Chinese, Greeks, Japanese, Russians, Indians, British, Germans, and French, not to mention the very much mixed Americans.

To be sure, some nationalities, like the Italians, seem to show a rather consistently inglorious record in recent wars. Yet there are reports that certain branches of the Italian forces, such as the field artillery, show a very high degree of competence and courage. We know that the Italian of antiquity or of the Renaissance was anything but a poor fighter, and that the youth of Italian descent in the American Army or Navy is as good a soldier or seaman as his fellow.

In this connection it might be noted also that there is no such thing as a naturally seafaring people. Man's natural habitat is the land, and he takes to the sea only as a result of various pressures or opportunities. The Phoenicians, Greeks, Venetians, Portuguese, and Dutch have at various times dominated the seas. If the Briton today excels in pursuits afloat, his aptitude comes to him not through inheritance but from the opportunities for pleasure and gain on the sea which are held out to him by his island environment. This aptitude stood the British in good stead at Dunkirk, where a thousand small boats gathered together at almost a moment's notice showed a remarkable ability to negotiate difficult approaches to the bombed beaches. But in the American Navy the boy from Iowa makes as good a seaman with a little training as the youth from Cape Cod, and if names on the roster mean anything, descent from such non-seafaring peoples as the Poles and the Bohemians is no disability. What constitutes a seaman other than experience afloat? If a chronic disposition to seasickness is taken as a criterion, then Nelson was no seaman.

Americans will do well to assume that so far as native courage and competence for waging war at sea are concerned, we start equal to other nations, and if our naval personnel demonstrate their superiority over those of other navies, it will be due not to God's gifts but to our own exertions. We must recognize that while it is a blessing to be an American, there is no particular virtue in being one—no virtue, that is, which releases us from the constant concern over the efficiency of our armed forces which all nations who wish to survive in today's world must maintain.

The history of most of our wars has been marked by the gradual evolution of fine leadership, but only at the cost of a long, costly period of the elimination of incompetents. In naval warfare such an exploratory period is often not permitted. Our naval strategy in the war with Spain was far from brilliant. At that time among the higher officers of our Navy there was scarcely any interest in the study of strategy. Mahan's career, it might be observed, was hindered rather than promoted by his penetrating and scholarly studies; ship officers were expected not to indulge in such trivial pursuits as book writing.

Things have changed a great deal since Mahan's time, but that does not mean we can rest in our efforts at improvement. It is not normal in any military service, with its overriding tradition of extravagant respect for and implicit obedience to higher authority, for junior officers who differ with their seniors on technical questions to get the hearing their ideas deserve. In his poem "The Laws of the Navy," Captain Hopwood of the Royal Navy thrice cautions the young officer who wishes to get ahead against differing in the slightest degree with his superiors. A capacity for original thinking is indeed valued, but only if it is combined with a fine sense of tact. It is a pity, but talent and tact do not always run together. Independent and incisive thinking therefore rarely receives the preferment it deserves in any navy, but we must see to it that ours is an exception.

The Royal Navy may be behind ours in certain respects, but in one it is definitely ahead. There is in England much less of that singular isolation of the Navy from the civilian community which is the experience of the American naval officer from the time he becomes a midshipman at Annapolis. British naval officers, both retired and in active service, frequently become members of Parliament, and their record there historically has been one of useful service. In Parliament and out, naval officers and civilians benefit reciprocally from a continuous exchange of views. Our public has traditionally considered its obligations with respect to the defense of the country fully redeemed by the voting of large appropriations in Congress. Even the members of our Congressional committees on military and naval affairs frequently betray a remarkable lack of information on the subjects which should be their special concern. In view of this indifference, the basic fault for the tragic error of Pearl Harbor must be ascribed not to a few officers but to the whole nation.

Open-mindedness and insistence upon vigorous thinking ought to reach down to the very beginning of the officer's career and influence the selection of cadets for the Naval Academy. It would seem logical that the midshipman corps at Annapolis, from which our admirals invariably issue, should be selected from the best of all the nation's youth who wish to enter the service. And yet by the allotment of appointments to senators and representatives we have what amounts to appointment on the fantastic basis of geographical distribution of residence. It is likely, too, that our physical qualifications for entry into the Academy are unduly rigorous, thereby eliminating many outstanding minds. The great German strategist General von Schlieffen would never have gained admission because of his defective eyesight to the peacetime officer corps of any of the American armed forces. An uncommonly good brain should be ample compensation for slight physical defects, but it is not now considered so.

The United States Navy is a splendid service in personnel as well as materiel, the best in the world in all but war experience—which at this writing it is rapidly gaining. We have not only wealth but a great fund of youth from which selection can be made, a democratic social system which permits selection to be untrammeled by class bias, and as one of our national traits a passion for efficiency. But since the world is so strangely constituted that the destiny of our own nation and of all the nations who look to us for salvation may hinge on the clear thinking of one man on a single afternoon, the constant pursuit of perfection is not an idle endeavor. No change that might improve even minutely the level of talent in our naval forces should be overlooked. We must remember always that the basic element of strength in any nation is not in its machines but in its manhood.

Reading List and Index

READING LIST

THE fact that this list is prepared for the layman rather than for the professional seaman or scholar explains the omission of a great many excellent books and articles. Highly technical or relatively abstruse works are in the main excluded, as are a great many fine contributions which deal chiefly with naval history. Most of the titles are of recently published books and articles, and all of them are in English. Of the hundreds of articles on naval affairs which have recently appeared in popular and professional journals the author has chosen only a few, and he cannot pretend that those which he has included are necessarily better than many which he has omitted. He had no choice but to use his own interest as a touchstone.

Air Ministry of Great Britain, *Bomber Command* (New York: Doubleday, Doran, 1941), pp. 128.

> An invaluable account of the achievements and problems of the Bomber Command of the R.A.F. during the first year and a half of war. Contains many authentic stories by bombing crews and some excellent photographs. A continuation was published in 1942.

Austin, A. B., *We Landed at Dawn* (New York: Harcourt, Brace, 1943), pp. 217.

Bacon, Admiral Sir Reginald *et al*, *The World Crisis by Winston Churchill: A Criticism* (London: Hutchinson, 1928), chap. v.

> A brilliant criticism of Churchill's account of the Battle of Jutland. Bacon is as much biased in favor of Jellicoe as Churchill is against him.

Bacon, Sir Reginald, and McMurtrie, Francis E., *Modern Naval Strategy* (London: Muller, 1940).

> This book falls far short of justifying its title, but it contains some shrewd observations on modern naval combat and on warship types.

Baldwin, Hanson W., *What the Citizen Should Know About the Navy* (New York: Norton, 1941), pp. 219.

A useful book of information about our Navy.

Brassey's Naval Annual, ed. by Rear-Admiral H. G. Thursfield (London: Clowes).

A yearbook which contains several articles, usually of the highest quality, as well as a good deal of data on the world's navies and of naval events.

British Seaman (pseud.), "The Bomb Hit the Cruiser," *Harper's Magazine* (December, 1941), pp. 18-21.

A vivid and illuminating account of what bombing attack means to the personnel of a cruiser.

Brodie, Bernard, *Sea Power in the Machine Age* (Princeton: Princeton University Press, 1941), pp. 466.

The story of the industrial revolution in sea power, with an interpretation of the consequences on strategy and politics of technological changes during the last century.

Cant, Gilbert, *The War at Sea* (New York: John Day, 1942), pp. 340.

A brilliant account of naval campaigns and battles of the Second World War up to the close of 1941.

Casey, R. J., *Torpedo Junction* (Indianapolis: Bobbs-Merrill, 1942), pp. 423.

The American Navy in action during the first six months of the Pacific war.

Churchill, Winston S., *The World Crisis, 1916–1918* (New York: Scribner's, 1927), Vol. I, chaps. v-vi.

The most readable of all accounts of Jutland, but biased against Jellicoe and contains many errors. Valuable chiefly because it provoked the excellent criticism by Admiral Bacon cited above.

Clarke, R. W. B., *Britain's Blockade* (Oxford: Clarendon Press, 1940), Oxford Pamphlets on World Affairs, No. 38, pp. 32.

An excellent discussion of the objectives of the British blockade in the Second World War. Shows the relationship between blockade and "strategic bombing."

Corbett, Julian S., *Some Principles of Maritime Strategy* (London: Longmans, Green & Co., 2nd ed., 1919), pp. 286.
A classic work on naval strategy, by a civilian British naval historian. Not easily digested by the layman.

Davis, Forrest, *The Atlantic System: The Story of Anglo-American Control of the Seas* (New York: Reynal & Hitchcock, 1941), pp. 363.
A discerning appraisal, based mainly on the teachings of Mahan, of the contribution of Great Britain to American security.

De Seversky, Alexander P., *Victory Through Air Power* (New York: Simon & Schuster, 1942), pp. 354.
A presentation of the extreme air-minded point of view. The author holds that fleets are obsolescent if not obsolete.

Divine, A. D., *Firedrake* (New York: E. P. Dutton, 1943), pp. 251.
A fine story of a British destroyer and the men who fight her.

Ellinger, Werner B., and Rosinski, H., *Sea Power in the Pacific, a Bibliography, 1936–1941* (Princeton: Princeton University Press, 1942), pp. 80.
This bibliography of books, articles, and maps from 1936 to 1941 is an invaluable contribution, indispensable to all serious students of naval problems in the Pacific.

Grenfell, Russell, *The Art of the Admiral* (London: Faber & Faber, 1937), pp. 255.
A popular discussion of naval strategy. Somewhat outdated by the events of the Second World War.

Harris, Murray, *Lifelines of Victory* (New York: G. P. Putnam's, 1942), pp. 160.
An excellent brief dissertation on the importance of communications in modern war—land, sea, and air.

Hase, Georg von, *Kiel & Jutland* (London: Skeffington & Son, 1927), pp. 128.
An exciting and instructive account of the Battle of Jutland as seen by the chief gunnery officer on the German battle cruiser *Derfflinger*.

Jane's All the World's Aircraft, ed. by Leonard Bridgman (American distributor: Macmillan & Co., New York).
The aviation counterpart of *Jane's Fighting Ships.*

Jane's Fighting Ships, ed. by Francis E. McMurtrie (American distributor: Macmillan & Co., New York).
The standard yearbook of the world's navies. Quite indispensable.

Johnston, Stanley, *Queen of the Flat-tops: The U.S.S. Lexington and the Coral Sea Battle* (New York: E. P. Dutton, 1942), pp. 280.
A superb piece of reporting. Brings us intimately into the lives of our fighting seamen and naval airmen, both in carefree leisure and in the feverish hour of battle.

Ley, Willy, *Bombs and Bombing* (New York: Modern Age Books, 1941).
An objective, considered analysis of the potentialities and limitations of aerial bombing.

Loening, Grover, "Ships Over the Sea," *Foreign Affairs,* Vol. 20, No. 3 (April, 1942), pp. 489-502.
A plea for the greater use of aircraft as transoceanic cargo carriers.

Lovett, Robert A., "Airplanes for Men and Freight in Wartime," *Proceedings of the Academy of Political Science,* Vol. 20, No. 20 (Jan. 1943), pp. 137-42.
More incisive than Loening's article, and a good supplement to it.

Mahan on Naval Warfare, ed. by Allan Westcott (Boston: Little, Brown & Co., 1942), pp. 372.
A well-selected collection of excerpts from Mahan's voluminous writings.

Mayers, Colin, *Submarines, Admirals, and Navies* (Los Angeles: Associated Publications, 1940), pp. 280.
A provocative discussion of the potentialities of submarines, by a former submarine officer in the British Navy. Contains also some interesting reflections on the personal consequences of heretical thinking in the Royal Navy.

Moorehead, Alan, *Mediterranean Front* (New York: Whittlesey, 1942), pp. 306.
Naval operations in the Mediterranean are only incidentally covered in this account, but it is one of the most brilliant pieces of reporting which has thus far come out of the Second World War.

Muller, Edwin, "On Board the *Bismarck*," *Harper's Magazine* (February, 1942), pp. 258-63.
An amazing story of what occurred aboard the *Bismarck* during her fateful cruise, as told by survivors taken by the British.

Puleston, William D., *The Armed Forces of the Pacific* (New Haven: Yale University Press, 1941), pp. 274.
Despite the recency of its publication, this book is now definitely out of date in many essential respects; but it is still useful for naval policies and organization.

Ricci, Lewis (pseud. "Bartimeus") *Action Stations!* (Boston: Little, Brown & Co., 1941), pp. 262.
A group of short stories about British naval men in the Second World War, by an officer in the Royal Navy. Gives intimate glimpses of life and action at sea in modern war.

Richmond, Admiral Sir Herbert, *War at Sea Today* (Oxford: Clarendon Press, 1942), Oxford Pamphlets on World Affairs, No. 60.
On the importance of naval warfare and the form it takes today.

Rimington, Critchell, *Fighting Fleets: A Survey of the Navies of the World* (New York: Dodd, Mead & Co., 1943), pp. 240.
A concisely written but copiously illustrated yearly review of the ships and planes of the world's navies. Arranged according to categories of craft.

Russell, Sir Herbert, *Sea Shepherds: Wardens of our Food Flocks* (London: John Murray, 1941), pp. 247.
The story of the convoy system. Begins with Elizabethan times but is concerned mainly with the two world wars.

Sprout, Harold and Margaret, *The Rise of American Naval Power, 1776–1918* (Princeton: Princeton University Press, 1939), pp. 398.

A valuable history of American naval policy.

Sprout, Harold and Margaret, *Toward a New Order of Sea Power; American Naval Policy and the World Scene, 1918–1922* (Princeton: Princeton University Press, 1940), pp. 332.

Devoted mainly to an account of the Washington Naval Conference of 1921, which will probably go down in history as the first and greatest naval victory of the Axis Powers in the Second World War.

United States Naval Institute Proceedings (Annapolis).

A monthly publication on naval matters. Especially interesting for the department in each issue called "Professional Notes."

Warner, Edward, "What Airplanes Can Do," *Foreign Affairs*, Vol. 20, No. 2 (January, 1942), pp. 339-58.

An essay by a distinguished American aeronautical engineer on the inherent limitations and potentialities of modern aircraft.

Walmsley, Leo, *Fishermen at War* (New York: Doubleday, 1941), pp. 302.

The great wartime role played by Britain's fishing fleet.

White, Wm. L., *They Were Expendable* (New York: Harcourt, Brace, 1942), pp. 209.

Tragedy and triumph in the opening moments of the Pacific war. An exciting and revealing story of an American PT-boat force.

Wolfert, Ira, *Battle for the Solomons* (Boston: Houghton Mifflin, 1943), pp. 199.

Woodbury, David O., *What the Citizen Should Know About Submarine Warfare* (New York: W. W. Norton & Co., 1942), pp. 225.

A good popular account of the subject.

INDEX

admiral, qualifications of the, 14*f.*, 180*f.*, 269*ff.*; *see also* "leadership"

Admiral Graf Spee, German pocket battleship, 33, 42, 44, 128, 232

Admiral Hipper class, German heavy cruisers, 127

Admiral Scheer, German pocket battleship, 42, 43, 128

Adventure, British minelayer, 77

aerial bombardment, limitations of, 7, 33-6, 54, 104*f.*, 185, 208-13

aerial transportation, 4*f.*, 190, 191, 201*n.*

Agincourt, British battleship, 30*n.*

air power, place of in naval warfare, 4*f.*, 50-59, 61*f.*, 99-102, 104, 105*f.*, 109, 126, 129-32, 139, 146, 149, 152, 154, 160, 162, 173*f.*, 176-214, 216, 218-27, 246

aircraft, naval, characteristics and functions of, 50-57, 64, 199-207, 209, 220, 224

aircraft carrier, characteristics and functions of, 57-64, 104, 198, 218-23, 224-7, 255*f.*

Alabama, Confederate raider, 119

Alberico da Barbiano, Italian light cruiser, 48

amphibious operations, 16, 109, 148-63, 186, 189, 223

Argus, British aircraft carrier, 58

Arizona, U.S. battleship, 181

Ark Royal, British aircraft carrier, 54, 61, 73, 100, 112, 181*n.*, 219

armor, on aircraft, 200; penetration of, 34-6; on warships, 22, 23-6, 48*f.*, 221*f.*

Asdic, 72; *see also* "submarine detection"

Atlanta class, U.S. cruisers, 47, 48

Atlantic, Battle of the, 11, 86, 113, 120, 134-42

Atlantic Ocean, strategy of the, 92*f.*, 96, 101, 113

Australia, strategic role of in World War II, 8, 110*f.*

auxiliary naval vessels, 77

Bacon, Admiral Sir Reginald, British naval officer, 254

Baltimore class, U.S. heavy cruisers, 47

Barham, British battleship, 73

Barnes, Franklin G., 220*n.*

Bartolomeo Colleoni, Italian light cruiser, 48

bases, air, 174; naval, 93, 109, 114, 159*f.*, 164-74

battle cruisers, characteristics and functions of, 40-42

battle fleet, function of, 3, 86-8, 107*f.*, 109, 116, 122*f.*, 144, 168, 215*f.*

battleships, building time of, 38*f.*; characteristics and functions of, 20-39, 88, 98, 107*f.*, 117, 183, 192-9, 201*f.*, 204, 207, 217*f.*, 233*ff.*; size of, 22*f.*, 44, 99, 173, 192*f.*, 195*f.*

Beatty, Admiral David, 232, 240, 244, 248

Bennett, British general, 179

Bismarck, German battleship, 22, 28, 31, 33, 36, 41, 54, 61, 81, 92, 99, 100, 112, 114, 129, 193,

INDEX